Picturebooks, Pedagogy and Philosophy

Routledge Research in Education

For a full list of titles in this series please visit www.routledge.com

Picturebooks, Pedagogy and Philosophy

Joanna Haynes and Karin Murris

Routledge
Taylor & Francis Group

NEW YORK   LONDON

First published 2012
by Routledge
711 Third Avenue, New York, NY 10017

Simultaneously published in the UK
by Routledge
2 Park Square, Milton Park, Abingdon, Oxon OX14 4RN

*Routledge is an imprint of the Taylor & Francis Group,
an informa business*

© 2012 Taylor & Francis

The right of Joanna Haynes and Karin Murris to be identified as authors of
this work has been asserted in accordance with sections 77 and 78 of the
Copyright, Designs and Patents Act 1988.

Typeset in Sabon by IBT Global.

Library of Congress Cataloging-in-Publication Data
Haynes, Joanna, 1953–
    Picturebooks, pedagogy, and philosophy / by Joanna Haynes and Karin
Murris.
        p. cm. — (Routledge research in education ; 60)
    Includes bibliographical references and index.
    1. Multicultural education. 2. Creative teaching. 3. Education—
Philosophy—Pictorial works. 4. Critical pedagogy—Pictorial works.
I. Murris, Karin. II. Title.
    LB14.7.H39 2011
    370.11'5—dc22
    2011004383

ISBN13: 978-0-415-88080-0 (hbk)
ISBN13: 978-0-203-80701-9 (ebk)

In loving memory of my mother, Muriel Haynes, 7th October, 1921–12th April, 2008

-Joanna-

For Simon, my life-long friend.

-Karin-

Contents

Figures, Diagrams and Tables

FIGURES

DIAGRAMS

TABLES

Acknowledgements

Many people have influenced the development and writing of this book. In particular, the thousands of teacher educators, teachers, students and learners we have had the privilege to work with for over the past twenty years. We are particularly grateful to postgraduate students at the University of the Witwatersrand Nicolette Anastasopolous, Lauren Rembach and Robyn Thompson for the inclusion of their work with learners in this book. Abigail Bothner, Hans van Heerden, Hope Tarita, Liam and Tim Geschwindt donated their powerful pictures to support the arguments we make and add a wonderful touch to the final product.

Our special thanks to Simon Geschwindt who edited a substantial part of this book and provided critical comments.

As co-authors, we are very fortunate to have both friendship and a creative and critical working partnership together. We have enjoyed happy times writing in different locations, punctuated by dog walks and swimming. We collaborated and contributed equally to the writing of this book. Thanks to the University of Plymouth for financial support to enable Joanna's involvement in this collaboration.

Our heartfelt appreciation goes to our respective families for their encouragement, care and practical support during the preparation of this manuscript. The use of picturebooks in our families has been the key for our passionate commitment to them and it is to our children, parents, partner and husband that this book is dedicated.

We would also like to thank the editors of Childhood and Philosophy for permission to include some material from two papers previously published in the journal.

Our thanks go to the following publishers for their generous free permission to reproduce the following illustrations: Andersen Press for the images from *Not Now Bernard*, copyright © 1980 David McKee, *Frog in Love*, copyright © 1989 Max Velthuijs, *Frog and the Birdsong*, copyright © 1991, *Frog is Frightened*, copyright © 1993 Max Velthuijs, *Michael*, copyright © 1990 Tony Ross and Tony Bradman. Random House Group Ltd. for the images in *Zoo*, copyright © 1993 Anthony Browne and images from *The Big Ugly Monster and the Little Stone*

Rabbit, copyright © 2004 Chris Wormell. Diogenes Verlag AG Zurich for the images on pages 26 and 32 in *Das Biest des Monsieur Racine,* copyright © 2006 Tomi Ungerer, images on page 23 in *Die Drei Räuber,* copyright © 2007 Tomi Ungerer, images on page 21 in *Der Mondmann*, copyright © 1996 Tomi Ungerer. HarperCollins Publishers for the images from *Where The Wild Things Are*, copyright © 1963,1991 Maurice Sendak and illustrations in *Outside Over There*, copyright © 1981 Maurice Sendak.

We are very grateful to the School of Education, University of the Witswatersrand, Johannesburg for their financial assistance with the reproduction of the following images. Thanks to David Higham Assoc. for one image in *The Princess and the Pea*, copyright © 2006 Lauren Child & Polly Borland. Reproduced with permission by Penguin Group (Australia) for the images in *John Brown, Rose and the Midnight Cat,* copyright © 1977 (text) Jenny Wagner, (illustration) Ron Brooks (published in London). Reprinted by permission of Disney•Hyperion, an imprint of Disney Book Group LLC (all rights reserved) one image and one sentence in Sam's Worries © 1990 by Maryann MacDonald, illustrated by Judith Riches.

Introduction
Censorship and Controversy in the Classroom

This book is born out of our deep enthusiasm for picturebooks and our experience of sharing them with children and adults. Earlier in our lives picturebooks were an important feature of Karin's work as a children's librarian and Joanna's work as a primary school teacher. As parents, we have enjoyed many picturebooks with our own children. For the last twenty years or more they have been at the heart of our professional work as philosophers in education, with children and teachers, in particular in the context of developing philosophy with children. We take delight in the philosophical thinking and dialogue that they arouse and we are intrigued by the controversy they cause. This book has grown out of this controversy and the sense of adventure that picturebooks provide.

Through our experience we have become aware that many adults, teachers, and teacher educators are anxious about discussing controversial issues with children and avoid open-ended dialogue about works of children's literature that might touch on taboo subjects. We recognise the climate of fear that is responsible for teachers' uncertainty in the face of controversial issues in classrooms. In this book we offer reasons to challenge censorship and risk avoidance, and we propose that exploring controversial subjects is of critical importance in education. Educators need to respond constructively to controversy to enrich knowledge and understanding through the extension of children's freedom of thought and exploration of ideas. In making our case, we refer to many picturebooks and various examples of dialogues with children. Picturebooks and philosophy with children (P4C) provide a sound framework to support adults' exploration with confidence and courage. P4C is an approach to teaching that encourages questioning, critical thinking, and open dialogue in a classroom 'community of enquiry' that aims to be democratic. We will explain and illustrate this approach to teaching throughout the book. Here we begin by describing experiences of some teachers' censorial responses to certain picturebooks.

TEACHER IN THE HOT SEAT

In our practice as teachers and teacher educators, we have often experienced disquiet or protest from teachers regarding the choice of certain books to begin philosophical enquiry. One London school refused to take part in any further sessions after a child had started crying during a philosophy lesson. The enquiry had opened with a child's question 'What happens when we die?' and the six year old girl who cried had recently lost her uncle. While the children were making their drawings at the end of the session, some of which included coffins with people crying next to them, their teacher left the room and informed the head teacher. She thought it 'inappropriate' for children to make drawings of coffins. When arranging this professional development session, the head teacher had intimated that the school was interested in embarking on 'emotional literacy programmes'. She justified the decision not to continue by saying 'the school isn't ready yet for philosophy'.

This head teacher's statement raises profound questions for us. What's involved in making judgments about what is 'appropriate' such as when and how a topic as significant as death and loss can be discussed? What exactly was meant by the phrase 'ready for philosophy' and who is included in the use of the term 'school'? Discussions of what is and isn't 'appropriate' often allude to 'givens' about children's development and learning, something Fendler has referred to as a discourse of developmentality (in Hultqvist & Dahlberg, 2001)[1]. The head teacher's decision reflects a climate in which children's safety and security are increasingly at the forefront of concern in educational practice. At what point does such protection turn into unwarranted control and regulation? On the one hand there is currently much talk about 'emotional intelligence' while on the other hand there is great confusion about where the exploration of sensitive and controversial matters might belong. As philosophers and educational practitioners, we are deeply interested in the place of emotions (Murris 2009a) and the 'upheavals of thought' that accompany them in the growth of our knowledge and understanding of the world (Nussbaum, after Proust, 2001).

Emotions are often regarded as a hindrance to learning, and it is implied that by understanding and 'managing' our emotions somehow the 'path' can be cleared for untroubled learning. Although there are undoubtedly occasions when emotions can cloud thinking, we have also found that the passion that picturebooks sometimes provoke in classrooms can open up unique possibilities for learning. In P4C, when offered a physical and metaphorical space in which to listen, to speak, or to remain silent, individuals *experience* what happens when they make choices and decisions about an enquiry, however complex or difficult this might be. They are faced with the consequences of participation and the responsibilities, choices, and decisions it throws up. They come to understand talk and participation as action in which they play a meaningful part.

   Philosophical enquiries can be playful, imaginative, fantastic, pertinent to current events, or concerned with the immediate and the everyday. Children's questions are wide-ranging and not necessarily controversial. What is important is that participants choose the questions that matters to them. Philosophy with children is not a detached intellectual exercise, although it certainly strengthens the intellect in all kinds of ways. But it does entail a passionate commitment to rigorous and reflective thinking. Participants experience perplexity, curiosity, and wonder. They experience the pleasure of agreement, as well as the frustration and challenge of disagreement. They meet confusion, struggle and disenchantment, excitement, disappointment, elation, and embarrassment. All these emotions can arise from the complex and unpredictable process of enquiry.

   In our practice the emotional and the cognitive are deliberately taken into account and prepared for. It is this characteristic which often takes teachers by surprise, especially if their initial interest in P4C was to teach 'thinking skills' or the currently popular 'emotional literacy'. In P4C there is a shift in responsibility for the lesson away from the teacher and towards the classroom community. Teachers may experience confusion, surprise, or unease when they realise the democratic nature of the practice in which children help to direct both the content and shape of a lesson.

DEMOCRATIC LABORATORY

In P4C, as we understand and practise it, the teacher needs to trust that when the structure of the classroom dialogue is firmly in place through democratic negotiation children are capable not only of taking responsibility for their own well-being and that of others, but enjoy doing so (Murris, 2008a). Philosophy lessons are structured, but not prescriptive. Detached youthworker Graeme Tiffany (2008:9) states that it is precisely when educational activities are not prescribed that they are attractive to young people, 'not least those who have rejected authoritarianism elsewhere'. Working democratically with young people is essential for initial engagement with the task at hand, especially when educators cannot rely on their authority or positions of power, as is the case in, for example, detached youthwork[2]. Tiffany argues that the pedagogic functions of democracy are often overlooked (2008:9). We believe that such principles should be extended to classrooms.

   In P4C there are strong elements of what Lipman identifies as autonomy and self-government (1991:72). Kennedy draws our attention to the educational and political consequences of attributing the capacity and natural tendency toward 'self-regulation' and 'self-organisation'. He equates this with attributing reason 'in the deepest sense' to children, elevating the status of 'child' to being regarded as a 'valuable stranger' and the 'outsider within' (Kennedy, 2006:148). In education we often bump into a

contradiction—psychological accounts of maturation, emotional development, and the capacity for reason which have tended to dominate views of
childhood versus the establishment of a framework for children's moral,
political, and social status as learners, as persons, and as citizens. We
question and challenge developmentality because it marginalises children
and limits education (Burman, 2008a; Dahlberg & Moss, 2005; Kennedy,
1992, 2006; Kohan, 2002). We are concerned with the ethical and political
dimensions of work with children. For Kennedy the consequence of attributing self-organising capacities to children is that more attention needs to
be paid to:

> the question of children's rights, and the transformation of child 'man-
> agement' methodologies from controlling, intrusive and unilateral to
> dialogical, collaborative and democratic ones (Kennedy, 2006:148).

The provision of a clear and confident framework in which children can
think and talk about problematic issues with support from adults and other
children is vital. In this book we demonstrate that philosophy offers a distinctive way of responding in the face of difficult questions. The community of enquiry pedagogy is not about a return to child-centredness: neither
teacher nor pupil is at the centre. The search for better understanding and
justified beliefs through collaborative reasoning and dialogue are at the centre. We are working for a more democratic pedagogy, where good judgement
and decision-making are a shared, negotiated, collaborative responsibility,
and where children's everyday proposals and actions are taken seriously
by the larger school community. A community of enquiry functions as a
political 'laboratory' (Tiffany, 2008), a place where the strengths and limits of a political system can be experienced first-hand and where reviewing
strategies support a continuous process of constructing and reconstructing
the community of enquiry as a micro-political system. There is no point of
'arrival' at a perfect process. In our classroom practice, and in our theorising, we have to constantly ask ourselves the question: what does it mean to
be democratic when teaching? What is the right thing to do by the children
and by the school community? Splitter and Sharp, who have written extensively on the pedagogy of P4C, prefer not to give a definition of a community of enquiry because it is one of those key concepts that

> takes on new aspects and dimensions as teachers and students apply
> it and modify it to their purposes. A *community of enquiry* is at once
> *immanent and transcendent*: it provides a framework which pervades
> the everyday life of its participants and it serves as an ideal to strive for
> (Splitter & Sharp, 1995:17, 18; our emphasis).

If we are serious about making schools more ethical and more democratic,
we need to re-examine the foundations of the everyday authority we claim

as adults. We need to look afresh at what it means to listen to children—a major focus in Part III of this book. We need to consider the intricate connections between democracy, theory of knowledge, and the assumptions we bring to concepts of 'child' or 'childhood'. Explaining and justifying our choice of picturebooks as starting points for P4C is a central part of this philosophical investigation. Our use of carefully selected picturebooks is primarily a philosophical choice, not a pragmatic one.

In this book we strongly emphasise the 'transformative' potential of the community of enquiry pedagogy. We hope that schools can become more ethical and democratic, and we believe it is within the power of practitioners and communities to make them so. At the same time, many advocates, including ourselves, have often been at pains to point out that P4C is consistent with many of the current policy aims for education, such as raising achievement, teaching thinking, creativity, teaching citizenship, inclusion, and emotional literacy. We adopt a cautious critical stance in relation to such political and social agendas. Justifying the introduction of P4C to classrooms by suggesting it can help to advance other educational goals is often motivated by the need or desire to secure funding to support 'innovations'. We live with such contradictions in our lives, along with the acceptance that we are caught up in the web of educational politics. How else might alternative approaches and ideas be introduced in mainstream education? Such an instrumental approach has been criticised (Vansieleghem, 2005; Long, 2005), but we believe that valuing P4C for its own sake and in instrumental terms are not necessarily mutually exclusive. P4C can be introduced as an essential part of, for example, the literacy curriculum and still retain its critical qualities. In some quarters philosophy with children generates fear. We hope that this book can make a small contribution towards challenging such fearfulness and will be a source of courage as well as a stimulus for wider debate.

BOOKS AS MESSAGE CARRIERS

Many educators are fearful, and some censorial, when it comes to the experiences and questions raised in open-ended dialogue in response to particular books. It is puzzling that some teachers are prepared to have the very same books on classroom shelves as long as they are used individually and are not for whole-class philosophical enquiries. Whilst the 'danger' seems to be located in *how* we use the literature, not necessarily in the content of the books themselves, there are certain themes that have proved to be sensitive. These include strangers, goblins and witches, dying and death, religious faith, race, the body, sex, and love (Haynes, 2007a). By contrast, teachers often suggest that certain books should be used as a vehicle for discussion of personal, emotional, and social issues that they see as pertinent, for example, conflict and bullying, friendship and power. They are used to doing so in the therapeutically orientated 'circle time' sessions popular, for example, in British schools. Those who come to P4C from such a perspective regard it as another teacher-led way of tackling such issues indirectly, while seeming to offer more room for students' views. Seen thus, the teacher's choice of book becomes another way to control the agenda for classroom discussion. We find this deeply worrying in the context of a process that is intended to shift power away from the teacher. As Dahlberg and Moss point out, 'empowerment approaches' that 'give the impression of reducing power . . . makes the workings of power relations more invisible and difficult to resist' (2005:149).

We distance ourselves from the practice of selecting picturebooks for P4C on the basis of any 'messages' they contain. We are always intrigued by what is involved in making sense of a picturebook and the topics for enquiry they generate. How important is the teacher's opinion about what the book is 'really about'? A central plank of P4C is that participants should learn to think for themselves and to determine the territory of dialogue through their questions and through democratic processes in a spirit of open-ended enquiry (Fisher, 1998; Lipman, 1991, 1993b; Murris & Haynes, 2002; Splitter & Sharp, 1995). The facilitator's role is to support and guide discussion, not to manipulate or steer it. This means that the choice of books or other starting points, as well as eliciting questions from children, are in themselves controversial (Haynes, 2007a).

Teachers have suggested that some of the stories we use for building communities of enquiry give the 'wrong message' or, even more significantly, not the 'right message' to children. Some teachers tell us that they want to steer children towards the 'right' moral position on particular issues, such as lying or bullying. They survey books for their potential to influence the agenda for discussion. When children produce questions based on the issues they want to discuss, teachers have told us that they are prepared to 'fix' the outcome of the voting in class to ensure a 'good' question is chosen for the enquiry. Such moves undermine the ethical base of P4C.

THOUGHT-PROVOKING PICTUREBOOKS

Certain books trigger in teachers an anxious and censorial reaction, cloaked as protectiveness, which seems to echo current moral panics regarding childhood. The picturebooks we use reflect a wide range of narratives and may portray events such as a robbery, children being taken from their homes, interaction between children and 'strangers', or characters such as goblins and witches. Some may provoke questions about good and evil, love or sex, or what happens when we die. Some children's stories contradict scientific truths, such as Tomi Ungerer's '*Moon Man*' (1966). A feature of the story is that that the moon itself changes size, rather than simply *appearing* smaller or larger, according to its phases (Figure 0.1).

Figure 0.1 Image from *Moon Man* by Tomi Ungerer.

There are also picturebooks that leave us in total confusion about their meaning (Shaun Tan's and Neil Gaiman's work spring to mind as examples). Certainty and security cannot always be assured. We deliberately avoid books that appear to be simple messengers for morals as these do not tend to generate thinking and discussion. Nor do we deliberately choose a book to provoke controversy or limit ourselves to a particular genre or style, such as, for example, postmodern picturebooks. We work with books of aesthetic quality that we have found to engage readers emotionally and cognitively, and we explore what the picturebooks we care about have in common. Children's literature can offer rich opportunities for deep engagement and philosophical reflection when the pedagogy of a community of enquiry is adopted in class. It is a pedagogy that seems to expose educators' tendency to censor certain picturebooks or to limit discussion of their content. As the author of the *Harry Potter* series, J. K. Rowling, commented[3], the issue is not so much *whether* children should be exposed to scary or upsetting topics, but rather it is the environment and context in which this takes place that determines its appropriateness. In classroom communities of enquiry trust is built up over a long period of time, and the fact that children themselves raise the questions is an indicator that such trust is present. This can neither be forced nor assumed.

FACILITATING PHILOSOPHICAL ENQUIRY

P4C is marked by a distinctive pedagogy. It can be the home of a complex mixture of educational ideas and philosophical traditions. Practitioners are bound to situate the approach in their own cultural context and infuse the practice with their own identity and philosophical beliefs. In a profound sense, what P4C *is* can be experienced only in practice, and it embraces a wide range of practices worldwide. In a Wittgensteinian sense, these approaches are united in the way members of a family share certain resemblances—any generalisations about P4C fail to do justice to what is unique about each family member (Murris, 2008)[4].

Whatever the philosophical, cultural, or educational setting, there is no doubt that P4C makes considerable demands on the teacher and requires special training and skills in philosophising, something covered by neither pre-service teacher training nor academic philosophy (see Murris & Haynes, 2002, 2010). Preparing for philosophy sessions is different from most other lessons because the content cannot be known in advance. An important part of the teacher's preparation is to try and remove any personal attachment to the story and to come to it afresh—as if one is reading it for the very first time. Given teachers' power and authority in the classroom, their disposition is hugely influential on the degree of freedom enjoyed by participants in an enquiry.

A philosophical facilitator creates a space in which there is both the desire and the drive to engage, both intellectually and emotionally. At best, participants lose themselves in pursuit of answering the question they have chosen, generating more questions in the process. The teacher is self-effacing and non-judgemental about the topics chosen. She asks open-ended questions where appropriate, guiding participants in their exploration of unexpected alleyways of thought, following the enquiry wherever it may lead, but without letting the enquiry drift or lose the agreed focus. In communities of enquiry, people generate their own questions from material chosen, at least initially, by the teacher. They are invited to ask whatever questions occur to them and to challenge and interrogate the material. Subsequently, they seek to answer these questions by listening to each others' points of view, thinking out loud, and building on each others' ideas. They are encouraged to clarify concepts, to develop lines of enquiry, and to use examples and counter examples to check the validity of their emerging arguments and perspectives. They are arguing their case, rather than simply airing an opinion or experience.

Participants are respected experts on the experience they bring to the sessions and as active participants in the creation of knowledge. Personal experiences are treated as examples that can help to illuminate the conceptual exploration in the movement back and forth between concrete and abstract forms. When effectively connected to concepts and values being considered in the enquiry, these experiences become sources of understanding. 'Disclosure', as in sharing confidences, is not a goal of philosophical dialogue, nor is it forbidden. But making room for personal knowledge is vital. The distinction here is that it is individual and shared meaning, truth, and significance that are sought in dialogue, rather than reparation, consolation, or healing. However, many participants in philosophical enquiry report that it is the freedom to speak about the issues that concern them and the respect that is shown for their expression of ideas that makes philosophical enquiry so valuable and useful in everyday life and can sometimes lead to a kind of resolution, or translation, of personal situations, either through action or reflection (Haynes, 2007a; 2008).

CONTROVERSIAL SUBJECTS AND THE 'WRONG MESSAGE'

Adverse reactions to certain books when working with children are varied, both in terms of their subject matter and the reasons given for a book being rejected as 'unsuitable'. In the story *Frog in Love* (Velthuijs, 1989) green Frog expresses his love for white Duck (Figure 0.2).

Whilst happy to have the book in the classroom, some teachers have expressed anxiety about how they might answer awkward questions about sex and reproduction, or about race, if the book were used in the open-ended way that we advocate. The anxiety might be about the possibility of discomfort, or expression of offensive or politically incorrect ideas, of losing control because of laughter at body talk, of parental complaints, of spontaneous and open discussion without prior preparation, or the introduction of more closed activities that allow the teacher to maintain control whenever 'sensitive' topics are tackled.

Ever since then, they have loved each other dearly.
A frog and a duck...
Green and white.
Love knows no boundaries.

Figure 0.2   Image from *Frog in Love* by Max Velthuijs.

Velthuijs' book, *Frog and the Birdsong* (1991), has provoked anxiety because the story includes the death of a blackbird and the other characters' reactions to it. The story is particularly valuable because it is humorous and does not focus exclusively on feelings. It encourages us to think about what death is and the different emotions and questions that it arouses. It plants the seeds for thinking about what happens after death. The dialogue provokes readers to explore the concept of death and to question 'truths' we take for granted, such as the belief that everything dies (Figure 0.3).

The moral of the story—that life goes on—is less relevant when children are allowed to construct their own meanings and are allowed the necessary space to speculate. Despite the clear morals of Velthuijs' stories, dialogues between the characters in his books allow divergent points of view.

He knelt beside the bird and said, "He's dead."
"Dead," said Frog. "What's that?"
Hare pointed up at the blue sky.

Figure 0.3   Image from *Frog and the Birdsong* by Max Velthuijs.

When anxiety about giving the single right answer disappears, children often surprise us with the theories they construct in order to make logical sense of a story. For example, children's explanations of how a blackbird can appear singing in a tree *after* it has been found dead and buried reveal fascinating theories about reincarnation. Many four to seven year olds have suggested that the blackbird that appears at the beginning of the story is the same as the one in the final picture of the book (Figure 0.4).

Death is something many teachers are uncertain about discussing in classrooms. They report that this is for fear of upsetting children. It is a subject that opens the chasm of uncertainty and inevitability as well as the diversity and plurality of beliefs that are usually avoided in schools.

Tomi Ungerer's picturebook *The Three Robbers* (1961) has provoked extremely strong reactions from some teachers, including the suggestion that this book should not appear at all in a primary classroom. In the story,

The tired friends set off happily for home.
As they passed the bottom of the hill, they heard a sound.
There in a tree was a blackbird singing a lovely song –
as always.

Figure 0.4   Second image from *Frog and the Birdsong* by Max Velthuijs.

three robbers come across an orphan girl who is on her way to live with
a wicked aunt. Since there is nothing else to steal they take the little girl
(Figure 0.5). Her arrival marks the beginning of their reform from thieves
to providers of an institution for lost, forgotten, and abandoned children,
funded from their robbing days. Teachers have told us that this book gives
the message that it is safe to go off with strangers, and that teachers should
point out that it is not safe to do so. This position expresses both the desire
to protect children and the suggestion that there is a clear and unambiguous way of identifying a dangerous adult. The teacher is supposedly the one
who helps to train the child in personal safety, and this can be reduced to
the simple instruction 'avoid strangers'.

Figure 0.5   Image from *The Three Robbers* by Tomi Ungerer.

Outside Over There (Sendak, 1981) has also caused disturbance among some adults. In this powerful and marvellously illustrated book the girl Ida's father is away at sea, and she is charged with helping to care for her younger sibling. The book hints at its content on the back cover: 'While Ida is busy playing her wonder horn, goblins come and kidnap her baby sister. In order to save her, Ida must go outside over there . . . ' (Figure 0.6).

Figure 0.6   Image from *Outside Over There* by Maurice Sendak.

Both language and imagery have fairy tale qualities and engage many themes such as paternal absence, guilt, darkness, responsibility, resentment, childhood, fear, courage, and adventure. The goblins first appear cloaked and fearsome but turn out to be 'babies just like her sister'. Sendak's inspiration for the book was the well publicised Lindbergh case, in which an American baby was kidnapped for a ransom but was never seen alive again. This real life event severely shook the young author's trust in happy endings. Significantly, he himself had been looked after many times by his older sister. The book is dark in places, is vividly imaginative, and provokes a sense of the uncanny, but the resolution of the story comes across as entirely happy for all concerned. 'Outside over there' is where Ida has to go in the story if she is to 'save' her baby sister. Wherever 'outside over there' is, it is certainly beyond the reach and supervision of adults, a critical feature that makes the narrative not only possible, but compelling.

This story has been found unsuitable on the grounds that it may frighten some children, particularly because of the inclusion of characters such as goblins. Elsewhere teachers have wanted to ban books that feature witches. Sometimes teachers report that they have had to remove such books under pressure from some parents who have insisted that they do not want their children to have access to such material. Another picture-book by the same author[5], *Where the Wild Things Are*, has also caused a similar disturbance.

Given the fears expressed, it is important to understand the sources of such anxieties and to develop a situated sense of adults' responsibilities in respect of children's access to literature and to opportunities to discuss the books and the complex questions they raise. Rather than going along with censorship of certain books or the discussion of certain topics, we argue that this should be resisted, and we explore the reasons behind these anxieties. As we conclude in Chapters 4 and 5, emotions are good indicators of implicit moral values. An awareness of and sensitivity to emotions generated in and through philosophical enquiry provide valuable insight into the philosophical and political dimensions of this practice.

Even if it were desirable, a sanitised curriculum is not realistic and can widen the gap between what happens inside and outside school. After all, children discuss these issues anyway because they want to know. But without structure or tactful facilitation, arguably this could cause *more* distress and harm and is a wasted opportunity to develop better judgements. Apart from this *pragmatic* argument, a *legal* argument can be put forward against censorship. The Convention on the Rights of the Child (1989), to which many countries are signatories, makes explicit reference to people's rights to information, freedom of thought, and conscience and religion, and this includes children. Participation Rights make provisions for children to take an active part in their communities. These include having a say and the freedom to express views, join groups, and assemble. The rights argument has its limitations, and some prefer the idea of adults taking proper responsibility to ensure children's participation to the idea of rights for children (Archard, 2004; Haynes, 2008). Either way, it is up to adults to create opportunities to listen to children and to support their exploration of difficult issues in educational settings. Whilst we recognise this as a process requiring considerable skill and sensitivity, we argue that it is one we have to be willing to embrace for many reasons. These reasons are explored in the chapters that follow, along with examples taken from our extensive experience of P4C with children and teachers.

This book offers a particular take on the urgent moral and political debate regarding children's freedom of expression, from perspectives other than the legal and pragmatic arguments above. Other arguments against censorship can be put forward (see Diagram 0.1). The ideas behind these arguments are complex and warrant careful unfolding—the reason why they have found a home in several different parts of the book.

We hope that this book will persuade readers of the importance of extending freedom of thought and exploration to children in classrooms and that it will provide a strong sense of the teaching approach that can give confidence to both participants and teachers alike in the face of controversial questions and issues. The book is divided into three parts. In Part I we explore picturebooks at length, making connections with a range of academic literature, drawing on many specific examples, and discussing the work of those authors whose pieces seem to be found particularly provocative or troublesome. The stories we choose as stimuli for enquiry are deliberately thought-provoking and ambiguous. A list of picturebooks that we have used for philosophical enquiry and feature in this book can be found in Appendix A.

In Chapter 3 we explain how our approach builds on, but also differs from, Matthew Lipman's P4C programme—internationally the most popular educational resource for the teaching of philosophy to children. We explain the significance of the adoption of picturebooks as starting points pioneered by one of us (Murris, 1992, 1997) and further developed through our shared teaching, our many conversations, and collaborative writing (see especially Murris & Haynes, 2002, 2010). We offer a philosophical perspective on children's literature, one that strengthens and complements the pedagogy and expresses our political and moral choices and our regard for children as philosophers.

Part II considers ideas of child and childhood, particularly from philosophical perspectives. We investigate the problems of responding authentically to children's claims to knowledge, particularly when ideas are expressed through playful and imaginative dialogues in the context of a flexible and creative philosophical space. This includes a look at ways in which children's engagement with philosophy challenges our understanding of what philosophy is. Part III of the book returns to the ethical and political dimensions of philosophical enquiry with children using picturebooks and explores the contribution that philosophical listening might make to educational practices that allow for more participation by the children (Haynes, 2007a; 2008).

The images in this book serve as carriers of abstract meaning and insight as well as contributing to the aesthetic delight and pleasure we hope the reader will experience. Our philosophical work with picturebooks is impossible to classify. It is neither literacy nor literary criticism; neither traditional philosophy nor art. It is also philosophically a radical departure from the P4C tradition that was its inspiration and starting point. We offer something new that we hope will contribute to these fields, but the main aim of this book is to support educators who have the courage to create a democratic space in which children are free to play with the ideas provoked by contemporary picturebooks, whatever the topic.

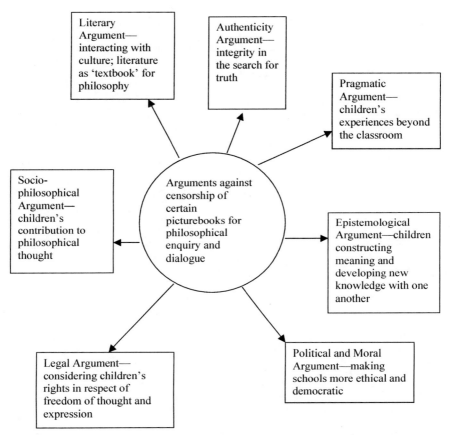

Diagram 0.1 Arguments against avoidance and censorship in dialogues around picturebooks.

Part I
Provocative Picturebooks

1 Playing with Dangerous Picturebooks

QUIET REVOLUTION

In this chapter we explore the characteristics of picturebooks we have found suitable for our philosophical work with children and adults. They open up a space between the 'real' world and other possible worlds and encourage a free exploration of philosophical ideas. Sometimes postmodern devices have been used that disturb readers' expectations. The books we use are often playful, lack seriousness, and contain humour. We argue that the ones most suited for philosophical enquiry are those that hold up a 'mirror' for the adult and encourage a self-critical stance. Teachers, whose usual role is to articulate certainty, sometimes struggle more with the indeterminacy of contemporary books than young people who have been born into a postmodern culture full of fragmented and indeterminate ironic images and ideas. So arguably the use of such resources for education puts children on a more equal footing with adults and appeals to children's sense of fun and willingness to play with philosophical ideas. It is not surprising therefore that the books we work with can provoke censorial reactions as adults are more likely to resist and censor books when their own habits, attitudes, and mores are under the spotlight. Enjoying books that are critical of other people or groups is easier, less painful, and without consequences.

In common with all literature, children's literature has always been highly controversial because of its potential to influence, to indoctrinate, or to subvert (see, for example, Hunt, Stephens, Tucker). Since the dawning of children's literature as a distinctive genre at the end of the seventeenth century, much of what falls under this heading has been concerned with inculcating family values (Cunningham, 2006; Townsend, 1996). Books were seen as instruments to instruct children—corrupted by original sin—to obey their elders and to help save their souls. However, in children's books blind obedience to authority slowly made way for the belief that consent should be based on good reasoning. This gradual departure from religious fundamentalism was influenced by British philosopher John Locke. His striking metaphor of the mind as a 'blank slate' (*tabula rasa*) continues to influence thinking about learning and teaching (for example, through reference to literacy lessons being 'delivered' to learners, a phrase that conjures up images of children as 'containers'). The metaphor of the blank slate, or translated in modern terms as 'blank page', expresses the idea that children are not 'condemned at birth' but can learn through experiences that are 'written' on this 'page' (the mind). John Townsend sums up how children's literature historically has expressed the changing relationships between young and old:

> Children had been presented in the seventeenth century as creatures of unearthly piety or as limbs of Satan, in the early eighteenth century as blank pages to be written on, and by Rousseauites as either wise children or foolish children. In books they were either good or bad examples to others. One would have to look rather hard to find between covers a child who could be described by such adjectives as frolicsome and mischievous (Townsend, 1996:81).

Whilst young people have increasingly taken centre stage in children's literature, parents still firmly rule, and, on the whole, the young continue to adjust to the authority of the adults[1]. Hierarchical relationships between adult and child remain the norm in literature, even in picturebooks that often provoke censorial reactions, such as Maurice Sendak's *Where the Wild Things Are*. Published in 1963, the boy's wild behaviour in the story incites his Mum to give him a 'time out' by sending him to his bedroom without supper. The subsequent solitary confinement allows him to deal with his emotions on his own terms. Although equilibrium appears restored at the end, the relationship subtly reinforces the balance of power and does not question the possible right and wrongs of the boy's punishment[2].

It is not until after the 1960s that a rapid loss of confidence in adults' wisdom and competence surfaces in children's narratives. Nowadays in literature, the young not only increasingly reject established adult values and mores, but are expected to 'face in fiction the harsh realities of life' (Townsend, 1996:85). As the title suggests, *The Day I Swapped My Dad for Two Goldfish* (1998) is a good example of a playful power shift between child and parent, and even more so in a picturebook by the same artists—Neil Gaiman and Dave McKean—called *The Wolves in the Walls* (2003) in which a young girl courageously takes the lead in rescuing her family home from the wolves. These books provoke censorial reactions, often justified by reference to the sinister and scary illustrations. We wonder to what extent the role young people play in both narratives influences these reactions. The children are central figures, making important decisions and wise judgements. The adults in these stories are not caricatures; they are easily recognisable and made to look ridiculous. Perhaps these aspects are perceived as threatening or uncomfortable for some adults[3]?

Awareness is growing that what Arizpe and Styles call a 'quiet revolution' has indeed taken place in the world of children's literature (Arizpe & Styles, 2003:22). Originally constructed for the early reader, images in picturebooks merely illustrated 'the early literary diet of sentimental animals or the neatly categorised, statistically and socially correct family unit' (Mawdsley, 1990:9). There are now an increasing number of picturebooks that offer complex frameworks demanding sophisticated interpretations through life experiences. However, this 'revolution' seems to have been so quiet that many educators are not aware of the wide potential of selected picturebooks as hugely enjoyable reading matter for *all* ages and also, more seriously, as aesthetic objects for philosophical exploration. We have found that adolescents, who might be expected to associate such books with teaching reading to the very young, respond enthusiastically to the visual and ambiguous nature[4] of these materials. Motivation is essential for critical engagement. We have had many philosophical enquiries with young people who were absolutely spellbound when they worked together to make sense of ideas arising from books such as Colin Thompson's *How to Live Forever* (1995) or Shaun Tan's *The Rabbits* (1998). The quality of the verbal and the visual, and the interaction between the two, compel the reader to explore the complex relationship of the whole work, to look at the detail, to think about the whole work again, while spiralling[5] into an extended process of deepening understanding.

Nikolajeva and Scott argue that:

> adults have lost the ability to read picturebooks in this way, because they ignore the whole and regard the illustrations as merely decorative. This most probably has to do with the dominant position of verbal, especially written, communication in our society, although this is on the wane in generations raised on television and now computers (Quoted in Arizpe & Styles, 2003:21).

In selecting our material, we do not avoid books that refer to painful, difficult, uncertain, surprising, or disturbing aspects of human experience or that may provoke enquiry about controversial social issues. The choice of books is important because both text and images either extend or limit the potential scope for enquiry. If we are overly cautious in our choice, we could inadvertently limit the opportunities for thinking. Through our approach to teaching we seek to build confidence in the process of enquiry and dialogue as a means to freely explore and illuminate a wide range of issues and questions.

DANGEROUS PICTUREBOOKS

Censorship in the classroom is not limited to book selection or decisions about their educational use. It also extends to decisions about their suitability for publication on economic or moral grounds. For publishers the moral and educational suitability of a book is high on their list of priorities as children's books are seldom bought on their artistic merits alone. Concern about moral suitability often overrides aesthetic value, and as a result some works of art never get published. Even when publishers are committed to publish picturebooks of high aesthetic quality, the real obstacle is to convince parents, librarians, teachers, and booksellers who ultimately decide which books children are allowed to read or explore.

Nowadays, parents are under enormous pressure to be actively involved with and partly made responsible for their children's acquisition of literacy. The children themselves are hardly ever included in these decision-making processes. They have little influence in the books they read. Nine year olds, who are often seen by parents to be old enough to choose their own clothes or toys, are not trusted to select the 'right' books. Even when choosing a book to take on holiday, children's pleasure or delight is often at the bottom of the parents' list of priorities, despite the fact that most adults themselves have access to a wide variety of books ranging from magazines and newspapers to 'lightweight' books and 'serious' novels.

The pre- and postpublication censorship of books may express a well-meant concern for children's welfare, but literary critic Peter Hunt warns that reading and interpreting children's books is far from simple, and that the 'reader' of children's literature is a much more immanent character than with other kinds of literature (Hunt, 1999:4,7). Hunt identifies in adults' concern the Romantic belief that children are 'impressionable and simple-minded, unable to take a balanced view of, for example, sexual or racial issues, unless the balance is explicitly stated' (Hunt, 1999:7). Our dialogues in classrooms contradict such beliefs about children's responses to literature. We continue to be struck[6] by the complexity and variety with which individual children make meaning of picturebooks.

Part of the planning for philosophy lessons includes the flexible use of the book an educator has carefully chosen and prepared for. Crucially, this 'letting go' or willingness to share the 'reins' is part of the preparation for the work. Responding to the needs or interests of the learners may result in 'unrelated' enquiries or going off 'on a tangent' as both children and adults sometimes describe it—challenging the idea of fixed learning outcomes and teaching objectives, and opening up possibilities to listen to what children believe and know. The forward movement of a philosophical dialogue leads to unexpected domains for further exploration even when books are used that appear to have a very clear message, such as 'be tolerant of differences', 'share possessions', or 'create a peaceful world'. Philosophy can be very frustrating for everyone in class when adults use philosophy with children (P4C) as an instrument to push, for example, the current global citizenship agenda, and the participants are puzzled about issues other than those the teacher had planned and anticipated.

THINKING BEFORE SWALLOWING

Adults have less control over the content of a lesson when picturebooks are used philosophically and meanings need to be negotiated with everyone in the room. With certain stories, adults are so fearful of children going off 'on a tangent' or touching on certain topics that they fiercely protect the children and censor their reactions. The picturebook authors mentioned in the Introduction of this book share certain characteristics and intentions as writers, and perhaps this offers clues as to why they appear to some as unsuitable. Velthuijs, Sendak, and Ungerer—born within eight years of each other between 1923 and 1931—all share a willingness to tackle challenging and complex subject matter with boldness, wit, and compassion. All three have earned wide international acclaim and won prizes for their contributions to children's literature and illustrations.

Sendak, who spent most of his life in North America, says that many of his stories are based on Jewish tales and his characters on family members. He has reported that what interests him is what children do when there are no rules, there are no laws, and they don't know what is expected of them emotionally. As a result of his frail constitution, he was terrified of death as a child and often speaks of 'the boredom and loneliness of children' (Sendak quoted in Lanes, 1980:16). He argues that those adults who claim to know what scares children do not know it at all. He despises schools and regards formal education as 'the sworn enemy of the imagination'. Schooling was the only part of his childhood, he says, 'that was truly punishing and suffering' (Sendak quoted in Lanes, 1980:22).

Ungerer, raised in Alsace, lost his father at the age of three. He lived with his mother in Strasbourg during the Nazi occupation. His mother tongue—French—was banned in school, and his independence of mind and spirit appear to date from this period of his life. He describes himself as '*a ferocious moralist and moulder of children's minds*' (Vincent, 1999). The moral 'messages' in his work, however, are not condescending towards children. Some of his picturebooks are poignant political satires that make us laugh with children about adults' behaviour. In both *Moon Man* (1966) and *The Beast of Monsieur Racine* (1971), for example, the children are the heroes and expose the behaviour of some adults as intolerant, greedy, irrational, pompous, violent, sexually abusive, selfish, and self-important. The reader is not spared the more basic facts of life. In *The Beast of Monsieur Racine* blood features in almost every page, once dripping from a mincemeat maker and later dripping from a cut off foot and a pierced skull. The bottles and glasses of 'wine' in the pictures may even contain blood too. The colour red is significant throughout Ungerer's work and is often questioned by the children we work with[7] (for example, the children in *The Three Robbers* (1961) are all dressed in red). *The Beast of Monsieur Racine* (Figure 1.0) is dedicated not only to Sendak, but there is also pictorial evidence that Ungerer appreciated his work. On the left hand side, in a crowd, almost hidden from view, an obscure character reads a newspaper with the following

Figure 1.0 Image from *The Beast of Monsieur Racine* by Tomi Ungerer.

headings: 'SENDAK A PARIS' (front page) and 'SCANDAL DU JOUR' (back page). The two may well be connected and hint at the controversial nature of Sendak's work.

Max Velthuijs was familiar with the art of Sendak and Ungerer (see Chapter 7). The moon is a significant feature in the work of all three authors. Velthuijs was born in The Hague, and his parents, both trained teachers, were interested in theosophy, mysticism, and psychoanalysis. Like Sendak, he hated school. He often felt embarrassed about his independent mother, whose eccentric behaviour included dressing up as a man and smoking cigars in public places. She cared little about what other people thought of her (Linders, 2003:16). One day after returning home from school, Velthuijs found that his mother (who was a fanatic collector of antiques) had sold all the family's furniture (Linders, 2003:16, 17). His Dad's solid wooden chair was the only exception, and it is this chair that features regularly in his stories. In a household of constant change, with a mother whose erratic behaviour was both exciting and threatening, this chair became a symbol of permanence, safety, reliability, but also of artistic freedom. In this chair, Velthuijs made his first flip-books[8]. Much later he became a graphic designer and created political prints, cartoons, posters, and book jackets. His breakthrough as a picturebook artist came late in life with the gradual emergence of his Frog character (Linders, 2003:152). His stories feature the same group of animals, and this continuity adds depth and development to the characters and their relationships. They are drawn simply but are capable of expressing subtle thoughts and emotions. The animal characters are the same size, making it possible for them to all sit around the same dining table—a natural forum for equal discussion (Carey, 2004). In *Frog Is Frightened*, the setting resembles famous paintings of 'The Last Supper' (Figure 1.1).

Figure 1.1   Image from *Frog Is Frightened* by Max Velthuijs.

Velthuijs' images reflect his modest lifestyle. His art is simple and childlike (not simplistic or childish) with a timeless quality inviting contemplation and philosophical questioning. His poetic dialogues do not shy away from controversial topics. They are what biographer Joke Linders calls 'philosophical reflections', 'lessons in life', or 'food for thought' (Linders, 2003:170; our translation). The work of Ungerer, Sendak, and Velthuijs and the comments and reviews of their biographers all suggest that they share a strong sense of responsibility and a desire to engage young readers with emotional and moral concerns. The power of all three authors is that they are a reminder of the difficulties of human existence, and, to some extent, they withhold decisive moral judgement. It is the quality of their artwork that invites us to think deeply about the links between our emotions and our moral standpoint, and they achieve this without preaching, moralising, or putting across a particular 'message' to be swallowed by children unthinkingly.

WHERE THE WILD THINGS ARE

Educationalist and specialist in picturebooks David Lewis refers to Maurice Sendak as a 'ground-breaking practitioner', and many literary critics regard *Where the Wild Things Are* (1963) as the first contemporary picturebook. It is interesting that Sendak himself regards Randolph Caldecott (1846–1886) as the inventor of the picturebook with his innovative juxtaposition of pictures and words: a delicate balancing act between leaving words out and letting the pictures do the work or leaving the pictures out and letting the words do the work (Lanes, 1980:110). Contemporary picturebooks are more than stories with illustrations; they are books in which the text and the pictures form an equal and totally *interdependent* partnership. The pictures fill in what the words leave unsaid, and the words, in turn, are indispensable in moving the narrative forward (Lanes, 1980:85). Adults working with children often report that children find the pictures more interesting than the words and that the words without the pictures would be 'boring' (Arizpe & Styles, 2003:109).

In *Where the Wild Things Are*, the main character, Max, dressed in wolf's clothing, hammers a nail into the wall, chases his dog with a fork, and threatens to eat his Mum up. It is left up to the reader to decide how serious or playful Max is. After Mum has sent him to bed without food as a punishment, a forest starts to grow in his bedroom (see Figure 1.2), and he travels to an island where he meets the Wild Things who make him their king.

After a Wild Rumpus, he tames the monsters by staring into their yellow eyes without blinking once. It is not clear whether he is dreaming or not.

Figure 1.2   Image from *Where the Wild Things Are* by Maurice Sendak.

Acting out a parental role, Max subsequently sends the monsters to bed without their supper. When Max is fed up with being king, he decides to return to the place where someone loves him best of all. But the monsters do not want him to leave and in turn threaten to eat him up because they love him so. Nevertheless he sails away in his private boat, and on arrival (when woken up?) his supper is waiting for him and is still hot (see Figure 1.3).

Lewis acknowledges the difference the interdependence of words and pictures makes in this book:

> the first adult readers of Maurice Sendak's Where the Wild Things Are were surprised not only by its apparently dangerous theme, but also by its formal inventiveness—the pictures that change size, page by page, and the boldly worldly rumpus at the heart of the book (Lewis, 2001:93).

Where the Wild Things Are pioneered a unique relationship between illustration and text. Sendak explains that for him illustrating means:

Figure 1.3   Second image from *Where the Wild Things Are* by Maurice Sendak.

having a passionate affair with the words. I hate to say that it's akin
to a mystic rite, but there is no other language to describe what happens. It is a sensual, deeply important experience. An illustration is
an enlargement, an interpretation of the text, so that the child will
comprehend the words better. . . . You must never illustrate exactly
what is written. You must find a space in the text so that pictures
can do the work. Then you must let the words take over where words
do it best. It's a funny kind of juggling act, which takes a lot of technique and experience to keep the rhythm going (Sendak quoted in
Lanes, 1980:109,110).

It is often the children who pick up cues from the pictures when constructing meaning out of picturebook narratives. For example, the picture of a
monster on the wall at the start of *Where the Wild Things Are* was believed
by a community of young enquirers to evidence their dream hypothesis. Max, the main character in the story, must have been dreaming as
'you dream about the things you have done during the day'. Max—the

*max*imum boy (Adams & Rabkin, 2006)—must have drawn the monster during the day and then dreamt about travelling to the island where the wild monsters live. Struggling with the same question, a group of teachers disagreed about how this picture helped to understand the story. A causal connection between the picture and the dream suggested a lack of control. As the enquiry continued they discovered that some people in the group could wake themselves up when their dreams get too scary. The facilitator's question *How much in control are we of our dreams?* assisted this group in clarifying the philosophical dimension of their disagreement and moved the enquiry onto the broader theme of 'free will' and how one can decide whether or not one is free to dream one's dreams.

The unique direction given to the investigation by its participants and the facilitator's interventions is typical of philosophical enquiries. No enquiry is ever similar to previous ones, even when the same book is used. Often, factual anomalies open up playful discourses. In *Where the Wild Things Are*, Max travels 'through night and day, and in and out of weeks, and almost over a year, to where the Wild Things are', and when his Mum put his dinner on the table 'it is still hot'. This certainly does not seem possible on a linear timeline. In an attempt to solve this logical problem, a profound philosophical dialogue emerged with a whole mixed-ability class of nine year olds:

Phillip:	You know that place [in the book] when he said that he smelled food from far across above, well, remember you said that he could travel around in a circle and came to the same place, but he couldn't have, because if it was from across the world there would be only a few miles when you come back to the same place.
George:	No, because you could circle round the world and come back to the same place.
Phillip:	If he had come round there to where the Wild Things are he would be near the same place so he wouldn't necessarily smell it from far away across the world.
Kieron:	If he had travelled a year, and a few weeks and a day, he would have gone all round the world.

[A conversation starts about journeys and beginnings.]

Teacher:	Do you think everything has got a beginning?
Christopher:	Yeah, it's like a story. A story needs an end and a beginning.
Russell:	It's like once upon a time there was a little boy and The End. You have to say what he did or . . . like he got eaten up in the middle bit.

> Gemma 2: You have to have a beginning, because otherwise
> things will go on forever and ever all the time and you
> wouldn't be able to see an end or anything, so everything
> must have a beginning and an end. The whole world
> wouldn't be here, if there wasn't a bit of a start, because
> if there wasn't a start, then nobody could have made a
> start, and that means nobody would have made it, and
> that means if nobody had made it, it wouldn't be there.
> (Murris, 1992)

For Gemma, there is more involved than just linguistic convention. She
means a beginning or ending in *time*, not *space*. If no one had started
the world, then it would not have been there. It is *there*, therefore there
must have been a beginning, and some adult philosophers and theologians have indeed argued that God was the cause and that therefore
God exists. This, known as the Cosmological Argument in philosophy
literature, raises further questions such as: 'If the universe is all there is,
can we experience what produced the universe?', and 'If God caused the
universe, who made God?'. The dialogue continued as follows:

> Gemma 1: Well, if there wasn't any starts, if no one invented starts or
> . . . then they would finish all the time. Everything would be
> a finish at the start.
> Teacher: Do you think the world, the universe, had a beginning?
> Kieron: Space goes on forever.
> Phillip: No, say somebody made the universe, the place where they
> made it . . . let's say you make the universe on that table, if
> you are making the universe from outside, there has got to
> be something outside, and then whoever built that outside
> would have to be outside something, and that would just go
> on forever and ever.

Phillip argues that the creation of the universe out of nothing is *logically
impossible*, that is, if you create the universe you have to be outside the
universe, and for creating the outside of the universe you have to be outside
the outside . . . *ad infinitum*.

> Teacher: Do we all understand this thought?
> Some: Yes.
> George: Say he was making the universe out of plasticine, someone
> would still have to make what *He* was in, and someone has
> to make what that was in, and it would go on forever.
> Teacher: Do we all agree with that?
> Russell: No, because the person who first started off might have
> fallen through the space . . . there is nothing there like a

blank piece of paper . . . and he had special powers and he quickly landed and started building round him and . . . .

Kelly: I disagree. I agree with Phillip, because you have to be in something to make something else, like otherwise if I wasn't here I wouldn't be able to make anything, because I would have no tools or anything, so. . . .

We have used *Where the Wild Things Are* for philosophical enquiries with all age groups. A very different aspect of the book puzzled a group of teachers. What is this place, this island where the Wild Things are? One teacher suggested it is the place where '*tax inspectors reside*'. Who *is* in control? Is it possible that love restricts our freedom because '*ultimately we always want to go to the people who love us best of all?*' or is it, as someone else proposed, that '*physical desires make us weak and give in*'? In its appeal to our basic fears and other emotions, the picturebook also provokes strong responses in adults. During one of our first workshops with a group of post-graduate students, a reception teacher opted out of the enquiry because, as she exclaimed, '*I hate the book and would never use it in class*'. Despite her efforts, she could not really explain the reasons for her antipathy. After observing the enquiry that followed, she volunteered that it had made her realise that the book instilled fears about what she termed '*the monsters residing in her self*'.

After its publication in 1963 in the United States, *Where the Wild Things Are* aroused great controversy. The 'rumpus'[9] only subsided when 'children themselves got hold of it and laughed with delight at the Wild Things' (Clark, 1993:67). Concern from librarians and parents alerted Sendak to the fact that he had created a controversial work, described by biographer Selma Lanes as follows:

> Long recognized as a highly talented and serious artist, he had now provided children with an unquestionable beautiful but—well—scary picture book. Max gets truly angry with his mother and escapes into a dream/fantasy containing possibly terrifying Wild Things. Many parents, educators, and librarians were confounded, and several self-styled guardians of childhood innocence began asking questions: Would the book upset small children? Would Max's bad behavior invite young listener-viewers to emulate him? Would the Wild Things induce nightmares in children or be psychologically harmful in other ways? (Lanes, 1980:104).

Child psychologist Bruno Bettelheim expressed his concern when he heard about the story's plot. Although he had not read the book himself, he condemned its content as follows:

The basic anxiety of the child is desertion. To be sent to bed alone is one desertion, and without food is the second desertion. The combination is the worst desertion that can threaten a child (Bettelheim quoted in Lanes, 1980:104).

Even Sendak's editor had initial reservations when seeing the pictures but then wrote to him:

It is always the adult we have to contend with—most children under the age of ten will react creatively to the best work of a truly creative person. But too often adults sift their reactions to creative picture books through their own adult experiences. And, as an editor who stands between the creative artist and the creative child, I am constantly terrified that I will react as a dull adult. But at least I try to remember this every minute (Nordstrom quoted in Lanes, 1980:106).

The editor's concern about responding to a work of art like a 'dull adult' is significant for our enquiry into censorship in education. Sendak himself insists that children should be allowed to choose their own books, as he believes that young people are resilient enough to put it aside if they find it too disturbing. He treasures a letter he received from an eight year old boy who wondered how much it costs to get to where the Wild Things are. If not too expensive, he and his sister would like to spend the summer there. Sendak observes that adults treat children in 'a very peculiar way' and insists that adults should treat children as 'the strong creatures they really are' and that what they yearn for most is 'a bit of truth somewhere' (Sendak quoted in Lanes, 1980:106, 107, 125).

In this book we will continue to explore what it is about 'troublesome' picturebooks such as *Where the Wild Things Are* that provokes such strong emotions and profound thoughts. Despite adult reservations about its suitability for child readers, millions of copies of the book have been sold, and Sendak continued to inspire many picturebook artists[10]. For example, a quarter of a century later, Anthony Browne in the picturebook *The Tunnel* (1997) uses Sendak-type palm trees in the forest in which the Big Bad Wolf and Little Red Riding Hood meet. The picture decorates the wall of Rose's bedroom—a girl who likes to read fairytales and whose fears are exploited by her older brother Jack. *The Tunnel* is a complex story full of symbolism and intertextual references[11], and the picture may well point at the wild and mischievous adventure the siblings will be embarking on when Rose has to journey through a damp and dark and slimy tunnel to save Jack (see Abigail Bothner's powerful depiction of the moment when Rose finally finds Jack who has turned into stone in Figure 1.4).

Browne's appreciation for Sendak is also apparent in his collaborative picturebook *The Night Shimmy* (Strauss & Browne, 1991), in which the main character—an elective mute—chooses the 'best stories' as bedtime

Figure 1.4 Drawing inspired by *The Tunnel* (Anthony Browne) made by Abigail Bothner (aged 8).

reading. The picture shows him holding Sendak's *In the Night Kitchen* (1970). A newly forged power relationship between adult and child is characteristic of contemporary picturebooks, with children's increasing independence from adult control.

SELF-CRITICAL AND PLAYFUL

The ideological positions, implicit in most literature for children, reflect Western values of children growing up as reasonable, autonomous, creative, and achieving human beings. But these often conflict with other ideals such as social cooperation, requiring children to obey (sometimes unreasonable) rules and accept subordinate roles in decision-making processes and conversational exchanges (Stephens, 1992:120). A break with this tradition started roughly speaking around 1960, with the emergence of 'carnivalesque texts' (Stephens, 1992:120). Carnaval is a short period of grotesque festivities and excesses preceding Lent and sanctioned by the authorities. It was Russian theorist and critic Mikhail Bakhtin who introduced the idea as a narrative device (Nikolajeva, 2009:10). Carnavalesque texts depict reality in a distorting mirror—a brief deviation from the existing order as well as freedom from the restrictions of society (Nikolajeva, 2009:10). John Stephens observes that such books feature 'child characters which interrogate the normal subject positions created for children within socially dominant ideological frames' (Stephens, 1992:120). They are grounded in playful opposition to authority, seriousness, and conformity. He explains that they 'mock and challenge authoritative figures and structures of the adult world—parents, teachers, political and religious institutions—and some of the (often traditionally male) values of society such as independence, individuality, and the activities of striving, aggression and conquest' (Stephens, 1992:122). Rules are broken or abandoned, but only temporarily.

Since then, it is also no longer the case that narrative structures require clear beginnings, middles, and reassuringly happy endings. A good example of a pop-up book that offers a glimpse of the possibility of a most gruesome ending to a picturebook is Sendak's *Mummy?* (2006). A baby—a tiny version of Max—crawls through the cellar of a cemetery in search for his Mummy. He passes various well-known monsters, such as Frankenstein, Dracula, and the Wild Things, but he moves on when it is obvious to him that they are not his Mum. Finally, he meets a woman monster who meets his tentative question '*Mummy?*' with a '*Baby!*' The laboratory and scientific equipment behind her may suggest that his end is near. Especially Sendak's later work breaks with a tradition that presupposes that books for children should have happy, reassuring endings, as for example in the Grimm fairytale *Dear Mily* (1988).

Many of the picturebooks we work with break conventional rules, such as providing happy endings or staying 'within' a story (see, for example, David Wiesner's *The Three Pigs*, 2001). They play with what is real, disturb readers' expectations, and can be 'unsettling, sometimes very funny and occasionally completely bewildering' (Lewis, 2001:93). However, the indeterminacy and uncertainty of these postmodern devices often clash with the instrumental nature of school pedagogy and the teaching of literacy in particular, which often focuses on teaching children what the author or illustrator intends or means. Children these days have been born into a postmodern culture full of fragmented and indeterminate ironic images and ideas. Using contemporary picturebooks 'levels the playing field' somewhat and appeals to children's sense of fun and willingness to play with philosophical ideas.

The choice of characters in such stories problematises social assumptions by blurring the borders between the serious and comic, the reality and fiction, creating in effect 'anti-heroes'. Sendak's *Max*, Ungerer's *Three Robbers*, and Velthuijs' *Frog* are all characters who forge new understandings and seem to break with stereotypes and social conventions. Teachers working philosophically with these narratives are challenged to question their most basic and precious habits of thought. They provoke them to consider whether robbers can be good people (*The Three Robbers*), whether a child's 'wild' behaviour can be caused by adult's interventions and inventions (*Where the Wild Things Are*), or whether an act of bravery can be foolhardy (*Frog Is a Hero*). It is not surprising that picturebooks featuring such characters provoke censorial reactions from adults with responsibilities for modelling socially acceptable behaviour.

By contrast, when such characters are regarded as useful *instruments* to start discussions about anti-social behaviour such as bullying, stereotyping, or intolerance (with the main purpose of changing such behaviour), such texts are often welcomed by adults. A good example of this is the character 'Willy' in Anthony Browne's *Willy and Hugh* (1991) and *Willy the Wimp* (1985), which may explain why they are popular resources for many teachers.

On the other hand, picturebooks that provide no easy answers to what counts as social or anti-social behaviour and that blur their boundaries can cause discomfort and disturbance with adults whose disciplinary role is to articulate certainty in this respect. It is easier to enjoy books that are critical of *other* adults than when texts require open-minded *self*-reflection and *self*-correction. When a narrative holds up a mirror for *any* adult reader—as the behaviour of Max's mother does in *Where the Wild Things Are*—censorial reactions are more likely. For instance, there will be very few parents who have never sent their children to their bedrooms as punishment.

HUNGRY BODIES (FOR LOVE)

Another characteristic of carnivalesque texts is the space given to the human body: food and drink, sexuality, and excretory functions (Stephens, 1992:122). We have noticed that the body is strongly present in the work of Ungerer, Velthuijs, and Sendak. This often evokes discussions about love, desire, and troubled consumption or abstinence among groups of teachers with whom we have worked. In Sendak's work, the interplay between food and love, animalistic desires, and human needs is unusually strong. His best childhood memories revolve around food and eating (Lanes, 1980:20). Food also inspired the shaping of his Wild Things. Determined to draw 'things', and because he couldn't draw wild horses, he explains that it was his visits to a Jewish family that became his inspiration for the Wild Things (see Figure 1.5):

> It was probably at this point that I remembered how I detested my Brooklyn relatives as a small child. They came almost every Sunday, and there was my week-long anxiety about their coming the next Sunday. My mother always cooked for them, and, as I saw it, they were eating up all our food. We had to wear good clothes for these aunts, uncles, and assorted cousins, and ugly plastics covers were put over the furniture. About the relatives, themselves, I remember how inept they were at making small talk with children. There you'd be sitting on a kitchen chair, totally helpless, while they cooed over you and pinched your cheeks. Or they'd lean way over with their bad teeth and hairy noses, and say something threatening like 'You're so cute I could eat you up'. And I knew if my mother didn't hurry up with the cooking, they probably would. So, on one level at least you could say that wild things are Jewish relatives' (Sendak quoted in Lanes, 1980:88).

Figure 1.5   Third image from *Where the Wild Things Are* by Maurice Sendak.

The rootedness of Sendak's narratives in human bodily needs and desires may explain part of his works' appeal to children, whose way of life includes more of the bodily as well as play. David Lewis emphasises the special relationship between the picturebook, the child reader, and the concept of play (Lewis, 2001:76). If adults are sufficiently receptive, children's sense of fun and playfulness can help adults break engrained habits of thought about picturebooks, he argues. Playing with what is *'im*proper' helps learning about what is 'proper', and this, says Lewis, is 'almost always funny'. As Bakhtin eloquently puts it, 'laughter delivers the object into the fearless hands of investigative experiment' (Quoted in Lewis, 2001:79).

In summary, contemporary picturebooks bend, stretch, or break the rules, and in this play with conventions, a space between the 'real' world and other possible worlds is opened up. In this space a free exploration of philosophical ideas becomes possible. Play and humour make picturebooks suitable for philosophical enquiry as they make it possible to become self-critical. It is the ability to 'bracket' seriousness that philosophers, artists, and child readers have in common and what they in turn bring to the medium of picturebooks. As Lewis puts it:

> Play is what children do, not because they are in a state of innocence, but because they are perpetually learning, perpetually becoming, and the best picturebook makers are their allies in this (Lewis, 2001:81).

The spaces that self-critical and playful picturebooks open up can be obscure, mysterious, everyday, or complex. But they are never innocent. They are always an expression of the workings of a culture and a mixture of cultures at large. John Stephens warns that even carnivalesque or interrogative texts can mask both conservative and liberal ideologies and hide didactic and educational purposes (Stephens, 1992:125).

The power relationship between adult and child is often questioned by either the picturebooks we choose or the dialogues they provoke. Teachers whose usual role is to 'deliver' certain knowledge may sometimes struggle with the indeterminacy of contemporary books, particularly in a classroom setting.

2   Not So Innocent Picturebooks

ADULTS IN CONTROL

In this chapter we continue to focus on the picturebook *Where the Wild Things Are* by Maurice Sendak to illustrate Jacqueline Rose's observation that adult writers help define the child outside the book, through the child inside the book. The censoring of some books demonstrates ignorance or denial of the fact that all literature expresses power differences between child and adult, so the deliberate withholding of such books is morally and politically significant. Censorship perpetuates not only many adults' assumptions about who and what children are but also reinforces the myth that speaking to children is simple. It is impossible for any picturebook to be 'innocent' because implicit and explicit expressions of ideology are present in all children's literature, including the self-critical and playful picturebooks we use. We claim that value positions can and should be questioned through educational activities that require readers to make a conscious effort 'to read against texts' and 'to deconstruct'.

All children's literature masks both conservative and liberal ideologies and hides didactic and educational purposes (Hunt, 1992, 1999; Stephens, 1992). Children's authors express (often unknowingly) the social, moral, and political values of their society. One way of dealing with ideology in picturebooks is to accept its inevitable presence. So rather than trying to control it, one could make a deliberate effort to understand it and to encourage all readers to be aware of its assumptions and to question them (Hollindale, 1988:10). We suggested in the introduction of this book that philosophy with children can be a natural home for collaborative interrogation of texts and pictures because the discipline of philosophy is the art of critical questioning and complex[1], meta-cognitive thinking. Philosophical facilitators can draw on the history of ideas as a major source of reference. In this chapter we will show how exploring philosophical ideas alongside children expresses our conviction that young children are people who can initiate, grasp, and initiate irony.

Sometimes ideology is *explicitly* present in children's literature, for example, when authors deliberately try 'to mould audience attitudes into desirable forms' (Stephens, 1992:3). Some picturebooks have been written especially to combat current environmental or social problems such as pollution, sexism, racism, or ageism. Judith Graham rejects those 'formula stories' about 'children of mixed race marriages whose mothers work and whose unemployed fathers happily child-mind, awaiting the West Indian milkman and entertaining the Asian neighbour before mother arrives home bearing a present of a non-sexist doctors' dressing up outfit' (Graham, 1990:116). She argues that it leaves children with little opportunity to identify with the fictional characters. Such stories can be so unlike everyday experiences that any potential pleasure is so overwhelmed by the message that they risk being irrelevant and meaningless to the reader. After all, 'isms', stereotyping, and 'otherising' are still part of the fabric of everyday life.

Where the Wild Things Are (1963) is the first book in what Sendak identifies as a trilogy, followed by *In the Night Kitchen* (1970) and *Outside Over There* (1981)[2]. Unlike Max's escapist jungle, Sendak's *In the Night Kitchen* offers a different kind of sanctuary from adult control. The night kitchen is a place much more anchored in the real world than the island where the Wild Things live, and the picturebook provokes the reader to explore why and how social labels function (Adams & Rabkin, 2006). Comic-book style characters include Mickey (after Mickey Mouse, but also 'mick', i.e. a child of uncertain ethnicity), who is an outsider falling into a new world. As all of Sendak's works, this story is semi-autobiographical and draws on his experiences as the son of Jewish Polish immigrants adapting to their new life in an economically struggling New York (Adams & Rabkin, 2006).

Clothing can be seen as a metaphor for alienation from nature, and it is only when Mickey happily takes off his pajamas that he can experience this new world with all his senses. Picturing frontal nudity is one of the reasons why this book is number twenty-five on the list of one hundred most challenged books between 1990 and 2000, compiled by the Office for Intellectual Freedom of the American Library Association (ALA)[3]. Some libraries stock only copies of the book showing Mickey with a painted-on nappy, and Sendak was told that showing a penis in a book frightens children. His response was that most adults find it perfectly acceptable that children see 'Roman statues with their dicks broken off'—something according to him would frighten children much more. Great artists would 'vomit', he claims, with the idea that art is desexualised in people's minds (Lanes, 1980:189).

DESEXUALISED ART

Jacqueline Rose in particular has drawn our attention to how the language spoken by the child as well as the language used by adults to speak to the child is desexualised and how it can be located within educational institutions where language is systematically taught. She challenges the idea that in children's literature 'there is a child who is simply there to be addressed and that speaking to it might be simple' (Rose, 1993:1). Language, and therefore literature itself, expresses power differences between adult and child (Sarland, 1992:38). Rose argues that the very existence of children's sexual abuse by adults has a *conceptual* cost. Historically, the idea of childhood innocence constitutes a 'wedge', a conceptual boundary between child and adult. But child sexual abuse starts to shake the status of children as 'stable and knowable entities'. Rose writes:

> Child abuse confronts us with the violence of limits flouted and transgressed. Bodies open where they should remain closed, and a defining space is invaded—the space which conceptually as well as physically is meant to keep children apart (Rose, 1993:xi).

As a result the child has been desexualised and the ideal of their 'innocence' perpetuated[4], as well as the innocence of the large majority of adults: such acts, after all, are committed by 'perverts'[5]. There is no language available to talk about child sexual abuse and childhood sexuality at the very same time. Rose explains the implications:

> if damage to children can be shown to stem from lone abusers, then the wider culture—with its responsibilities, trials and dangers in relation to children—can be absolved. Thus childhood returns to a pre-Freudian state of sexual innocence and families, that is, families without abusers, revert to the ideal. Oddly labile as a concept (contrary to first appearances) innocence stretches its meanings and contracts (Rose, 1993:xi).

For Rose innocence is not a property of childhood but of adults' desire. Desire is a form of investment by the adult in the child—the act of constructing the child as the object of its speech. It is in this way that children's literature is far from innocent because it secures, places, and frames the child. It creates an image of the child inside a book, and 'it does so in order to secure the child who is outside the book, the one who does not come so easily within its grasp' (Rose, 1993:2).

If we put this in the context of *Where the Wild Things Are*, Max is 'secured, placed, and framed' as a 'wild' child whose solitary confinement will help him deal with his anger. Social and cultural values express themselves in Max's characterisation, as well as the story's plot, and the book is therefore—as all literature—far from innocent. Child readers learn to regard themselves as 'wild' through adult language. The adult writer has secured the child outside the book, through the child inside the book. The basic structure also contains a familiar sequence in children's fiction, that of 'home-adventure-home' in which both home and the adventure are safe. Max's exploration is 'held in place by the world which we recognise and know as real' (Rose, 1993:33, 34, 84, 146n9). Similarly the classic structure in fairytales is that the protagonist journeys outwards beyond the threshold of the home in order to return to its safety, stability, and familiarity.

It is what Maria Nikolajeva calls 'the wheel of power' that has gone 'full circle', and 'adult normativity is irreversibly cemented' (Nikolajeva, 2009:25). Although Nikolajeva herself identifies the great potential of picturebooks to subvert adult power and to interrogate the existing order, it is ironic that we have found her particular reading of *Where the Wild Things* perpetuating some common oppressive discourse about children—in particular what Dahlberg and Moss call 'developmentality' (2005:17). Nikolajeva's *explanation* rather than tentative exploration of what this picturebook 'is about', is far from innocent. Literary critics and teacher educators substantially influence how books 'should be' understood and subsequently taught in class, and in the process fix or affirm beliefs about child and childhood. Nikolajeva's psychological and psycho-analytical reading of the story and Rose's claim of the desexualisation of child and childhood in literature provoke profound questions about *what* and *who* literature is for—an enquiry we will pick up again in Chapter 6. First we will return to the picturebook *Where the Wild Things* and its various possible readings, including the one by Nikolajeva and other literary critics. They provide useful examples of how professed knowledge and expertise can get in the way of using picturebooks in an open-ended, exploratory, potentially philosophical manner.

AMBIGUITY OF MEANING

Often regarded as a carnivalesque text[6], *Where the Wild Things Are* offers a brief respite from social norms. In the company of the Wild Things, who live significantly on an island, Max is free from the usual social constraints, which define his behaviour in the world (mainland) as 'mischief'. After all, he has caused damage to property, attacked the dog with a fork, and 'hanged' his teddy bear. Literary critic John Stephens claims that Max 'has not yet learnt the first principle of freedom—that freedom of action is bounded by the rights of others' (Stephens, 1992:135). Those boundaries are breached in carnivalesque texts but not necessarily redrawn. For Stephens this classic picturebook examines power in parent–child relationships in an imaginative and emotionally satisfying way. He comments:

> the carnivalesque has been used not to question the values of the official world but to define the values which may be at most implicit in some of the puzzling actions performed by those in power. In this respect, it is important to see that Max's return and his mother's gift of 'supper' are not causally linked but contiguous, since each is unconditional (Stephens, 1992:137).

The role of food here may be more ambiguous than Stephens and others make it out to be. After all, it is when Max smells good food to eat that he decides to return to the place where someone loves him best of all, suggesting a causal connection. Selma Lanes also claims that Max's supper on the table—with a large piece of cake for dessert—suggests that his mother has forgiven him (Lanes, 1980:93), but it is not clear at all that what is drawn is indeed a piece of cake and/or that the relationship has been restored. Is it indeed cake we see in the picture, or maybe they are just sandwiches to go with the soup (also on the table; see Figure 1.3). Instead of forgiveness and resolution, loneliness could be read into the picture depending on who is constructing meaning. The giving of food may provide some kind of closure, but we do not believe that this necessarily implies growth in the parent–child relationship. Stephens claims that the Wild Things are:

> comic and droll, rather than frightening, though this was not always perceived when the book was first published. And yet this is important, since *one way in which the book invites to be read* is as a coming to terms with the potential wildness of one's own inner being. By giving comically grotesque forms to inner fears, the illustrations image the defeat of that fear. Moreover, Max is always in control (Stephens, 1992:136; our emphasis).

What strikes us in the story, however, is Max's self-sufficiency. He deals with his wildness on his own terms, and this is conceptually depicted by Sendak's perceptive use of the visual space when Max is moved to the foreground of the illustration when the wildness seems to get out of control (Goldstone, 2008). Max, himself, decides to give up his crown when purged of what many critics describe as 'rage', subtly signified by the wolf suit slipping off his head (Lanes, 1980:93). We wonder whether Max is indeed angry and not just playfully wild—a good illustration of the difficulty in which human emotions can be categorised neatly and with certainty. Subtle ambiguities and differences of opinion about the meaning of this book make it so suitable for generating open-ended questions. Most literary critics use psychological insight into Max's character as an instrument to help construct the work's meaning.

Nikolajeva claims that the visual art enables Max to express emotions that he himself cannot yet(!) articulate. The deficient child character exclaims 'I'll eat you up', but *as a matter of fact* what he is 'trying to express' is a 'wide range of emotions', from 'I hate you-right now' to 'I love you and I know that you will always love me no matter what' (Nikolajeva, 2009:170). The adult (literary critic) seems to know better and best. Like young children in the real world, Max is treated as 'too young to be able to verbalise his contradictory feelings'. Moreover, Nikolajeva suggests that the way this young boy treats his teddy is evidence that he is emotionally disturbed. The boy's 'improper behaviour' goes by unnoticed by the 'indifferent' mother (Nikolajeva, 2009:170). The child is portrayed as an emotionally, (still) immature creature that needs moral and spiritual guidance from adults. Fantasy can play a significant role in this maturation process as children, Nikolajeva continues, have 'not yet discovered any firm distinction between reality and imagination' and their fantasy does not dismiss magical worlds and events as implausible' (Nikolajeva, 2009:42). Fantasy is regarded as an adult tool to 'deal with important psychological, ethical, and existential questions in a slightly detached manner, which frequently proves to be more effective with young readers than straightforward realism' (Nikolajeva, 2009:42). This instrumental use of children's literature serves adults well: they can remain detached and firmly in control of the meaning of text and images. There is no doubt expressed about the correct reading or about the claims made about children (through an explanation of the child character's behaviour). General scientific theories are the lenses through which instances and concrete examples are interpreted. Counter examples are ignored. Despite Nikolajeva's observation that his bedroom looks like a 'prison' with 'gloomy colours' and an 'absence of toys', she still believes that the 'setting does not support' the idea that there could be no happy ending to this story. With an uncertain ending the claim that it is a carnavalesque text becomes problematic. A popular approach to reading texts in education is using psychological and psycho-analytical insights, but it often leaves no room for sincere ambiguity and uncertainty when reading texts. A theme throughout our book is how such a dominant discourse can block listening to children.

A BOURGEOIS TRADE

We called Max an *anti-hero* in the previous chapter[7] as he seems to break with stereotypes and social conventions and forges new understandings. In contrast, some literary critics regard Max as a *hero*, not because of his role in the plot, but because of something in his psychological make-up that makes him heroic (Sarland, 1999:44, 45). It is claimed that he is 'strong-willed' enough to take 'a private boat' to the island, tame the Wild Things, and, when they beg him to stay, he makes the independent-minded decision to go back to the place were someone loves him best of all. Evaluating the quality and value of literature in terms of psychological traits is regarded as a Leavisite practice, after the influential work of F. R. Leavis, who focused on characteristics such as 'intelligence', 'vitality', 'sensibility', and 'depth, range and subtlety in the presentment of human experience'. Others have added other values to this list such as: 'sincerity', 'integrity', 'freedom', and 'authenticity' (Sarland, 1999:43, 44). Since the 1960s, literary critics have made an effort to establish criteria for judging the quality and value of children's fiction, although Sarland critiques the reluctance of critics to justify the liberal humanist consensus in their choice of values. In an excellent article about ideology in literature, Sarland (1999) specifies that enthusiasm for psychological characterisation as a book's source of meaning is 'a bourgeois trade' that fails to acknowledge the political significance of escapist responses to the bourgeois materialism of capitalism, as expressed through literature.

Following Sarland's line of thought, *Where the Wild Things Are* can indeed be understood as a celebration of autonomy, freedom, and courage involving exploration away from the secure home to which Max returns. From a liberal humanist perspective, the characters in this story create their own actions, and therefore their own history, and the meaning of the book is the product of Sendak's intentions. It has indeed become commonplace to speculate what the intentions of an author are, in readers' efforts to make sense of a story. But this is what critics call the 'intentional fallacy' (Sarland, 1999:47) which hides, it is claimed, the conscious and unconscious ideological context of a picturebook such as *Where the Wild Things Are*.

One could indeed maintain that one of the tasks of the critical reader is to expose the 'underlying' ideology of a picturebook and to explore a whole range of codes that operate in texts and help construct a work's meaning. This could also include critical reflection on the structural elements of a story that reflect the structural elements in society (Sarland, 1999:45). For instance, the power structure between Max and his mother expresses a typical modern parent–child relationship: when a child is naughty it is the parent who can justifiably use his or her power to, for example, send a child to its bedroom without eating. But reading for meaning is of course far from straightforward. Research on readers' behaviour suggests that children are not passive victims of, for example, identifying with the characters in a story (Sarland, 1999). Implicit and explicit value positions can and should be questioned through educational activities that require readers to make a conscious effort 'to read against texts' and 'to deconstruct them' (Sarland, 1999:52).

It is here that philosophy can play a vital role with its familiarity of how ideas have shaped and continue to shape people's everyday belief frameworks. Often stories tempt the reader to draw certain morals from a story. In philosophy the facilitator can encourage children to think for themselves and to critique the implicit and explicit assumptions of a story.

KNOWING WHAT IS GOOD FOR CHILDREN

The various interpretations that have been given to *Where the Wild Things* by children and adults, including teachers, parents, and literary critics, show the book's ambiguity of meaning. To remove this classic from class would constitute ignorance or denial of the overt or covert ideology present in *all* children's literature. All writing, producing, or reading of books takes place within a social, political, and cultural framework, which is in and by itself inevitably suffused with values (Sarland, 1999:41). Censorship not only fails to regard *Where the Wild Things Are* as a work of visual and literary art in its own right, but also shows no faith in young children's ability to grasp and initiate irony. The author and illustrator, Maurice Sendak, explains *his* take on censorship:

> Certainly we want to protect our children from new and painful experiences that are beyond their emotional comprehension and that intensify anxiety; and to a point we can prevent premature exposure to such experiences. That is obvious. But what is just as obvious—and what is too often overlooked—is the fact that from their earliest years children live on familiar terms with disrupting emotions, that fear and anxiety are an intrinsic part of their everyday lives, that they continually cope with frustration as best they can. And it is through fantasy that children achieve catharsis. It is the best means they have for taming Wild Things. It is my involvement with this inescapable fact of childhood— the awful vulnerability of children and their struggle to make themselves King of all Wild Things—that gives my work whatever truth and passion it may have' (Sendak quoted in Clark, 1993:67).

When censoring books, the certainty of some adults in prescribing what is good for children is rather disconcerting. Sendak challenges the idea that children cannot tolerate ambiguities, peculiarities, and illogicalities. Like other adults, he says, artists too are concerned about protecting children from danger, but what 'the specialist' regards as right or wrong may not conform with what an artist believes is right or wrong. Artists' inspiration comes from their 'deepest selves', drawing on what Sendak poetically describes as 'a particular vein from their own childhoods that is always open and alive' (Lanes, 1980:125).

Philosophical dialogues with children continue to surprise us and challenge the idea that knowing which books are good for children is straightforward. Thinking moves in unexpected directions, as was the case when eight year old James Galvin held a 'meta' position when exploring the meaning of *Where the Wild Things Are* in class. He clearly realised that it was 'just' a book and interpreted the meaning of the story with this in mind. The children had generated and chosen the following question for enquiry: 'Did Max in *Where the Wild Things Are* go on holiday'? They started their investigation by exploring the meaning of the concepts 'money' and 'work'. Going on holiday means spending money and also not being 'at work'. A counter example became the focus of their thinking: playing a computer game at home. It could be understood as going on holiday. The new idea unfolded that you do not need to travel physically in order to be on holiday. For Gavin, *Where the Wild Things Are* was a holiday, a 'spiritual journey'. During some silent time to encourage private reflection, he wrote:

> I think Max had a spiritual journey because a bed canott turn into a boat in the phiscal world and you cannot control your dreams. So Max moved from one world to another.

When asked to explain what he meant by 'spiritual journey', he wrote:

> A spritual journey is a journey in which you do not move phiscally . . . because your spirit is the only part of you that moves.

Again, when asked to explain what he meant exactly, he showed frustration with his inability to write quickly, so one of us wrote his thoughts down as follows:

> The spirit is the only part that survives death. It's the only thing that forms a person, what they look like and who they are and also tells you what you are going to do, because it is part of you. It's the thing that sets out what you're going to do, because the brain can't do that. The brain can't do that, because it only tells your body to move, but not what you are going to do. I don't believe in science to the end (Haynes & Murris, 2004:69).

This eight year old seems to be pointing at the limits of science. Gavin speculates that intentionality can only be understood with the help of a spirit that tells the brain what to do. A scientific, causal connection between brain events and physical movement may describe the event, but not explain the reasons for the movement. More is needed, according to Gavin, for instance, human purpose and intentions. Children rarely have opportunities to express such profound thinking in school.

SIDESHADOWING

Gavin's thinking in the previous section is a good example of *philosophical* thinking. Typically hard to define, philosopher Evgenia Cherkasova describes philosophical thinking as 'sideshadowing' (Cherkasova, 2004:201). She puts it succinctly as 'the idea that every situation, imaginary or real, comprises not only what happens but also what might have happened' and therefore points at 'the elemental openness of events and champions the concrete, random and inassimilable'. Especially when using contemporary picturebooks for philosophy, neither the moral effect nor the emotional effect can be manipulated or predicted, even if it were justifiable to do so. Evgenia Cherkasova explains:

> Philosophy is a sideshadowing activity, for it is never satisfied with the apparent state of affairs but wants to explore all the latent, invisible

and even unthinkable options. This philosophical play with possibilities disrupts our natural tendency to finalize our experience and give fixed meaning to our actions and practices. Moreover, in its persistent attempts to think-out-of-the-ordinary, think 'otherwise', philosophy aspires to question the very practice of thinking (Cherkasova, 2004:203).

We have often experienced young people's uncompromising readiness to play with the limits and boundaries of thought and language. We treasure these moments of philosophical play. In Gavin's case, the classroom community had clearly been given space to think aloud and play with ideas. The community aspect adds an invaluable dimension to the activity of philosophising. Children and teacher alike were engaged in the kind of philosophical reflection and self-reflection which help to develop habits and skills of critical *self-correction*[8]. The classroom community was holding up a 'mirror', and individuals were directly experiencing the consequences of their own thoughts, whether spoken, written, or expressed physically. Disagreement was celebrated, and Gavin's contributions made us all stop in our tracks. Whether we agreed with him or not, we had to give his contributions attention and had to place ourselves philosophically in relation to his position. What is the 'it' that tells the brain to do things? A spirit? A transcendental[9] ego? What is the 'I' that reflects on the interaction between brain and mind? Can a scientific theory of hard-wired brains and firing neurons be satisfactory to explain human intention? The views expressed in that class could have upset some members of class, especially if Gavin had expressed an opposite perspective, such as an atheistic one, as children in our experience sometimes do[10].

We do not concern ourselves with the right moral message in our choice of books or in our teaching. Neither do we aim for emotional catharsis, which of course is not the same as saying that we are not concerned about children's welfare. We agree with pioneer of Philosophy for Children (P4C), Matthew Lipman, who recognises the value and necessity of dissent and disagreement when teaching philosophical thinking (Lipman, 1991:64). It takes time to build a community of enquiry in a class, and Gavin and his classmates had made a very promising start. Gavin's response to *Where the Wild Things Are* was striking, but such striking thinking is not unusual in philosophical enquiry. We have found that the responses to picturebooks we work with are as unpredictable as life itself, and they profoundly question any kind of certainty about adults' claims about what is right or wrong for children.

Our interest and energy as educators are directed towards creating environments that maximise engagement and interest of people of all ages to explore ideas dialogically[11] and philosophically. Contemporary picturebooks have become an essential part of this environment as they complement and strengthen our practice. The unique value of picturebooks is eloquently put by educationalist and picturebooks specialist David Lewis:

> there is no picturebook house style or fixed approach, no set of genre conventions, no preferred forms of text. The picturebook is thus emphatically not itself a genre. It is an omnivorous creature, ingesting, absorbing, co-opting pre-existent genres—other ways of speaking, writing, picturing—in order to make its texts, and as these genres change and mutate within society, so does the picturebook. . . . We can never be sure exactly what the picturebook will do next as it is forever becoming and never completed (Lewis, 2001:74).

We have found that picturebooks provide an aesthetically rich context for our teaching, and we advocate the pedagogical method of a *community of enquiry* as a way to establish and sustain high quality thinking and dialogue in classrooms.

COMMUNITY OF PHILOSOPHICAL ENQUIRY

Our work is located in the field and practice of P4C and the pedagogy of building a community of enquiry. In the early stages of working together, the main activity of the 'community of philosophical enquiry' (Cam, 1995; Haynes, 2008; Lipman, 1991, 1993b; Murris, 1992; Splitter & Sharp, 1995) is a whole-class discussion where classroom organisation may vary from week to week. A topic may be carried forward for several sittings, often enhanced by the interludes that provide time for digestion of ideas. During the enquiries, participants usually sit together in a way that enables each of them to hear and see all the others, although they will also move in and out of this arrangement for paired and group work of various types. Ground rules for working together may be agreed on and can be modified as the group develops. Rules include all the obvious pre-requisites for ordered and fair deliberation: listen carefully, avoid interrupting or dominating, respect one another, and do not ridicule. Silence is accepted, although the reticent are gently encouraged to participate. Once internalised, groups of children and their teachers seem to be quite empowered and are able to move in and out of this 'enquiry mode' to suit their thinking and learning at other times. The way of working becomes a flexible point of reference available for use whenever it is needed.

In the early stages, the teacher usually provides a starting point for questions. Teachers present picturebooks carefully for their power to express ambiguity, to produce puzzlement, or to evoke a deep response. The illustrations in books are just as important as the text in prompting questions and establishing reference points for discussion. Once the material has been introduced and made accessible to all the pupils, there is plenty of time to think. This may be spent in silence or in talking to a peer. Depending on age, language competence, and mood, children can draw or write notes. Drawing is also encouraged with older learners. Children are then invited to consider their own responses and formulate them into the kind of questions that the 'Internet cannot find the answer to'. It is the examination and pursuit of the children's questions that form the substantial part of each enquiry. The teacher does not normally offer questions. The class adapts or modifies the process to suit its needs.

A range of activities, such as drawing, writing, painting, and drama, can provide a vital part of the philosophical enterprise. Movement and change in the focus of the children's attention is a natural habit. Classroom philosophy is often a practical activity as well as an intellectual one. Its practice is collaborative and collective as well as individual. In the same way as adults, individual children have strengths in different areas, such as logical reasoning, imaginative ideas, the ability to see the whole, awareness of others, the capacity for empathy, the ability to spot patterns and connections, and to see flaws in a line of argument. Successful engagement depends on the freedom of interaction of such divergent and complementary strengths within a group.

Attention needs to be paid, not only to how we reason and listen, but also to *how* and *what* we question in classrooms. In philosophical enquiry the precise content of a lesson is not known in advance but is determined by the children's questions. This has implications for planning and preparation as well as for the styles of teaching. Teachers have to be willing to treat learners' questions without prejudice, to genuinely commit to the enquiry, while resisting the desire to drive the discussion in a pre-planned direction. The teacher's presence, attention, and responsiveness during the enquiry are of utmost importance to support the children's experience of thinking (Murris & Haynes, 2002, 2010; Haynes 2008). The role of the teacher is to assist children to take the enquiry wherever it may lead, while resisting the temptation to unnecessarily return to the text, or to turn to the ideas, themes, or morals that the adult finds important. The enquiry's direction or purpose is to answer the questions the children themselves have raised from the narrative. Using picturebooks in this way differs significantly from a conventional, more didactic, use in the classroom.

Such enquiry is more than just discussion. It differs in the way in which concepts are explored, shaped, and reshaped, in line with the belief that children should not *learn*, but *do* philosophy. Walter Kohan speaks of philosophy as an experience of thinking, rather than a way to 'form' the child (Kennedy & Kohan, 2008). Each community of enquiry is unique in that it constructs its own rules and procedures. However, it is successful only when all contributors work together in their search for understanding or, more specifically, when they all use each other's ideas as building blocks to form beliefs that are more accurate or balanced.

The teacher's role is to help the children to build a so-called 'community of enquiry'. The idea of teaching philosophy through the community of enquiry pedagogy needs to be attributed to American philosopher Matthew Lipman. He acknowledges philosopher Charles Sanders Peirce as his source in understanding a 'community of enquiry' as a practice of self-criticism and self-correction through internalisation of the social practice of thinking with others. As Lipman sees it, the aim of a community of enquiry is 'to discover its own weakness and rectify what is at fault in its own procedures' (Lipman, 1991:72 footnote 4). Members of the classroom community are critical of their own methods and procedures as well as those of others and subsequently correct them (Lipman, 1991:121). The dialogical movement and deepening of thinking is visualised in Diagram 2.3[12] below and contrasted with more traditional teacher–learner interactions as represented in the first and second diagram. In more traditional education (Diagram 2.1), the teacher prepares for the lesson by fixing in advance the questions and answers that need to be explored in relation to a particular picturebook. Merely changing the seating will not make a significant difference (Diagram 2.2) until learners themselves are allowed to ask the questions and are encouraged to build on each other's ideas through responsive listening (Diagram 2.3). Ownership of the initial questions about a picturebook narrative opens up possibilities for learners to express the ideas *they* find interesting or valuable, which makes it more likely they will engage and respond to the thinking of the others in the community.

Traditional Education

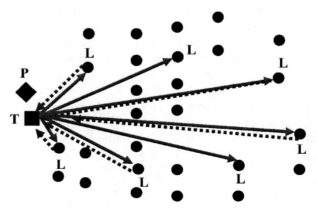

T   = Teacher

L   = Learner

P   = Picturebook

··▶ = Talk

➡ = Questioning

Diagram 2.1   Traditional education.

Circular, but teacher still asks the questions

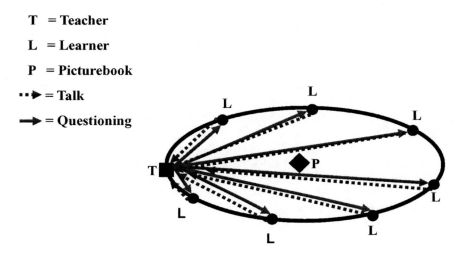

T = Teacher
L = Learner
P = Picturebook
··▶ = Talk
➔ = Questioning

Diagram 2.2   Circular, but teacher still asks the questions.

Exploring picturebooks in a Community of Enquiry

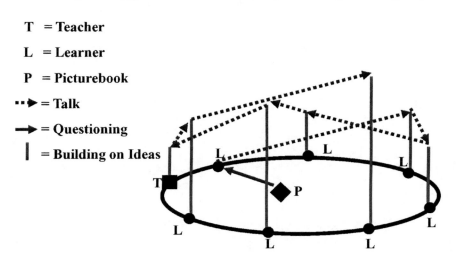

T = Teacher
L = Learner
P = Picturebook
··▶ = Talk
➔ = Questioning
| = Building on Ideas

Diagram 2.3   Exploring picturebooks in a community of enquiry.

CONCLUSION

Drawing on various sources such as the ideas of adult literary critics, authors, illustrators, and children, we have shown how the meaning of a particular picturebook—that of Sendak's *Where the Wild Things Are*—is not only complex and ambiguous, but also implicitly and explicitly expresses ideology and is therefore far from innocent. The analysis of this particular case serves to illustrate the more general point we make, that is, the idea that *all* picturebooks contain ideology of some kind or another, and that censoring just some of them misses significant educational opportunities to involve learners in a process of 'sideshadowing'—the philosophical activity of deconstructing texts through alternative readings and reflective thinking. We propose in the final part of this chapter that this thinking other-*wise* flourishes when communities of enquiry are built in classrooms. This critical pedagogy is the cornerstone of an approach to teaching philosophy called P4C. Despite the similarities between the open-ended nature of philosophical enquiry and the self-critical and playful picturebooks we use in school and university classrooms (and argued for in Chapter 1) the use of such picturebooks remains controversial. Philosophers often deliberately use classroom materials that are text-based and avoid the visual, the sensory, and the bodily—even when committed to teaching in communities of enquiry as an alternative to 'delivery' or 'transmission' models of teaching and learning. It is to their critique we will now turn in the next chapter. In particular we will explore some of the philosophical and educational assumptions that those critics bring to their ideas and their practices.

3 From Philosophical Novels to Picturebooks

THE PHILOSOPHY FOR CHILDREN PROGRAMME

Teachers' selection of suitable educational resources expresses their moral values, epistemological assumptions, implicit theories of childhood, and aesthetic beliefs. Validation of the picturebooks as a philosophy teaching resource needs to be considered against the backdrop of the pioneering work of Matthew Lipman and colleagues at the Institute for the Advancement of Philosophy for Children (IAPC), Montclair State University, Montclair, New Jersey, United States. His Philosophy for Children (P4C) programme provided the confidence and conceptual background for others to create a variety of resources to support teachers in their innovative work—teaching philosophy to young children was a revolutionary idea. Lipman's programme paved the way for an international response by practitioners, often trained initially with Lipman, to 'deliver' the P4C programme. Different cultural settings and fields of expertise that trainers have brought to P4C theory and practice have culminated in diverse philosophical practices and resources worldwide. We will mention some of them, but as the P4C programme (translated into many foreign languages) is probably the most popular worldwide, our critical evaluation of the programme will clarify our own views on picturebooks as philosophical texts. Initially the use of picturebooks for philosophical enquiry was a creative and practical response to the P4C programme (Murris, 1992). The philosophical dimension became apparent later (Murris, 1997) and has developed since, especially through our shared teaching, our many conversations, and our collaborative writing.

In the late 1960s, Matthew Lipman—then Professor in Philosophy at Columbia University in New York, United States—was struck by his college students' incapacity to think and express themselves creatively, critically, and with confidence. In an interview Lipman says:

> when my own children were about 10 or 11 years old, the school they were attending did not give them the instruction in reasoning that I thought they needed. I was teaching logic at the college level at the

time, and I felt that I wasn't accomplishing very much with my students because it was too late; they should have had instruction on reasoning much earlier. So I decided I would do something to help children (Lipman, interviewed by Brandt, 1988:34).

Inspired by his own childhood memories of schooling as a 'tedious' and 'dull space' (Lipman, 2008:2), Lipman devoted the rest of his career to strengthening children's capacity to enquire and to make philosophy accessible to children and teachers (Lipman, 1988b:144; 1993b). Thinking skills-building and value-formation are intertwined in the programme to counter criticisms that better thinking skills might be abused by people with poor judgement or deficient moral values (Lipman, 1997). Partly co-written, the programme consists of seven specially constructed philosophical novels with accompanying teacher manuals, each one of them targeting a different age group (see e.g. Lipman and Sharp, 1984, 1985, 1986). The novels are not a narrative version of the history of philosophy, but classical philosophical ideas, themes, and questions that have been 'injected into' the text without the use of technical jargon. In order to provoke philosophical questioning they deliberately contain 'the perplexing aspects of natural language that they are bound to encounter in daily life' (Lipman, 1988b:144). In practice, children read short episodes of a novel aloud together. For example, in the philosophical novel *Elfie*, six year olds are introduced to Cartesian dualism[1] as follows:

> Last night I woke up, in the middle of the night, and I said to myself, 'Elfie, are you asleep?' I touched my eyes, and they were open, so I said, 'No, I'm not asleep.' But that could be wrong. Maybe a person could sleep with her eyes open. Then I said to myself, 'At this moment, **am I thinking**? I really wonder'. And I answered myself, 'Dummy! If you can wonder, you **must** be thinking! And if you're thinking then, no matter what Seth says, you're for real' (Lipman, 1988a:4, 5).

After reading an episode such as this[2], the children are asked to raise questions from the text. The teacher writes their questions on the board or flipchart, and the children subsequently discuss what they (rather than the teacher) find puzzling and interesting in the story. The fictional characters in the philosophical novels model the community of enquiry structure (see Chapter 2)—one of the major *advantages* of the P4C programme. There is an ongoing dialogue between the fictional children and their peers and between those children and adults. In his autobiography, Lipman explains that P4C is about process not content. The emancipatory idea is that children 'develop their own philosophy, their own way of thinking about the world' (Lipman, 2008:166). Inspired by the philosophical practice of Socrates, the dialogue structure encourages readers to think critically about issues and arguments raised in the text and to develop their own answers to philosophical questions. When reading and discussing the philosophical novels, the children immerse themselves and become part of the novel's community of enquiry. Thinking is understood as a social practice, so thinking together with others in 'external' dialogue develops thinking for oneself in 'internal' dialogue. Exposure to diverse thinking styles and immersion in intelligent conversations nurture reasonable thinking. The novels' purpose of modelling the practice of communities of enquiry explains why the fictional characters in the novels are quite unlike 'normal' children. They are 'thinkers' not 'doers'[3].

Lipman argues strongly against the use of children's literature because if the aim of education is to 'produce' thoughtful children, then educational material should model thoughtful children, and publishers and editors, he claims, deliberately 'exclude thoughtfulness from their depiction of fictional children . . . [because, in contrast to adults] . . . children are thought to inhabit a world whose security is ensured by adults, a world into which the threat of problematicity does not intrude, with the result that, under such circumstances, active thinking on the child's part is hardly necessary' (Lipman, 1988b:187). This is his justification for writing particular kinds of stories for philosophy education which 'portray the thought process itself as it occurs among children . . . [and] . . . depict fictional children giving thought to *their* lives as well as to the world that surrounds them' (Lipman, 1988b:186, 187). The novels' focus on the everyday and the familiar is further explored in Chapter 7.

The P4C curriculum includes instructional manuals containing substantial exercises, games, and discussion plans. They are designed to teach children a reconstructed body of philosophical knowledge. Unlike normal worksheets or educational materials, they do not focus on the production of answers, but provoke further open-ended questioning and increase awareness of the complexity involved in conceptual knowledge. Abstract concepts that are familiar territory in the work of adult philosophers are embedded in the novels. The manuals are designed to 'maintain the inquisitive momentum to which the novel gave the initial impetus' (Lipman, 1988b:148). For example, to help six year olds explore the above episode from *Elfie*, the teacher has four pages of support to explore the concepts 'real' and 'thinking' philosophically (Lipman & Gazzard, 1988:35–39).

With so many exercises and discussion plans for only a few paragraphs of the novel, the practicality of getting through the manuals in a sequenced curriculum is a daunting task for teachers. However, Lipman emphasises the importance of teachers using the instructional manuals to guarantee the philosophical quality of the enquiry. He explains:

> Would-be classroom teachers of philosophy need models of *doing philosophy* that are clear, practical and specific. They need to be able to distinguish essentially decidable concepts from essentially contestable concepts, if they are to understand why only the latter are truly philosophical (Lipman, 1997:1).

He suggests that exercises and discussion plans should be 'integral parts of the elementary level philosophy curriculum, and without a curriculum of some kind, the chances that one will be able to do philosophy at all are greatly reduced' (Lipman, 1997:1). The exercises and discussion plans in the different manuals are sequenced *logically*, and the P4C programme is a *logically* and not an *empirically* sequenced curriculum. Lipman stresses that an empirical sequence would involve a correspondence 'to already existing stages of cognitive development derived from descriptions of children's behaviour in non-educational contexts' (Lipman, 1988b:147). By-passing the need for any stage-theory of children's cognitive development, the P4C programme sequences practice in a range of thinking skills rather than competences. In later publications, especially in *Thinking in Education* (1991), Lipman focuses almost exclusively on thinking *skills*, thereby inadvertently pushing controversial content to the background. The focus on skills tends to 'neutralise' philosophical enquiry when all the evidence is that situated dialogue that includes communication about class, cultural, racial, and gendered positions is at the heart of educational and social transformation[4].

PEDAGOGICAL INCONSISTENCY

It is difficult to conceptualise how the dialogical pedagogy of a community of enquiry[5] and the didactically constructed P4C curriculum can work in harmony. In a community of enquiry, participants set the agenda by raising their own questions and philosophical problems. They take responsibility for the process and content of the enquiry. The likelihood that questions from the manual can be 'injected' into the dialogue without disturbing the flow of enquiry is slim, especially with young children. Facilitating enquiries requires philosophical listening that creates space for children's own voices[6]. Aware of the problem of balancing the open-endedness of the method with the directedness of the manuals, Lipman suggests that teachers should be discreet in utilising discussion plans and exercises. His advice is to employ them 'sparingly', for it could 'restrict . . . [the discussion's] . . . open flow' (Lipman, 1997:8, 9). However, he suggests they can be useful to 'channel and discipline' an enquiry that is not going anywhere (Lipman, 1997:9). The delicate balance between pushing for philosophical depth and giving power and trust to the children is endangered when relying on discussion plans. This raises the question of how often they have to be used to ensure logical 'progress'. Moreover, Lipman stipulates that 'the sequence of questions in a discussion plan generally proceeds from *simple* to *difficult* and from *clear-cut* cases to *fuzzy* cases' (Lipman, 1997:6). It means that the teacher has to ask a whole series of pre-planned questions, while possibly ignoring the one question (for example, the first) that may lead the enquiry. It is also implied that it is vital to reach the last questions in the discussion plan because 'the questions towards the end seek greater impartiality and generality' (Lipman, 1997:6). This is clearly demonstrated by the following exercise from the manual designed to help teachers to explore the above episode from *Elfie*:

EXERCISE: Does thinking imply a thinker?

1. If there's a painting, must there be a painter of that painting?
2. If there's a book, must there be a writer of that book?
3. If there's smoke, must there be a smoker around?
4. If it's raining, does that mean there's someone making it rain?
5. If it's snowing, does that mean there's a snower causing the snow?
6. If there are puddles, does that mean it rained?
7. If there was a sound, does that mean there was a listener?
8. If there are thoughts, does that mean they were made up by a thinker?
    (Lipman & Gazzard, 1988:38)

The exercise, and in particular the last question, is aimed at exploring Descartes' 'I think, therefore I am'. Descartes argued that we can doubt the certainty of knowledge claims about the 'external world' as sense perception can deceive us. His solution was to epistemologically ground certain knowledge through the following thinking move: an individual may doubt the external world, but in this process of doubting, there is certainty about the subject who is doing all this doubting. So, asking question 8 (from the above list) could indeed be very useful (in addressing the question, you must be thinking, therefore you must exist). Our concern is not so much to critique the purpose of any such exercises but the pedagogical timing of them. In order to arrive at the last question of this exercise, the teacher has to be directive, but this presupposes a teacher–learner interaction at odds with the community of enquiry pedagogy. In the previous chapter we suggested that the teaching needs to be responsive to learners and democratic in its practice when supporting the building of ideas. If teachers prepare philosophy lessons with the clear intention of asking a series of questions, as above, they risk the practice resembling a discussion as visualised in Diagram 2.2 (see Chapter 2), rather than that of a community of enquiry as in Diagram 2.3.

We fully acknowledge that Lipman's P4C programme offers support to teachers without a background in academic philosophy. The issue of how to adequately support teachers in facilitating *philosophically* is a recurring problem in terms of P4C teacher education internationally. This question is particularly urgent in countries where the P4C programme is not used systematically in schools, but alternatives are used such as picturebooks, photographs, poems, paintings, music, and outdoor activities. We argue elsewhere that incorporating P4C in a school's curriculum can have substantial educational benefits, even when the teachers have little or no background in academic philosophy. P4C puts philosophy *of* education firmly on the agenda of *all* educators, not just teachers of philosophy (Murris, 2009a; Haynes & Murris, 2011). There is a danger, however, in relying heavily on the P4C programme for the teaching of philosophy. As put forward in Chapter 2, philosophy encourages a kind of meta-thinking, the ability to 'sideshadow', an urge to think other-*wise*. The choice of philosophical content that is implicitly or explicitly contained within educational material for teaching philosophy positions the teacher within the academic philosophical tradition. Such teachers are unlikely to be able to draw independently on a range of philoso-phies. The danger is that without prior philosophical knowledge, they may introduce a philosophy curriculum such as the P4C programme in an uncritical way. 'The' philosophy would be spoon-fed to the teacher and drip-fed to the learners.

So, would it be better to use academic philosophers as facilitators of classroom philosophy? An academic background in philosophy can be a hindrance to actively listening to what the children are saying—a prob-lem addressed elsewhere through a critical analysis of transcripts (Murris, 1999, 2000b). In Chapter 8, we also explore the complexity of 'reading' transcripts. How we view our own role as facilitator is critical. For McCall, the facilitator is not a 'co-enquirer' and therefore remains physically out-side the circle of the group. The democratic nature of the practice is seen as less important than the rational, logical moves the community makes, and which the facilitator needs to safeguard. The teacher is the expert adult who creates the conditions of the possibility for an enquiry to be philo-sophical (McCall, 2009; Cassidy, 2007:130).

Although most P4C practitioners are in agreement about the use of stories[7] for teaching philosophy, there are some profound disagreements about the use of literature. Lipman is not alone in his rejection of litera-ture for philosophy teaching: Danish philosopher, Soren Kierkegaard has called children's literature 'poetic rinsewater'—it does not encourage chil-dren to enquire or to think for themselves (Kierkegaard in Lipman, 1993c). Some academic philosophers, however, have been publicly and consistently appreciative of children's literature. Gareth Matthews observes that chil-dren's authors are more likely to be sensitive to philosophical thought in young children than psychologists or educational theorists (Matthews, 1980: 56). Matthews' interest in using literature for philosophy, however, differs substantially from our own. He focuses on classical philosophical themes in existing children's books (Matthews, 1992, 1993b, 2006, 2009), and recently he has also been writing specially written 'story beginnings' inspired by classical philosophical texts (Matthews, 2009:28). By compar-ing the issues raised by professional adult philosophers and those raised by children, he has provided what he calls 'evidence' that children can do philosophy and enjoy doing it (Matthews, 1978, 1980, 1984, 1994). Mat-thews' message is that academics should not look down on children's litera-ture. Very good children's poems and stories contain the kind of perplexity that 'demands to be worried over, and worked through, and discussed, and reasoned out, and linked up with each other, and with life' (Matthews, 1993b:279). We agree with Matthews that the possibility of doing this kind of philosophical work depends on whether the adult holds on to a deficit conception of childhood, as beliefs about children lacking certain cognitive competencies profoundly influence our expectations about the kinds of conversations we can have with them (Matthews, 1980, 1993a, 1994, 2009). Matthews observes:

> Being in a real philosophical discussion with children offers both child and adult an opportunity for mutual exchange and mutual respect that is otherwise rare in our society (Matthews, 2009:40)

Another academic philosopher, Thomas Wartenberg, uses children's literature didactically with the overall aim of communicating moral messages (Wartenberg, 2009). His book's title—*Big Ideas for Little Kids*—and much of its moralising language also frames the child. His political agenda is apparent in sentences such as: 'In discussing this book with the children, *our* goal is to get them to think about . . . ', or '*Our* aim here is twofold. First, *we* want to make sure that the children focus on the aspect of the story that is relevant for *our* discussion' (Wartenberg, 2009:98, 9; our emphasis). The use of 'we', 'our', and 'them' functions to unify (the adults) and fragment (adults from children) (Janks, 2010).

Although grounded in academic philosophy, our interest in picturebooks for the teaching of philosophy does not hinge on possible links with academic philosophical themes or on finding similarities between children's responses and those of adult philosophers (Murris, 1997). Our paradigm is not adult philosophy, but we suggest a more 'expanded' notion of rationality that critiques modernist and rationalist philosophies. We are particularly interested in children's philosophical perspectives and what they can bring to academic philosophy as a discipline (see especially Chapter 9). Our use of literature is integral to such a project and not accidental to it. What facilitators use as a starting point for enquiries expresses different philosophies of childhood, as well as epistemological and educational beliefs. In particular we are concerned here with the relationship between theory and practice, the concrete and the abstract. Literature that contains both the everyday and the strange and unfamiliar mediates philosophical understanding. Philosophical enquiry requires delicate facilitation between the abstract and the concrete, otherwise learners and teachers lose them-*selves* in meaningless abstractions. French philosopher Jean-François Lyotard reminds us that reading a text is not philosophical just because the texts are philosophical. They could equally have been written by artists. A reading is only philosophical, Lyotard continues, when:

> it is autodidactic, when it is an exercise in discomposure in relation to the text. . . . Teaching philosophy is not the transmission of a 'body' of

knowledge, knowledge of how things should be done or what to feel—but simply that it is in action (Lyotard, 1992:115, 117).

The history of philosophy is open for re-interpretation and re-thinking. We are interested in a pedagogy that includes children of all ages in processes where not only the learner but also the teacher 'numbs' and 'gets numbed', as if the facilitator were a 'stingray' (Murris, 2009a). As educators we are committed to letting thinking occur (in a responsive sense), and we have found that the self-critical, playful picturebooks we choose to work with readily offer fertile ground for learners and teachers to 'sideshadow' and to think other*wise*.

COBWEBS TO CATCH FLIES

It is our experience that carefully selected picturebooks have the ability 'to numb' and 'to be numbed by' when used philosophically. The revolution in quality picturebooks has been so quiet that it seems to have escaped the general notice of philosophers, including many P4C practitioners worldwide. For this reason we need to look elsewhere for theoretical arguments for their use as philosophical texts and their educational value. Even in the field of literacy teaching, picturebooks are generally not regarded as aesthetic objects provoking philosophical responses, but as 'cobwebs to catch flies', that is, they are there as an instrumental aid to develop children's reading abilities. As soon as children are literate, the illustrations gradually disappear from books, and 'real' reading can start (Graham, 1990:8, 9; Moss, 1988:4). One of the forerunners in valuing pictures and the process of picturing when teaching children to read was Judith Graham, who wrote that the act of reading is not 'a mechanical unpicking of the written code and relies much more on what's in our heads already in terms of knowledge about language and life' and involves the ability to 'picture it in your mind' (Graham, 1990:13). Lipman believes that it is better that children do this picturing themselves—adding illustrations would obstruct this personal meaning-making process.

The rejection of the use of illustrations for philosophy is also spelled out in the book that justifies the P4C curriculum—*Philosophy in the Classroom* (Lipman et al, 1980). The authors distinguish among children's yearning for *literal* meanings (scientific explanations), *symbolic* meanings (fairytales, fantasy, and folklore), and *philosophical* meanings, which they claim are neither literal nor symbolic. This, they maintain, makes existing children's literature unsuitable for teaching philosophy to children. Their main critique is summed up in the following statement:

> children's literature is generally written for children rather than by children. . . . The parent who invents stories for children . . . runs the risk of so indulging his own imagination as to pre-empt the child's imagination. We find delight in the creativity with which we express ourselves in such stories (and in the illustrations that go with them). But to what

extent do we rob children of their creativity by doing their imagining for them? . . . We have resisted putting illustrations in the children's books we publish because we feel that to do so is to do for children what they should do for themselves: provide the imagery that accompanies reading and interpretation. . . . There is something unwholesome, even parasitical, in the thought of adults seeking to hold on to their own creativity by pre-empting the creativity of their own children (Lipman et al, 1980:35, 36).

The quote takes us into two separate, but related, directions for further analysis. Firstly, in the next section we will engage with the P4C programme's implicit theory of meaning. Secondly, in the last section of this chapter we will examine the authors' equating 'imagination' and 'imagery'.

PREGNANT PICTURES

The programme's philosophical novels are steeped in topics and exercises that are part of academic philosophy courses in formal and informal logic. Even children's moral responses need to be 'disciplined by logic' (Lipman, 2003:92). It is assumed that this is the case, '[s]ince to *a great extent what a statement means* consists in the inferences that can *logically* be drawn from it' (Lipman et al, 1980:16; our emphasis), and, '[i]nference is reasoning from what is given literally to what is suggested or implied' (Lipman et al, 1980:17). But we wonder what makes 'what is given literally' meaningful to us? Do we receive *passively* literal input and then construct meaning by making logical connections, drawing inferences, etc., or, do we *actively* construct meaning when the 'literal is given to us' as, for example, Lakoff and Johnson (1980, 1999) suggest? And what is the role of the imagination and emotions at this basic level of giving meaning to our experiences?

Traditional semantics focuses only on the meaning of *words* and *sentences*—a reflection of some deeply rooted dichotomies in the history of Western thought: the split between mind and body, reason and imagination, science and art, cognition and emotion. It is not accidental that in most educational settings (especially in Higher Education), it is still common practice to centre teaching on solitary reading of texts with no or very few pictures. The P4C programme is no exception. Current changes in learning and teaching practices, technologies, and theories reflect a change to embrace other means of meaning making that include the visual, the aesthetic, and the kinaesthetic (Johnson, 1987, 2007). The thinking body is also a feeling body. Who we are, where we live, and what we feel affect our reasoning processes. Our body is not only an object of knowledge but also a knowing, sentient being (Burkitt, 1999:61). The body and its location are significant for how knowledge is constructed. This contrasts starkly with the Cartesian view referred to earlier in this chapter which assumes that the

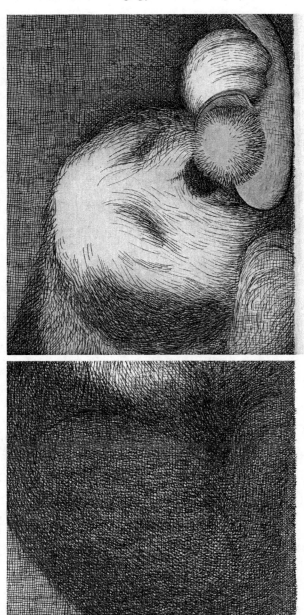

John Brown thought.
He thought all through lunch time

and when supper time came, he was still thinking.

Figure 3.1   Image from *John Brown, Rose, and the Midnight Cat* by Jenny Wagner.

thinking body is still and passive, poignantly illustrated by the dog John Brown in Jenny Wagner's and Ron Brooks' *John Brown, Rose, and the Midnight Cat* (1977) (Figure 3.1)[8].

The dog John Brown symbolises the stereotypical philosopher: male, middle-class, and white. Faced with an ethical dilemma—with his nose on Rose's slipper—he 'thought all through lunch time and when supper time came, he was still thinking'. His *mind* (or brain) is thinking but not (the rest of) his body. Leaving out the body in reason and rationality, and therefore feelings, emotions, and imagination, is *disembodied* rationality, which is clearly expressed in Cartesian dualism, i.e. by mere *thinking* one knows one exists, not by the fact that we *are* bodies and find ourselves in a world with others (*Mitsein*)[9].

The P4C programme has never gained much ground in certain countries (e.g. Britain, Germany), and we suggest that one of the reasons might be those countries' easy access to good quality children's literature as workable alternatives[10]. Also, we have found that many teachers we have worked with prefer pictorial resources over text-based materials, mainly for aesthetic but also political and pedagogical reasons such as inclusion and participation. As picturebook author and illustrator Anthony Browne confirms:

> children's sophisticated reactions didn't surprise me as I've known for some time how we often undervalue the abilities of children to see and understand, I was particularly struck by how below-average readers of print were often excellent readers of pictures. . . . Children are wonderful readers of visual metaphors (Anthony Browne interviewed in Arizpe & Styles, 2003:Afterword).

One of the aims of this book is to engage with some theoretical perspectives on the use of picturebooks for P4C. Although picturebooks are arguably the most popular resource for P4C with younger children in a country such as Britain, reasons for their philosophical use are predominantly practical and instrumental. This has implications for the kind of picturebooks chosen. Some teachers tend to choose their resources for P4C on the basis of themes perceived *in* the text and whether these 'fit in' with the curriculum of a country, or the topic or other school generated concerns. But using contemporary picturebooks philosophically demands that educators think afresh about pedagogy and how people make meaning when presented with a complex and interdependent mixture of images and text, regardless of age. The meaning of contemporary picturebooks is far from fixed and, as David Lewis explains metaphorically:

> words are never 'just words', they are always words-as-influenced-by-pictures. Similarly, the pictures are never just pictures, they are pictures-as-influenced-by-words. Thus the words on their own are always

partial, incomplete, unfinished, awaiting the flesh of the pictures. Similarly the pictures are perpetually pregnant with potential narrative meaning, indeterminate, unfinished, awaiting the closure provided by the words. But the words and pictures come from outside the picture-book (Lewis, 2001:74).

In other words, readers are not empty of images when they open a picture-book any more than they are empty of ideas when they open a text. As with words, 'because readers bring meaning to them . . . children filter art as they do all life experiences through their own perspectives' (Graham, 1990:18). Picturebooks are more than books with illustrations, the narra-tive is a complex web of words and images, and we return to this question in Chapter 6 in the context of literacy teaching.

Matthew Lipman and colleagues wrongly assume that children's minds are *passive* when they look at illustrations, that they do not have to actively construct meaning when they see a picture, and that the meaning is 'given' without having to think imaginatively. This renders the P4C programme philosophically incoherent. After all the suggested pedagogy for the teach-ing of the P4C programme—the 'community of enquiry' method—assumes that the making of meaning is a dynamic, social, historical, and linguistic *activity* (Sharp, 1991:34). But this is at odds with the belief that children's minds *passively* absorb the meaning of illustrations, without the need for the *activity* to fit the meaning of the picture into their own meaning-struc-tures. We argue throughout this book that the theory of meaning implicit in one's pedagogical practice has implications for the kind of resources educators choose for philosophical practice.

IMAGERY OR IMAGINATION?

The authors of the P4C programme conflate 'imagery' with 'imagination' when they claim that philosophical novels should not contain images because children must 'provide [themselves] the imagery that accompanies reading and interpretation'. 'Imagination' is frequently equated with 'visualisation'. It is often conceptualised as the faculty of the mind to create pictures 'in' the mind, but the etymological root of the word imagination is 'imago', and although in Latin this means 'image', it also means 'representation'. For example, in our aesthetic judgements about Willy's fabulous goal against a gorilla goalkeeper in Anthony Browne's *Willy the Wizard* (1995), the reader re-presents the goal, that is, has a visual image, but this process *also* involves knowledge about football: the speed of the ball, the positioning of Willy's body, and the anticipation of what the goalkeeper is likely to do next. The *experience* is extraordinary. It stands out on the basis of a whole myriad of background beliefs the reader needs to consult to understand what is possi-ble on a football pitch. More generally, imagination allows flexible rehearsal of possible situations, and to combine knowledge in unusual ways as, for example, in thought experiments. It is therefore wrong to think of imagination as being at odds with reason (Blackburn, 1996).

The outdated but widely held belief that imagination is nothing more than the capacity to form images has strong roots in the Platonic tradition, which has carved up 'reality' into the rational and the irrational. For example, the Greek *logos* was the term used not only for 'reason', but also for 'word' or 'speech'. In other words, rational understanding takes place when we can articulate it in words. Meaning, in this view, is something that only words and sentences have. People look (passively) at pictures in books. In contrast, David Lewis places contemporary picturebooks in the context of wider postmodern culture and identifies some distinctive characteristics that help explain why these narratives can be so emotionally and cognitively demanding (Lewis, 2001:Chapter 6). The interaction between image and text is neither stable nor predictable and requires members of the community of thinkers to actively construe meaning. 'Boundaries have dissolved', writes Lewis, 'inviting a promiscuous mixing of forms' (Lewis, 2001:90). When using such works of art with children they are not 'spoon-fed' by ready-made products of other people's imaginations. It takes a different kind of effort to read pictures. Constructing meaning is not just the process of finding out what the pictures denote or literally represent. The reader is pulled in two different directions of meaning-making by the use of the different sign systems, creating a 'kind of miniature ecosystem' (Lewis, 2001:48, 54). The linear direction of the text invites us to continue reading while the pictures compel us to ponder. Importantly, the 'gaps' between text and image may be experienced differently as we grow older and as we bring our established habits of thought to the reading of the narrative, forging a new relationship between teacher and learner.

Modern education still celebrates the Platonic idea of true knowledge (*episteme*) as being contemplative, rational, and theoretical. For Plato, truth and art do not meet. Art has little to do with truth. For rationalists, the senses and emotions have no place in objectivity and in acquiring real knowledge. On the contrary, the body gets in the way by 'contaminating' philosophical thinking that needs to be impartial, generalisable, and abstract. In Western culture, in the pursuit of objective and real knowledge, philosophers have traditionally rejected art and images as a means to arrive at or reveal truth. It explains philosopher John Locke's contempt for figurative speech, which he saw as an enemy of the truth (Lakoff & Johnson, 1980:189, 190). An alternative way of understanding art is to regard images, especially the more abstract ones, as putting a real cognitive and emotional burden of interpretation on the reader. The simpler the representation of an object, the further it is removed from reality and therefore the more challenging it is to make sense of it (Hunt, 2001:288; Bosch, 2001). Artists' decisions about what to *leave out* in their work seem to intensify aesthetic responses and make picturebooks such powerful starting points for philosophical enquiry (Murris, 1993, 1994). Contemporary picture-books invite openness to a more 'expanded' notion of rationality, one that attaches high value to art and emotions in philosophical thinking.

Throughout this chapter we have put forward an alternative to the well-known P4C programme as a resource for doing philosophy. Critical of Lipman's idea that the thinking-moves involved in following the carefully constructed arguments in his specially written philosophical novels are mainly logical, we have hinted at the idea (further developed in later chapters) that authentic democratic deliberation required for building communities of enquiry assume freedom of thought and a theory of meaning that draws on the imagination and moral values, as well as the emotions *as an essential part of* the process of making reasonable judgements. We have argued that the P4C programme and many practitioners conflate 'imagination' with 'imagery'. Drawing on insights from contemporary linguistics and philosophy of language we suggest a more 'expanded' notion of rationality. We are particularly interested in children's accounts of their embodied experiences and what their philosophical perspectives can bring to academic philosophy as a discipline. It takes a different kind of effort to read books in which pictures are pregnant with words. The meanings we bring to core concepts such as 'meaning', 'imagination', and 'emotion' have implications for the particular picturebooks we select and how we choose to use them. We see it as our challenge to use educational resources that generate philosophical questions and topics worth exploring, even in and by communities whose members have nothing in common (Biesta, 2006). In a sense it is ironic that the more ambiguous and the less culturally, historically, politically, and morally specific a starting point for enquiry is, the more likely it is that members of a community will experience a sense of freedom to connect with the picturebook narrative on the basis of their own cultural and personal identities. When learners are allowed to construct their *own* questions, they imbue the material with the specific context that makes the narrative meaningful for them. It is this continuous movement between the specific and the general that helps to make the practice philosophical. In reaching beyond the meanings of words themselves, and to include embodied experiences in meaning-making, opens up spaces where imaginative philosophising becomes possible. This is further explored in more detail in Chapter 8. Narrative context and emotional engagement are characteristic of meaningful philosophical encounters. It is to these features of our philosophical work with picturebook narratives that we now turn.

4   Picturebooks as Philosophical Texts

NARRATIVES AND PHILOSOPHY WITH CHILDREN

This chapter explores the view that narrative is a fundamental organising structure, implicitly and explicitly applied when people try to make sense of their lives and their experiences. We investigate the idea that making sense of stories involves not only making logical connections between abstract concepts but also making imaginative, affective connections. This is an idea only recently appreciated in the field of philosophy. Many philosophical texts in the Western tradition tend to be devoid of wonder, complexity, and mystery, and are inattentive to particulars, the concrete, and the everyday. But the everyday and the unfamiliar can be topics for philosophical investigation when offered in the contexts of a narrative and people's own storied experiences. Offering de-contextualised arguments for logical analysis strips philosophical practice of meaning and can lead to meaningless abstractions. We propose that emotions aid engagement with philosophical ideas. With the help of the picturebook *Frog in Love* (1989) by Max Velthuijs we argue that experience is paramount for reasonable, practical judgements, and that the body and emotions are central to the process of meaning-making. It is these features of contemporary philosophical practice that seem to provoke censorship in teaching, as they involve children's lived experiences and embodiment.

Whilst curriculum and pedagogical policy does not always reflect the most recent theoretical developments, ideas about teaching and learning have shifted from implicit beliefs about the importance of teachers transmitting content to learners to an acknowledgement that much learning takes place in the interaction *between* people (with the teacher as a learner too) and a recognition of the central role of language in meaning-making. This new focus on linguistic and social practice implies a move away from learning as knowledge representation to a focus on understanding. The idea that human experience is expressed and mediated through *language* is significant for teaching and learning, and this includes both spoken and written language. We do not have 'direct' access to the '*world*' when we study the universe, work out how to build a bridge, or do a psychological experiment, but we think *about the language we use when we think* about the universe, a bridge, or other people. Thinking always has this social and linguistic element.

As meaning is a function of the endless web of language itself, the importance of dialogue and how people use metaphors implicitly and explicitly in their thinking has come to the fore. One such central organising metaphor is narrative. Since Roland Barthes, many have argued that narratives are central to human lives. Narrativity is the principle way that human beings organise their experience in time (Worth, 2008:42). Philosopher Mark Johnson explains that:

> Not only are we born into complex communal narratives, we also experience, understand, and order our lives as stories that we are living out (Johnson, 1987:171, 172).

It is the narrative structure that makes our life intelligible, with its beginning (birth), middle (maturity), end (death), and the need for coherence within one's own story (life). The 'life-is-a-story' metaphor involves understanding one's life in terms of *stages*, *causal* connections among its parts, and *plans* to achieve a goal or set of goals. We see our 'selves' as the main figures in the stories of our lives (Jaynes, 1990:63). In this sense, narratives shape not only self-identity, but also group identity, and can be used explicitly in conversation, teaching, training, therapy, surgery, or consultancy. Narrative in the broad sense includes spoken or written language, pictures (still or moving), gestures, myth, legend, fairytale, short story, dance, history, tragedy, comedy, opera, pantomime, painting, glass stained windows, cinema, cartoons, internet chat rooms, text messages, computer games, newspaper articles, memories, dreams, and conversation. Important for learning and teaching is that narrative context gives *meaning* to an event. This is by and large an interpretative and imaginative exercise.

Narrative understanding taken in this broad sense even includes what Bruner calls 'logico-scientific understanding'[1]. The narrative structuring of our thinking and understanding is in a sense so implicit to how we make sense of the world that we stumble when seeking for a definition of what differentiates a narrative from an argument or a recipe (Bruner, 2002: 3, 4). In the broadest sense, narrative refers to 'any spoken or written presentation' (Polkinghorne, 1988:13), as opposed to narrative, in the narrow sense, which is equivalent to a true or fictitious tale or *story*—usually in the form of a causally-linked set of events (Polkinghorne, 1988:13).

Philosophers of education Smeyers, Smith, and Standish warn against the dangers of the recent narrative turn in contemporary thinking. They claim that much confusion has arisen (ironically) as a result of not taking narrative seriously enough (Smeyers, Smith, & Standish, 2007:57). Narratives are often assumed to have unity; they are linear and have an internal coherence with beginnings, middles, and endings (the narrow definition of narrative as described above) (Smeyers, Smith, & Standish, 2007:62). They radically challenge the familiar conceptions of self-identity assumed, e.g. the implicit need for certainty by imposing coherence on a narrative (rather than going back to what Dunne calls 'the rough ground'[2]). If not careful, the narrative turn tends to reinforce the notion of individuals as atomic and separate from others. In contrast, they stipulate that our lives are interwoven in textures of dependencies, vulnerabilities, and relationships. The idea of the authentic self, they claim, is romanticised and sentimentalised, and this has implications for how we read narratives. An alternative, they propose, is a wider sensitivity to what language does. For example, a poem allows us to 'sit alongside with', 'listen to', 'walk with'. Even isolated words (e.g. 'projection') may open a doorway and enable us to think differently and to *be* different (Smeyers, Smith, & Standish, 2007:62, 63). They suggest we should not look for beginnings and endings in narrative accounts, but for a 'centring from which to move out' (Smeyers, Smith, & Standish, 2007:63).

The narrative structuring of our thinking and being-in-the-world has implications for pedagogy. Every life can be seen as a story, and through the writing or telling of stories we create other possible worlds. In Philosophy for Children (P4C), however, use of narrative is discussed mainly in the context of choosing starting points for enquiry. As we have seen in the previous chapter, Matthew Lipman acknowledges the power of stories. The novels that are part of his internationally popular P4C programme contain words only and deliberately no pictures. Guidelines for their use include reading the text aloud together with infants[3], and older children take turns in reading a paragraph of the text out aloud, with an option to 'pass'. Both practices are designed to create a communally shared reading experience. Since learners have to be motivated to raise questions themselves, it is important that teachers make a conscious effort to select material that appeals to as many learners as possible.

A lack of interest in traditional forms of text is common for a variety of complex reasons. Some associate them with the sort of 'work' you have to do at school and 'switch' off before they have had the opportunity to 'connect' with the narrative. Some are more visually or kinaesthetically orientated and/or less able to make sense of print. Changes in technology reflect the ease with which many young people access ideas and information visually. The move away from specially written texts has arguably widened access to narratives—historically available only to an elite minority, as well as giving rise to a much wider range of narratives. Narratives are now presented and constructed through television, film, computers, computer games, and even mobile phones. Its medium does not make the narrative more or less inferior—each has to be judged on its own merits and purposes. Many visual narratives demand emotionally and intellectually sophisticated 'reading'. At the same time, there are many written texts not worth reading. So which criteria should we use for selecting narratives for philosophical enquiry?

HORIZONTAL AND VERTICAL IMAGINATION

The 'life-as-a-story' metaphor highlights how events, actions, and behaviour acquire meaning because of their place in the story we live out (Egan, 1992:70). The so-called objective, logical reasons we give for our beliefs and actions are in fact embedded in a narrative structure created by ourselves. Julian Jaynes gives the following example:

> A child cries in the street and we narratize the event into a mental picture of a lost child and a parent searching for it (Jaynes, 1990:64).

By drawing on our own experiences, we make connections to help fit events into meaningful, coherent wholes (Lakoff & Johnson, 1980:172–175). The crucial point seems to be that the mind creates connections and therefore meaning out of narratives, not by *causally* linking earlier events *logically* with later events (Worth, 2008:44), but the information and cues in text and images require the reader to fill in the explanatory 'gap' between events in a story. Narratives are never purely descriptive but always contain an element of justification—not *causally*, but morally, socially, or psychologically (Goodson et al, 2010:11).

To understand the connection between Max being sent to bed and his subsequent travel to the island in Sendak's *Where the Wild Things Are*[4], multiple explanations are involved, and by using one's *reasoning* some explanations will have more 'explanatory force' (Worth, 2008:45) than others. The power of a narrative does not depend on whether it is factually true or not, but on how the story functions (Goodson et al, 2010:12). The particular details of text and illustrations, and the emotional depth of Max's imaginary journey to the island where the Wild Things are, give the picturebook 'narrative intensity' (Goodson et al, 2010:12).

Reading narratives, fictional or non-fictional, necessarily involves a particular human perspective. Philosopher Hans-Georg Gadamer's groundbreaking work *Truth and Method* (1975) is a powerful challenge to the idea that texts can be interpreted objectively and from a certain external, secure vantage point by an educator or a literary critic. The process of making sense of a narrative always involves a 'fusion of the contexts of both interpreter and text' and requires a 'relationship of vulnerability to the text' and an attempt to be 'fully open' in the conversation between reader and text (Dunne, 1993:105, 115). Gadamer's 'hermeneutics'[5] implies that meanings are not already contained 'in' the text, but 'the meaning of the text has its *being* in the conversations in which it is brought into partnership'. A text, Joseph Dunne, continues:

> is always released into a semantic field, beyond the reach of its author, and is charged with possibilities of meaning that become actual only in virtue of movements in the rest of the field. It is the dynamism of

history itself that constitutes this field and within it there is the meaning of the text. It is in this sense that Gadamer speaks of time (i.e. the time elapsed between the production of a text and its subsequent interpretation) not as a 'gulf' but as a 'supportive ground (Dunne, 1993:118).

The past is always active in reading a text in the present, even when humans are not conscious of this fact. Readers bring their own historicity and temporality to their interpretations of a narrative. In a sense it is confusing to use the in-vogue phrase 'bringing meaning to the text' as if text were a 'thing', 'an object' injected with meaning by the reader. Humans always already find themselves 'in'[6] time and space, and therefore they bring to any meaning-making processes their own prejudices and socially, culturally, and historically situated understandings[7]. From the situatedness of such encounters between text and readers it follows that when young people are allowed to participate in such conversations, unique opportunities emerge for different readings of texts, readings that are sometimes extra-ordinary, unusual, or disturbing. Writers and readers are temporal beings. Therefore claims to a distanced, objective, meta-narrative perspective on texts are no longer credible. Outdated epistemologies still prevail in much literacy teaching and literary criticism[8]. The influence of Gadamer's hermeneutics includes a revival in the interest and relevance of the Aristotelian distinction between *phronesis* and *techne* for teaching and learning, to which we return later in this chapter.

If knowledge is always part of being, it not only involves a 'knowing how' or a 'knowing that' (Gilbert Ryle's famous typology[9]), but also a 'knowing what 'x' is like'. Literature offers a potent source of knowledge— knowing what experience is like from a character's perspective (Stroud, 2008:21, 22). Characters in literature are viewed through the lenses of the authors and illustrators. Neo-Aristotelian American philosopher Martha Nussbaum claims a distinct and unique role for artists in the forceful way in which they can represent characters. She writes:

> literature is an extension of life not only *horizontally*, bringing the reader into contact with events or locations or persons or problems he or she has not otherwise met, but also, so to speak, *vertically*, giving the reader experience that is deeper, sharper, and more precise than much of what takes place in life (Nussbaum, 1990:48; our emphasis).

It is by engaging with literature 'horizontally' and 'vertically' that our moral imaginations are engaged and expanded. Moreover, she stresses that as narratives put readers in positions unlike real life, readers are free to relate more ethically to fictional characters. She explains:

> Since the story is not ours, we do not find ourselves caught up in the 'vulgar heat' of our personal jealousies or angers or in the sometimes blinding violence of our loves (Nussbaum, 1990:48).

As picturebook settings are often beyond anything we could ever experience, genuine altruism seems possible when, for example, we connect with the plight of a monster (Figure 7.2) who is so terribly ugly that all living creatures flee, the natural world turns grey, leaves shrivel up, and the only friend he has is a stone rabbit (Wormell, 2004). Agonisingly poignant, the world returns to its previous beauty only after the monster's death. For Nussbaum, our moral concern is genuine only because there is no possibility that such a creature could ever compete for the attention of our loved ones or compete with us in any other way, and therefore there is space in our heart to empathise and sympathise fully[10]. The act of reading, she writes, 'is exemplary for conduct' (Nussbaum, 1990:48). In her work, the choice of narratives as philosophical texts and morality are intricately intertwined.

Another important connection between narratives and morality is made by Neo-Aristotelian philosopher Alasdair MacIntyre. In his influential work *After Virtue* (1985), MacIntyre draws our attention to the link between life-as-a-story and moral agency. In order to answer the fundamental ethical question 'What am I to do?' moral agents need to answer the preceding question 'Of what story or stories do I find myself a part?' It is through stories, he says, that:

> children learn or mislearn both what a child and what a parent is, what the cast of characters may be in the drama into which they have been born and what the ways of the world are. Deprive children of stories and you leave them unscripted, anxious stutterers in their actions as in their words (MacIntyre, 1985:216).

Attributing such an important meaning-making role to stories is relatively new in the history of ideas. For centuries it has been assumed that the productive and properly functioning mind works with abstract concepts in a logical manner (Egan, 1992:62). But the *whole* mind—not just the logico-mathematical part of the mind—is involved when making sense of stories. Rationality cannot be reduced to a set of skills, to be trained like muscles (e.g. brain), but is intrinsically 'tied up with all these hitherto neglected attics, basements, and hidden rooms of the mind, in which emotions, intentions, metaphors, and the imagination cavort' (Egan, 1992:63). The implications of a broader conception of rationality for choosing picturebooks as philosophical texts are explored in the next section.

AFFECTIVE JUMPS

Whilst Lipman emphasises the power of logic in making sense of stories[11], Kieran Egan emphasises that an integration of the cognitive and the affective is needed in order to understand the causality which holds stories together. In the fairytale *Cinderella*, for example, the reader has to make an affective 'jump' in the story from when Cinderella's sisters have left for the ball until the Fairy Godmother arrives. Egan explains:

Following a purely logical causal sequence we might have to witness some dish-washing or dusting or coal-heaving or whatever, but the affective causality makes the connection between the two scenes immediate and directly comprehensible (Egan, 1992:63).

In picturebooks even more demanding thinking is called on because of the interdependency between words and pictures[12]. In David McKee's *Not Now, Bernard* (1980), the pictures show a monster, but in the text the monster is called 'Bernard'—the name of the boy who has just been gobbled up (Figure 4.1). Significantly, learners often spot that the eyes of Bernard's parents are closed when talking to their son. The story makes little sense unless readers draw imaginatively on emotions such as loneliness, sadness, alienation, and vulnerability; and in turn these emotions are always embedded in the story the reader is living out. Their own experiences of family relationships help construct meaning and provoke imaginative speculation of other possible relationships between parents and children. The quality of the art facilitates this process of creating other possible worlds through 'the metaphoric transformation of the ordinary and the conventionally 'given' ' (Bruner, 1986:49).

Figure 4.1 Image from *Not Now, Bernard* by David McKee.

The mind functions as a 'whole', and it is imagination that gives reason 'flexibility, energy, and vividness' (Egan, 1992:65). The mind also includes the body and is not separate from it as John Brown's body was when he had to solve an important moral dilemma (see Figure 3.1, Chapter 3). For classroom resource material to engage thinking meaningfully, narrative context is often essential. In a community of enquiry, learners are motivated to give meaning to picturebook narratives when the imagination is engaged. Imagination is necessary to make connections in enquiry: it helps connect personal knowledge to public knowledge and vice versa. Imaginative rationality creates insight and understanding out of the complex mix of emotions, words, and pictures. This process generates new ideas cherished by learners who are co-constructers of fresh knowledge. We will argue in the next section that the emotions in the high quality picturebooks we choose to work with play a significant role in how meaningful, inclusive, and participatory P4C can be.

FROG IN LOVE

As seen in the previous chapter, Lipman explicitly rejects the use of children's literature for philosophy as children are seldom portrayed as 'thoughtful, analytical, critical, or speculative', but as 'happy or sad, beautiful or homely, obedient or disobedient' (Lipman, 1988b:186). We respond to Lipman's concern through detailed analysis of one of our favourite picturebook narratives and explore whether focusing on emotions does indeed hinder philosophical thinking.

In common with many of Max Velthuijs' picturebooks, *Frog in Love* (1989) can provoke censorship by educators. The story begins with the narrator commenting that the main character Frog does not know whether he is happy or sad. He just feels odd. Walking about in a dream all week, he feels like both laughing and crying at the same time. Sometimes turning cold, sometimes turning hot, he points to his chest and says that there is *'something going thump-thump inside me'*. Having been 'diagnosed' by the 'doctor' Hare as being in love, Frog realises that he doesn't know *who* he is in love with. When he finally finds out that he is in love with Duck, Piglet comments: 'A *frog can't be in love with a duck. You're green and she is white'*. Frog is undetered and declares his love to Duck. This deceptively simple story written for young children can raise profound philosophical questions: *Can you be in love without knowing it? Can a doctor diagnose love? Is it possible to be in love without knowing who you are in love with? Can you be mistaken in thinking you are in love? What does it mean to be 'in' love?* With eight year olds in a school in Johannesburg, the story provoked questions such as: *Was frog really in love? How did he know he*

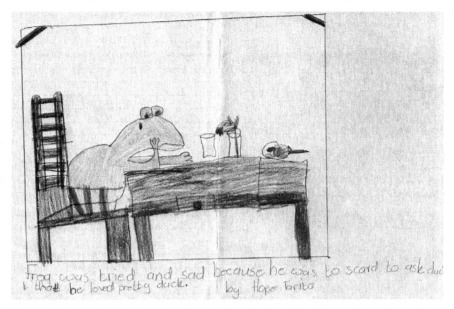

Figure 4.2 Drawing inspired by *Frog in Love* (Max Velthuijs) made by Hope Tarita (aged 10).

was in love with duck? Why didn't he sign his name under his drawing so duck would know who it was? How can you just look at someone and fall in love? and *Why did Piglet say it was wrong to love a duck?*[13] One learner in this class, Hope Tarita, expressed Frog's distress in a beautiful drawing (Figure 4.2).

The book has been met with censorial reactions by some teachers for not giving the 'right' message—frogs do not fall in love with ducks—and the story has provoked many enquiries about skin colour and race and whether mixed-race love is possible.

One teacher and postgraduate student Robyn hints at her own initial unease in her diary:

> It was only towards the end of the session, once I felt a bit more comfortable with the process, that I started asking more open-ended questions. Although I was still in control, this questioning technique elicited a more natural response from the children and I was able to get a glimpse of what their understanding of love was.

When asking her learners open-ended questions, unexpected answers were given:

T—'Can doctors diagnose whether you are in love or not?'

'Doctors can't tell that you are in love because he doesn't always know you—he sees a lot of people each day so how would he know your exact feelings? He can't see inside you or see your feelings' (Mark, age eight).

T—'Can a book tell you about being in love?'

'Not always, it can be wrong for you—how does the person writing the book know what you are feeling?' (Angela, age eight).

'Sometimes people write a book about love for fun and love isn't fun it's a serious thing or they write about themselves and not other people's feelings' (James, age seven)[14].

Robyn comments as follows:

> From the last two responses, children felt that the emotion of love is a serious thing and at the same time, those in authority, like doctors and authors, cannot know and therefore tell you how to feel love or behave when in love as each person is different. I was surprised that Jack acknowledged love was serious. Also, I was astonished that at that age they had an understanding of the magnitude of the emotion. Up until this point, I felt that they were too young to understand or perhaps experience the notion of love of another human who isn't a care giver or parent.

Children's responses often take us by surprise because a *philosophical* investigation into the meaning of 'love' necessitates that everyone (including the teacher) draws on his or her own concrete experiences of loving relationships. For example, a five year old expressed his disagreement with the narrative when he stated: '*I am in love with Rebecca, but my heart doesn't go thump-thump!*' This imaginative connection with personal experience engages the self and makes the reasoning passionate. There is *care* about the focus of the investigation; it matters what love *is*. The interdependency between words and images provokes further questioning and opens up opportunities to sympathise and empathise. Frog's experiences are like our own, or maybe not, or just a little bit. We need to find out. Hare's chair and his raised hand tell us something about their unequal relationship, a powerful portrayal of doctors' status in society. There is nothing about that in the text. Frog's bodily expression doesn't make it clear whether he feels uncomfortable standing there—the kind of discomfort one can experience when visiting a doctor (Figure 4.3). The

Hare thought hard, just like a real doctor.
"I see," he said. "It's your heart. Mine goes thump-thump too."
"But mine sometimes thumps faster than usual," said Frog.
"It goes one-two, one-two, one-two."
Hare took a big book down from his bookshelf and turned the pages.
"Aha!" he said. "Listen to this. Heartbeat, speeded up, hot and cold
turns...it means you're in love!"
"In love?" said Frog, surprised. "Wow! I'm in love!"

Figure 4.3   Image from *Frog in Love* by Max Velthuijs.

picture on a previous page may suggest a different reading—he doesn't
know whether he is 'happy or sad' (Figures 4.4).

Are the expressions indeed similar in both pages? How easy is it to distinguish between 'being happy' and 'being sad', or any emotions for that
matter? How accurate a portrayal of love is it? Such invitations to question the things we perhaps normally take for granted are characteristic
of Velthuijs' dialogues. This is why they make exciting starting points for
philosophical enquiry. The difference between feeling happy and sad is far
from straightforward and deserves further exploration. We will take this

Frog was sitting on the river bank.
He felt funny.
He didn't know if he was happy or sad.

Figure 4.4   Second image from *Frog in Love* by Max Velthuijs.

up in the following two chapters (see in particular Table 6.1). A further complexity is that emotions are not static, but dynamic and can fluctuate from one moment to the next. The ambiguous and open-ended nature of his narratives provokes speculation of an imaginative, hypothetical kind—there are no right or wrong answers in text or drawings.

Frog in Love shows the philosophical potential of stories that involve fictional characters who are happy or sad and *at the very same time* thoughtful creatures, inviting reflective reasoned responses from the reader. Initially through artful[15] adult facilitation, members of a community of enquiry problematise the meaning of 'love' and other philosophical concepts that describe feelings and emotions. This probably would not convince philosophers who believe enquiry into the meaning of emotions has no place in *philosophy*. Teaching philosophy through narratives in schools and universities is highly innovative.

THE EYES OF THE SKIN

Most Western philosophical texts have been surprisingly devoid of wonder, complexity, and mystery, and inattentive to particulars, the concrete, and the everyday. The removal of emotion from thought is not untypical in philosophy, and the root of this belief goes back as far as Ancient Greek philosopher Plato. In the dialogue *Phaedrus* Plato claims that certain emotions (e.g. desire) bind 'the soul to its bodily prison house and forces it to view everything from within that distorting enclosure' (Nussbaum, 1990:263). Plato's view that art and emotion corrupt reason discourages the use of picturebook narratives for philosophical enquiry.

The author and illustrator of the first contemporary picturebook, Maurice Sendak[16], believes that his unusual gift (if he has one, he says) is not in writing and drawing, but

> [r]ather, it's that I remember things other people don't recall: the sounds and feelings and images—the emotional quality—of particular moments in childhood (Sendak quoted in Lane, 1980:7).

The emotional context of this story makes us care about characters such as Max in *Where the Wild Things Are*. The linguistic medium necessitates reflection on the meaning of the various concepts embedded in the story and opens up possibilities to explore their complex nature. As stated before, philosophy is not about 'the world', but starts with enquiries about the *language* we use when we make sense of the world, including our 'inner' world and our embodied experiences. In Max's case, examples of emotions that emerge in the experience of reading are 'anger', 'loneliness', and 'power' and how these are experienced through and with *his* body.

Nussbaum is sympathetic to the idea of using narratives to teach philosophy and for philosophers to write differently. In *Love's Knowledge* (1990) she offers an alternative form of philosophical text. She explains:

> Style itself makes its claims, expresses its own sense of what matters. Literary form is not separable from philosophical content, but is, itself, a part of content—an integral part, then, of the search for and the statement of truth (Nussbaum, 1990:3)

For Nussbaum the alternative to Anglo-American philosophical prose does not sacrifice precision and completeness even if it refuses to be 'scientific, abstract, hygienically pallid' or has a style that is like 'a kind of all-purpose solvent in which philosophical issues of any kind at all could be efficiently disentangled, any and all conclusions neatly disengaged' (Nussbaum, 1990:19). *Love's Knowledge* challenges philosophers to write differently, and the book's own form is a good example of an expression of truth 'dictated by the heart'. No clear guidelines are given, or arrived at, for the use of certain literature or books, and that is a deliberate part of the Aristotelian point. The method of practical philosophy, *phronesis*, requires the practice of attending to particulars, respect for emotions, and a 'non-dogmatic attitude to the bewildering multiplicities of life' (Nussbaum, 1990:27). This highly influential notion of practical reason from Aristotle's *Nichomachean Ethics* requires a kind of reason that is personal and experiential, flexible, and not formulable, as opposed to *techne*, a mode of reason that requires the making of a product or state of affairs which can be exactly specified before the activity and provides it with an end or purpose (*telos*) (Dunne, 1997:9). Many modern teaching practices are good examples of *techne*, such as the goal orientated curriculum and predetermined teaching outcomes.

Nussbaum argues that *phronesis* demands resources of a particular kind. An abstract philosophical treatise about the concept 'love' would lead us into darkness. It is misleading to think that we can only access the abstract through the abstract (e.g. few philosophy texts contain concrete examples or illustrations), but fictional concrete settings and characters provide the means to highlight abstract truths. The powerful portrayal of Frog's plight in *Frog in Love* is a concrete expression of what Nussbaum describes as '*that strange unmanageable phenomenon or form of life, source at once of illumination and confusion, agony and beauty*' (Nussbaum, 1990:4). Frog's contradictory emotions and mad behaviour in the text, images, and the 'gaps' in between (e.g. his effort to make the biggest jump in history to impress duck despite the health risks involved) set up a dialectical relationship with the reader. The reader needs to consult the characteristics of his or her own concrete experiences of loving relationships to respond to the narrative. It is in this way that Marcel Proust thought that the literary text is an 'optical instrument' through which the reader becomes a reader of his or her own heart' (quoted in Nussbaum, 1990:47).

Proust's use of a visual metaphor is not unusual to describe the insights (another visual metaphor) literature makes possible. In a fascinating book on architecture, Juhani Pallasmaa makes the case that the emphasis on the visual in our history of ideas has led to architectural designs (e.g. schools) that house the intellect and the eye but have left the body and the other senses homeless. By contrast, through focusing on the sensory mode of touch, a kind of architecture becomes possible that 'makes us experience ourselves as complete embodied and spiritual beings' (Pallasmaa, 2005:11, 19). He explains:

> All the senses, including vision, can be regarded as extensions of the sense of touch—as specialisations of the skin. They define the interface between the skin and the environment—between the opaque interiority of the body and the exteriority of the world (Pallasmaa, 2005:44).

The thin layer of skin over the eye 'confronts' the world in 'focused vision', but 'peripheral unfocused vision' moulds the 'very essence of the lived experience' and therefore touch is the sensory mode that integrates our experience of the world with that of ourselves, and thus 'vision reveals what the touch already knows' (Pallasmaa, 2005:10, 44). When entering a school building peripheral unfocused vision will generate an indivisible complex of impressions (Pallasmaa, 2005:44). In this phenomenological approach the human body is the centre of the experiential world. The meanings incorporated in any work of art, whether a school building or a picturebook, are pre-verbal and lived, rather than merely understood intellectually.

Understanding a picturebook such as *Frog in Love* takes place on what Pallasmaa calls the 'threshold of language' (Pallasmaa, 2005:25). Understanding what love is for Frog, as well as our own sentiments about Frog, involves a myriad of our senses, especially touch. Embodiment bridges the gap between the reader (the subject who is reading using her eyes) and the picturebook (the object). The reader is a unity of past, present, and future, and therefore to understand what love means now (in the present) we bring to our reading our past experiences, and also imaginations, desires, and future projections. This temporality is crucial in understanding emotions because simply measuring Frog's faster heart-beat or his lack of appetite at any particular moment in time does not help to understand what love *means*. Past experiences can be accessed through memories[17]. According to phenomenologists, in order to understand love in the story we start with our own personal experiences of love. In order to say something about love that also has validity for others it is important to try and abandon personal and cultural prejudices, as well as scientific concepts, because many have lost the original connection between language and embodiment (Levering, 2006:455, 456; Lakoff & Johnson, 1999; Johnson, 2007).

For phenomenologists, an individual has no privileged access to his or her own 'inner' self. From this perspective, it is indeed possible that Hare can diagnose Frog as being in love. We can be strangers to ourselves. The fact that we find ourselves (bodily) existing ontologically precedes our individual 'essence', for example being an introvert or extrovert. We know about ourselves through our interaction with others and the language others use about us. Understanding our self and others is an incomplete, dynamic, ongoing, and developing communicational experience (Levering, 2006). So a pedagogy that revolves around the testing of personal opinions in a community of enquiry seems appropriate because it assists in the process of making personal views more inter-subjective and supports the process of getting to know ourselves better—not only what we think, but also who we are. Why this may seem counter-intuitive or against 'common sense' has to do with certain habits of thought or internalised psychological and physiological accounts of self. This is explained further in Chapter 5.

FROG IN CONTEXT

In P4C, it is common practice to use narratives as starting points for enquiry. They are referred to, in behaviouristic terms, as 'stimuli'. Often regarded merely as *instruments* to provoke philosophical lines of thinking, their artistic quality is often seen as incidental to the depth of thinking provoked. They are chosen mainly on the basis of content and the links between what the story is about (according to adults) and, for example, curriculum links or learning outcomes. In this chapter we suggest other ways of thinking about the reasons for the use of narratives to teach philosophy.

It is only when we free ourselves from the narrow interpretation of narratives as stories with unity—with beginning, middle, and ending structures—that a different way of thinking about P4C starting points opens up. As argued in this chapter, there is a complex connection between narrative and self. The human mind constructs narratives to makes sense of its own self. Experiences are made intelligible and coherent by using a narrative structure. In a profound sense we *are* the stories we are living out. To understand stories we use an intricate mixture of reason, emotions, imagination, and also the body. We *feel* our ways into stories through touch, sight, smell, and hearing. What are the implications?

Frog's love of Duck makes no sense in isolation. We need to understand Frog in the context of the community of which he is a part—his relationships with Hare and Pig and Rat and Duck. Not only his memories and imaginings of who he wants to be, but also the space he wants to carve out for himself within that community make him what he is, which is always changing. It is a continuous process of self-construction.

We need to understand Frog in the context of the reader–text relationship whereby the reader brings her own cultural, social, and historical narrative to the reading process. The information and cues in the text and images require the reader to 'fill in' the explanatory 'gap' between events in a story. This is not a logical, causal linking of earlier events with later events. Narratives always contain an element of moral, social, or psychological justification. Reading narratives necessarily involves a particular human perspective. In reading (and writing) texts in the present, humans bring their own historicity and temporality to their interpretations.

Finally, we need to understand Frog in the context of the environment in which the reading takes place: the walls, the furniture in the room, the weather, the presence of other bodies in the room; their smells, their size, their clothing. The expressions on their faces, what these bodies say, what they do, how they listen. We not only get to know Frog better, but also ourselves through such relationships with others and our environment.

This less narrow interpretation of *Frog in Love*, and of narrative more generally, makes it possible to develop a different interpretation of self: a self that is embodied, and whose essence depends on its existence with others (through bodily interaction and communicative relationships). Exploring such stories with others in an environment that actively nourishes and encourages dialogical talk about thinking and emotions helps students (and teachers) to construct more profound self-narratives and understanding of others, provided concepts such as 'love' are presented in all their ambiguity. Teachers need to encourage learners to question the meaning of such concepts from an early age in a community of enquiry, before meanings become too heavily anchored and solidified in self-narratives and narrative accounts of others.

It is in this sense that psychological approaches to emotional literacy are unhelpful and morally questionable. They present the vocabulary of emotions as if it were straightforward, enabling adults to explain and teach their meanings as though they were unambiguous. They discourage generation of possibly new ways of thinking about emotions through spoon-feeding adults' perspectives. Presenting children only with popular beliefs about emotions (e.g. as inner, mental states or as physiological reactions in the body) is a reductionist option. Frog's love is more than dopamine, norepinephrine, and serotonin 'reward and motivation pathways' in his brain (Goldie, 2010), even if these chemicals could indeed be detected in his little green body when he is in love with Duck.

The situatedness of encounters between text and readers implies that when young people are allowed to participate in such conversations, unique opportunities emerge for different readings of texts. The inclusion of children can create anxiety because the role of experience and therefore the role of the body and emotions are included in the making of practical judgements. Children's directness and frankness in such encounters often provokes censorship. Adults have become more socialised in suppressing their emotions especially when engaged in a practice that aspires to be philosophical. Traditionally associated with rationality, 'headwork', and 'being brainy', an approach to philosophy through art and literature acknowledges the central role that emotions and imagination play in philosophical meaning-making. Children's lack of self-consciousness in imaginative thought experiments, drawings, metaphors, as well as their expression of emotions *as an essential part* of making practical judgements, are faculties that adults themselves could learn from.

In the next chapter we continue to contrast our understanding of emotions with more popular theories of emotions in educational theory and practice. Frog continues to be our companion in that chapter. Max Velthuijs' artwork may appear to be simple and is often judged as simplistic and therefore appropriate for young readers only. But let us not be deceived. The complexity of emotions portrayed by simple line-drawings and poignant open-ended dialogues between characters in Velthuijs' stories are far from simplistic, and his talent provides excellent material for philosophical contemplation at all ages. The reasons put forward in this chapter for using a narrative such as *Frog in Love* as a philosophical text can be summarised as follows:

- The reader can engage *horizontally* with Frog—we are introduced to another possible logical world and encounter previously unknown characters, problems, and events.

- Frog can be engaged with *vertically*—the experience is deeper, sharper, and more precise than much of what takes place in life.
- Our moral imaginations are therefore engaged and expanded.
- Readers are free to relate more ethically to Frog. Genuine altruism is possible as Frog is not in any competition with the reader. He is not a threat to our own love life, for example.
- *Frog in Love* is itself a love story. The form itself is part of the philosophical content, that is, a search for what can and cannot be claimed about love.
- The fictional concrete settings and characters in the story are a means to highlight abstract truths. Meaning-making and understanding involve a continuous interaction between the abstract and the concrete, and not between the abstract and the abstract.
- The situated, emotional context of a story makes us care about characters such as Frog and motivates the reader to find out what will happen to him. Emotion is not an enemy of reason but gives energy and life to our philosophical thinking.
- *Frog in Love*'s content is far from 'smooth' and does not contain clear, disentangled arguments. It contains contradictions as well as conclusions. As in real life, meanings are uncertain, and the story's humorous complexity provokes cognitive conflict. The story invites its readers to play on 'rough ground' (see Chapter 13).

5   Emotions and Picturebooks

THE SHEPHERD CALLS HIS DOG

This chapter continues with a further exploration of the moral dimension of emotions through a detailed analysis of love, explained and illustrated with the help of the picturebook *Frog in Love* by Max Velthuijs and *Love's Knowledge* by Martha Nussbaum. We start with an overview of various theories of emotions and critique the popular psychological and neuro-physiological approaches to emotions, prevalent in education today. We argue that such approaches are based on a profound misunderstanding of Aristotle's Golden Means Rule, and that emotions are not mental, inner states to be 'controlled' and 'managed' with the help of experts. Emotions are constructive, moral indicators and intelligent responses to situations. We conclude that this indeterminacy and uncertainty corresponds well with the ambiguity and complexity of the contemporary picturebooks with which we choose to work. The 'gaps' between words and pictures require imagination and empathetic understanding, offering a distinct kind of (emotional) knowledge.

One of the sources of a currently popular view of emotion was originally conceptualised by Plato: emotions are regarded as mental states in need of mastery and control. As a result, some adults argue that their age and experience puts them in an advantageous position to tame youngsters' 'wild sides' and to help them 'mature' into adults who understand and manage their emotions and become so-called emotionally 'literate' or emotionally 'intelligent'. For many educators it offers an appealing promise of empowerment for all (Miller, 2009:222).

Philosophy with children (P4C) is sometimes promoted and adopted in schools as a vehicle for emotional 'intelligence' or emotional 'literacy' (see e.g. Lewis, 2007). The caring thinking it encourages is often interpreted *psychologically* without acknowledging its moral and political dimensions. As an alternative to such a view, we argue that emotions are informative expressions of, and responses to, dynamic social relationships.

In his complex dialogue *Phaedrus*, Plato describes the efforts of a person to be a philosopher. He makes an analogy between passion for philosophical enquiry and falling in love with someone. Out of all of his dialogues, this is the only one in which the protagonist Socrates leaves the city of Athens (the embodiment of reason) and travels to the countryside to engage in philosophical conversation. It may be no coincidence that the topic explored by Socrates and his partner-in-dialogue Glaucon is love, and that the journey can be characterised by his discovery of 'monsters that come from *within*' (Plato, 1995:ix, x; our emphasis). For Plato the self[1] consists of three distinct drives: the lowest are the appetites (e.g. various bodily needs) and the highest is reason (e.g. curiosity to solve a mathematical puzzle). In between those two are what we call the passions or emotions, which are distinct from appetite and reason. They are irrational, not expressions of physiological needs. The self is likened to a winged two-horse chariot driven by a charioteer (reason), who has difficulty with one of the horses, a wild, disobedient animal (Plato, 1995:246a–246d).

Plato's moral theory focuses on the struggle 'inside' an individual. The wider context, such as the social or political, is not involved in understanding the emotions. Plato seems to assume a distinct 'within' and 'without', 'inner' and 'outer', although it has been argued that the ontological status of the three 'elements' of the self vary in the dialogues. In the *Phaedrus* he speaks of distinct 'parts' of self. In the *Symposium*, however, he regards it as 'a single stream of mental energy'. A translator and commentator of *The Republic*, Desmond Lee, reminds his reader that Plato's intention is not to speak 'with scientific precision, but rather on the level of ordinary conversation' and that he is more concerned about ethics than psychology; about motives of self and its impulses to action. Lee is convinced that much of Plato's language, when he speaks of 'parts', 'elements', or 'faculties' of self, is metaphorical (Plato, 1987:207). Plato's concern is to describe the conflicts people encounter within when making decisions to act. In dialogue with Glaucon, Socrates explains:

'The mind of the thirsty man, therefore, in so far as he is thirsty, simply wants to drink, and it is to that end that its energies are directed.'

'Clearly.'

'If therefore there is something in it that resists its thirst, it must be something in it other than the thirsty impulse which is dragging it like a wild animal to drink. For we have agreed that the same thing cannot act in opposite ways with the same part of itself towards the same object.'

'That is impossible.'

'For instance, it is not fair to say that an archer's hands are pulling and pushing the bow at the same time, but that one hand is pushing it, the other pulling.'

'Certainly.'

'Now, can we say that men are sometimes unwilling to drink even though they are thirsty?'

'Oh yes; that is often true of many people,' he said.

'Then how are we to describe such cases?' I asked. 'Must we not say that there is one element in their minds which bids them drink, and a second which prevents them and masters the first?'

'So it seems.'

'And isn't the element of prevention, when present, due to our reason, while the urges and impulses are due to our feelings and unhealthy cravings' (Plato, 1987, 439b–439e).

Socrates continues to define the nature of the third 'part' of self. He wonders what happens when a person believes he has been wronged. He explains to Glaucon:

> And what if he thinks he's been wronged? Then his indignation boils over and fights obstinately for what he thinks right, persevering and winning through hunger, cold and all similar trials. It won't give up the struggle till death or victory, or till reason calls it back to heel and calms it, like a shepherd calls his dog (Plato, 1987:440d, 440e).

The influence of Plato's moral philosophy on the history of ideas has been truly remarkable. But in contemporary philosophy, radically different ontologies have emerged that have rendered misleading the simile of mastery, that of a 'shepherd' (reason) in control of his 'dog' (emotion).

EMOTIONAL INTELLIGENCE

Broadly speaking, there are two distinct theories of understanding emotions—*cognitive* and *non-cognitive*. Non-cognitive theories of emotion identify emotional states with states of bodily arousal combined with a certain affect. An emotion can be identified as a feeling of being in a particular physiological state. For example, an increased heart rate and tense jaw muscles don't just *accompany* anger, but anger *is* the sensation of being in those physical states. In contrast, *cognitive* theories hold that an emotion necessarily involves a judgement, an idea, or a perception. During the past thirty years or so, many cognitive theorists agree that emotions are forms of cognition, sometimes called 'appraisals' (Meadows, 2006). They involve evaluative judgements about something 'in' the world (Schleiffer & McCormick, 2006:17). We get angry, jealous, or sad on the basis of beliefs about how things are and what is important to us.

The central question here for some philosophers of education (see e.g. Kristjansson, 2010) is whether emotions are 'donors' of moral value or merely 'recorders', that is, do moral facts exist independently of human beings feeling them? A commitment to the individualistic view (e.g. Kristjansson, 2010; Goldie, 2010) is problematic as the question already assumes a 'gap' between the world 'out there' and human beings experiencing 'this world', with moral judgements and emotions somehow bridging this 'gap' (or not). As temporal thinking and feeling bodies, we always find ourselves 'in' this world already, and we regard emotions as part of the intricate, complex web of the aesthetic, the social, the ethical, and the political. When, as our starting point for thinking about emotions, we use the idea developed by Hannah Arendt that individuals *are* always *with* others (Heidegger's *Mitsein*) a different picture emerges of what the relationship is between an individual and the community (see e.g. Todd, 2009; see also Chapters 3 & 4). The question of whether emotions are 'donors' or 'recorders' simply becomes irrelevant.

Cognitive theories of emotion come in many variations. An influential position is that of Robert Solomon and Neo-Aristotelian philosopher Martha Nussbaum who argue that emotions are *judgements* (Solomon, 1993, 2004; Nussbaum, 2001, 2004). In an oft quoted work on the roles of emotions in philosophy, Solomon argues that they are not only *evaluative* judgements, but also *constitutive* judgements: emotions do not just *find* interpretations and evaluations of the world, but they *construct* them. Emotions *supply* the standards by which we interpret our experiences and are meaningful to us (Solomon, 1993:132–134). For Nussbaum emotions are informative expressions of, and responses to, dynamic social relationships. Emotions arrest the intellect to pause and reflect, are part of the mind's moral course, and contain evaluative appraisals of situations (Bonnett, 1994; Donaldson, 1993; Nussbaum, 1990, 2001, 2004).

Social and cultural factors have a significant effect on how people develop, experience, and show emotions—a position called social interactionism (Hochschild, 1983:211). From this position emotions are social constructions and serve to defend social norms, values, and beliefs and to shape personal identity. Feminists focus on questions of how the experience and display of emotion may be a site of social control or political transformation; how emotions may serve to maintain the *status quo* of dominant patriarchal, hierarchical, capitalist systems; or how emotions may be used to disrupt these systems (Winograd, 2003:1643). Historically women have been associated with feelings, which, although valued in the private sphere, are often frowned on when expressed freely in the public sphere of gendered institutions such as schools (Winograd, 2003:1645). Ken Winograd distinguishes between *functional* and *dysfunctional* uses of emotions (Winograd, 2003:1642). Functional uses alert teachers to problems that can and need to be solved. Dysfunctional uses of emotions, in contrast:

> reflect situations in which teachers' emotions (especially dark emotions like anger and disgust) do not lead to positive action but, instead, lead to blaming of either self, students, parents, or the system (Winograd, 2003:1642).

In P4C, fearful emotions provoked by philosophical enquiries are functional when they are seen as moral and political signposts and motivators for (political) action. Teachers often suppress or change their 'dark emotions' rather than critiquing structural problems in the workplace, putting considerable strain on their own mental health and well-being. Similarly, children's 'troublesome' emotions are seldom understood as criticism of the set-up at school. The profound moral conflict female teachers face daily is to conform to the ideal of being maternal, nurturing, and patient on the one hand, and to comply with school bureaucracy with its demands for rationality and the control of students and teachers, on the other hand. Much emotional upheaval in schools is the result of the construction of relationships between adults and children. Participation in a community of enquiry requires vulnerability, epistemological tentativeness, and modesty, so it is not surprising that the practice of philosophical enquiry in community settings often invites censorship. For transformation to take place, however, Zembylas reminds us that vulnerability to negotiate new affective connections is necessary (Zembylas, 2007:305). The 'darker emotions' that sometimes surface in communities of enquiry challenge the idea that emotions are divorced from rationality and knowledge acquisition. Emotions can be described as '*a way of knowing* and as a distinct realm in which meaning is constructed' (Zembylas, 2007:297; our emphasis).

It is only very recently that the interface between ethics, social relationships, emotions, and cognitive models of the world has come to the fore in educational research. Emotions are not only a private matter but also a *political space*, in that prescriptions about which emotions are allowed to be expressed and by whom and under what circumstances locate power in emotional expression (Winograd, 2003; Zembylas, 2007:296).

Unfortunately, with Plato as one of their major influences, emotions are still mostly regarded as individual, subjective, inner mental states in educational contexts. Such an essentialist, psychological base strips the individual subject from its context. The assumption is that learners are confused about their emotions. Guided by the expert-in-emotions adult and through structured talk, the idea is that specially designed exercises and worksheets will fix this confusion and restore order. Our use of self-critical and playful picturebooks[2] is an alternative to behaviour management and competence/skill approaches to emotional literacy. In our practice we seek opportunities to explore the role various emotions play in experience philosophically and acknowledge their complex role in practical judgement.

INTELLIGENCE OF EMOTIONS

'Emotional intelligence' (EI) has been popularised by Daniel Goleman. He describes it as the capacity to recognise our own feelings and those of others for motivating ourselves, and for managing emotions well in ourselves and in our relationships (Goleman, 1995:42–45). As is the case in Plato's moral theory, there is an assumption that understanding our emotions (e.g.

through brain research) will help to control and *manage* them and avoid their 'spillage' into an otherwise more objective reasoning process. He talks about the importance of controlling impulses and regulating one's moods. Distress should be kept from *'swamping the ability to think'* (Goleman, 1995:34) as a means to, for example, prevent violence (Schleiffer & McCormick, 2006:15).

Sophie Rietti (2009) cautions educators that such an approach to emotional intelligence can become a form of social control and indoctrination. She explains that the original inspiration for the concept of emotional intelligence, the work of psychologists John D. Mayer and Peter Salovey, was not intended as a measure of personality or character, but as value-neutral knowledge or skills (Rietti, 2009:260). She critiques the clear moral and political agenda of EI as conceptualised by Goleman and others (e.g. Reuven Bar-On). Without rejecting EI altogether, she points at the lack of a fact/value distinction in Goleman's theoretical account and the blurring of lines between applied science and moral education. A theorist has to *justify* why the proposed values and virtues are desirable. Simply conforming to a particular value system that happens to have widespread consensus is not satisfactory (Rietti, 2009:269).

Grounding the choice of educational material on certain beliefs about EI confuses the emotionally literate person with the morally good person (Gardner, 1999:206). Accounts of EI or emotional literacy make no references to class, gender, and race in a highly individualistic conceptualisation of emotions. The child skilled and drilled for self-control is stripped away from its context. In the capitalist labour market, emotions are commodities (Burman, 2008b:274–277). Erika Burman critiques Goleman and others for depoliticising EI, reducing emotional literacy to a personal growth and self-awareness exercise. By connecting it with mental health, well-being, moral agency, and good citizenship, EI has become a politically conservative tool (Burman, 2009). According to Burman, the metaphor emotional *literacy* suggests the educational alternative would be to focus on educational interventions that develop

> a discourse about emotion, rather than the discovery or recognition of some essential inner, individual feelings that require naming in order either to be better tamed or communicated (although these may happen too) (Burman, 2009:150).

She suggests that one way of putting the social origin and moral dimensions of emotions on the agenda is to:

> become interested in children's emotional experiences, rather than in trying to manage them or make uncomfortable emotions disappear, then we have to engage with them, and with our own responses to them (Burman, 2008b:277).

Although many cognitive theorists in the psychological and philosophical literature (including Daniel Goleman) justify their approaches by referring to Ancient Greek philosopher Aristotle, he has been profoundly misunderstood (Kristjansson, 2005, 2007, 2010). Aristotle did not claim that emotions need to be 'managed' through self-discipline and willpower as tools to keep emotions under the control of reason. For Aristotle self-control is not a virtue. Kristjansson explains:

> Only the virtuous person has his emotions, as well as his actions, in a mean; he does not need to control them since he is a manifestation of his own properly felt emotions (Kristjansson, 2005:681).

For Aristotle, bringing intelligence to our emotions means infusing the emotions with intelligence, rather than policing them from above with intelligence (Kristjansson, 2005:680; 2010). Anger, for example, is not like a horse that needs to be tamed by a charioteer[3], but it can be virtuous if felt at the right time and expressed towards 'the right people, with the right motive, and in the right way' (Aristotle, 1973:378 [1106b]).

Aristotle compares this to good works of art: it is impossible to either take away or add anything as excess or deficiency will destroy the goodness of art. Similarly, the mean preserves the goodness of anger. Anger should not be eradicated or controlled, but making sense of the multiplicity of meanings of such an emotion informs decisions about the actions we take. Emotions are a judgement or set of judgements that embody our dynamic relationships and express the values, ideals, structures, and mythologies through which we experience and evaluate our lives (Solomon, 1993:126).

In contrast to *emotional intelligence*, the phrase *intelligence of emotions* (Nussbaum, 2001) suggests that we can learn from our emotions—that they can point out truths that are otherwise not available to us. Emotions express moral values. As *subtle* and *sophisticated* responses to others and events, they provide information about the world and others. Anger, for example, can *tell* us about a situation in a different way and make us think differently about it. We may have been wronged or damaged—information that perhaps would otherwise not be available to us.

THE HOOK TO CATCH FLIES?

There is an intricate link in Nussbaum's work between the intelligence of emotions and literature. Authors' artistic ability to display life's events as they unfold and happen to their characters makes the reader care about the events. Inspired by Marcel Proust she reminds us that:

one of the primary aims of literary art is to show us moments in which habit is cut through by the unexpected, and to engender in the reader a similar upsurge of true, surprised feeling (Nussbaum, 1990:43).

The emotions are not just the 'hook' to 'catch' the reader into the cognitive work required in, for example, a philosophical enquiry. It is the emotional itself that provides understanding, as we will now illustrate with a detailed analysis of the picturebook *Frog in Love* (1989) by Max Velthuijs. When Frog makes the highest jump in history to impress the duck he has fallen in love with, the careful description of the unexpected event that follows makes us care about Frog's bumpy ride 'back to earth' and illuminates love's painful trials:

> At thirteen minutes past two on Friday morning, things went wrong. Frog was doing his highest jump in history when he lost his balance and fell to the ground. Duck, who happened to be passing at the time, came hurrying up to help him (Velthuijs, 1989).

This is a key moment in the story—a sudden reversal in circumstances, or what Aristotle calls *peripeteia* (Bruner, 2002:5).The specificity of the timing and the place of the accident draws the reader even more into Frog's predicament.

We see here an interesting link between the community of enquiry pedagogy and the use of literature in Aristotelian conceptions of learning and teaching. Nussbaum writes:

> A large part of learning takes place in the experience of the concrete. This experiential learning, in turn, requires the cultivation of perception and responsiveness: the ability to read a situation, singling out what is relevant for thought and action. This active task is not a technique; one learns it by guidance rather than by a formula (Nussbaum, 1990:44).

We suggest that in the school context such 'guidance' involves listening and dialogue, and that these are not problem free (see Part III). Novels can exemplify and offer experiential learning. The dialogical relationship between narrative and reader is extended to a similarly dialogical relationship among members of a community of enquirers. This also includes the facilitator who acts as a guide in 'the cultivation of perception'[4]. We learn about the meaning of love through our dwelling on and dialogical responsiveness to Frog's particular predicament. It is the unexpectedness of the 'twists and turns' in literature that surprise and compel the reader. Emotions are not simply 'hooks' to 'catch' students' attention and commitment to the construction of new ideas, but the emotional dimension of a narrative provides insight into its meanings—meanings that are as ambiguous as life itself: finite and full of events outside our control.

Frog is not alone in not knowing who he is in love with. Nussbaum expresses the complexity involved beautifully:

> We deceive ourselves about love—about who; and how; and when; and whether. We also discover and correct our self-deceptions. The forces making for both deception and unmasking here are various and powerful: the unsurpassed danger, the urgent need for protection and self-sufficiency, the opposite and equal need for joy and communication and connection. Any of these can serve either truth or falsity, as the occasion demands. The difficulty then becomes: how in the midst of this confusion (and delight and pain) do we know what view of ourselves, what parts of ourselves, to trust? Which stories about the condition of the heart are the reliable ones and which the self-deceiving fictions? We find ourselves asking where, in this plurality of discordant voices with which we address ourselves on this topic of perennial self-interest, is the criterion of truth? (And what does it mean to look for a criterion here? Could that demand itself be a tool of self-deception?) (Nussbaum, 1990:261).

Although she finds Proust's answer attractive that 'knowledge of the heart comes from the heart' (Nussbaum, 1990:262), she prefers a more radical, non-scientific solution (a scientific solution could be symbolised through the character Hare, who carefully attends to Frog's symptoms, analysing and categorising, unifying and generalising). Frog's predicament poses fascinating questions about the nature of love and how we do indeed *know* we are in love. To what extent are we passive victims in our love for others? Does our love reveal itself, as it does for Frog, through our inability to eat or sleep and through self-conscious embarrassment when in the company of our loved one? Do we have a choice in our desire to express love through art and extraordinary deeds to impress our sweetheart? Most importantly, to what extent can we deceive ourselves that we do indeed love someone?

Frog seems powerless in his love. The story suggests that he cannot help but love Duck and that he cannot deceive himself about his love. Nussbaum would have difficulty with the idea that self-deception is not possible. Is Frog simply confused or, for example, expressing egocentric needs? Nussbaum insists that in order to be sure that this pain we experience is love— and not, for example, fear or grief or envy—other beliefs and circumstances need to be examined (Nussbaum, 1990:269, 270).

The difficulty in establishing whether Frog really is in love has to do with the possible circularity of Frog's knowledge. Frog knows he is in love because of his suffering: he cannot eat or sleep and cannot address Duck directly. In this way, love is defined as the very things revealed to Frog. Frog's analysis of his 'condition' seems a solitary affair; Duck is not in the vicinity. He does not know whether his love is reciprocated or not. Knowledge or trust in the feelings of the other appear to be irrelevant for what love *is*. Nussbaum would probably disagree with such a portrayal of love. We suspect that she would say that Frog's love is an interesting relation with himself, rather than '*a source of dangerous openness*' (Nussbaum, 1990:272).

At first sight Frog's gender may not be accidental (Frog's creator is also male). Nussbaum speculates that her discussions about love with undergraduate students confirm Carol Gilligan's related observations in her influential work *In a Different Voice*: the emphasis on autonomy and control in the education of males seems to make men more interested in views of love that promise self-sufficiency (Nussbaum, 1990:276, footnotes 20, 21). Women are more likely to agree with a conception of love as not a state or function of the solitary person, but '*a complex way of being, feeling, and interacting with another person. To know one's love is to trust it, to allow oneself to be exposed*' and '*to fear being criticised, deceived and mocked*'. Above all, '*it is to trust the other person*' (Nussbaum, 1990:274, 276, footnote 21). For Nussbaum, love is a relationship. Frog's love is *about* Duck. This *aboutness*—how he sees and interprets her—is part of the emotion itself. His perception of her may change over time. He may start to perceive her as a threat or a source of embarrassment. He may start to hate or pity her. Frog's beliefs and judgements about Duck and the values he attaches to her are crucial to the identity of the emotion itself (Nussbaum, 2004:188, 189).

RE-COGNISING LOVE

Characters in literature transcend particularity: Frog helps us mediate between individual, concrete experiences of love and the abstract concept of love. He *is* a frog and, at the same time, he is *not*; he is Frog, neither animal nor human. Love's inter-relational nature and vulnerability are apparent throughout the text, especially when he finally plucks up the courage to admit to Duck his feelings for her. But more than anything else, it is the *pictures* that pull on the heartstrings of young and old; his facial expressions and bodily movements re-*mind* us of love's delights and suffering and help us re-*cognise* love.

What can we learn from Nussbaum's analysis of love and the way in which we have applied some of her ideas about emotions to the *Frog in Love* picturebook? It seems that *defining* love by an analytic summing up of necessary and sufficient conditions is impossible. In doing so, we would miss what love *is*. Nussbaum urges us to turn to stories, as 'knowledge of love is a love story' (Nussbaum, 2004:274). Thought experiments or philosophical text books miss the human contextualisation. We need to know much more about Frog to decide, for example, whether he really is in love or whether it is self-deception. Like cognition, emotions have no privileged place of trust, and their truth or falsity involves a continuous dialogical checking of relevance and consistency in picture, text, the temporal history of both author and artefact, and one's own complex history of emotions. This dialogical process can be enriched by verbalising thoughtful emotion and passionate thoughts in a community of others[5]. This is *not* the same as the idea that children need to 'master' the vocabulary that exists with regards to the emotional life as Ann Margaret Sharp (a former colleague and associate of Lipman) proposes. She explains:

> I might experience a sensation, such as what seems a pain in my stomach, but if I cannot put a word to the sensation, e.g. jealousy or envy, there is a real sense in which I cannot reflect on it. Just as there is a specific vocabulary identified with the cognitive life, so such a vocabulary exists with the emotional life. And somehow children must master this vocabulary (Sharp, 2007:255; our emphasis).

For Sharp, the educational aim of Philosophy for Children (P4C) is to bring about 'emotional maturity' (another form of management), and, significantly, it is the teachers' role to 'refine their understanding' by providing opportunities to 'identify the nouns, verbs and adjectives that describe emotions' (Sharp, 2007:255). The idea is that we can identify only complex emotions and think about them if we have learned the necessary language. Is it true that concepts are the 'tools' to 'uncover' the existence of various emotions, and are adults indeed in a better position to do so? How context specific is this language? Could young children offer unique perspectives relative to their 'form of life' (see in particular Murris, 2000a)?

An alternative view is to understand our re-cognition of love and associated behaviours as *products* of our own categorisations, that the language itself brings certain emotions into existence. By calling particular experiences 'love', certain socially, culturally, and historically influenced patterns of behaviour are set in motion. Take, for example, Frog's lack of appetite, creative art-attacks, and giving of flowers to Duck. Without Hare's 'diagnosis', would Frog have behaved in a similar vein? Would he have felt the same 'thing'?

Discomfort with uncertainty, however, tends to steer teachers into the direction of educational approaches that offer a scientific (but false) sense of security. Psychological approaches tend to look for *causes*, and the effect (e.g. disruptive behaviour) can be modified by changing the cause. In *Frog Is Sad* (2003), also by Max Velthuijs, a more complex picture emerges. In the story, Frog wakes up feeling sad. He feels like crying but does not know why. He simply cannot be happy. His friends try to cheer him up, but all efforts are in vain. When Rat plays him a tune so beautiful that Frog begins to cry, Rat laughs and laughs until Frog's smile grows and grows until he is laughing and singing and dancing with Rat. All his sadness is gone. When Little Bear asks him: '*But why were you so sad in the first place?*' Frog responds, '*I don't know . . . I just was*' (Velthuijs, 2003).

As emotions are not fixed entities, not just feelings 'inside' ourselves that need to be managed or controlled, but informative expressions of and responses to dynamic social relationships, the role P4C could play in the education of the emotions becomes visible. Identification of how and what we feel is far from straightforward, and, as Nussbaum suggests, we could even deceive ourselves about the love (we think) we feel for a person. Our emotions are constructed through our language, our morals, our history, our culture, and our thinking, and they are in constant flux.

Exploring stories with others in an environment that actively nourishes and encourages talk about thinking and emotions helps learners (and teachers) to construct complex self-narratives and understanding of others. As participants in a community of enquiry listen to the diverse descriptions of what falls under umbrella terms such as 'love', 'anger', or 'jealousy', they become accustomed to the need to reflect on such descriptions and the experiences they express. They start to question the meaning of such words before such meanings become more anchored and solidified in self-narratives and narrative accounts of others. It is in this sense that psychological approaches to emotional literacy can be unhelpful. They merely present the vocabulary and meaning of the emotions as though straightforward, explicable, and unambiguous, as if all you need to understand them is to know the word that represents them. In contrast, participants in philosophical enquiry have the opportunity to embrace the uncertainty that comes with philosophical thinking.

Philosophical dialogues increase children's and teachers' vocabulary, but also, and more importantly, they help to develop a critical, meta-cognitive stance towards the meaning of core concepts and the role emotions play in thinking and everyday living.

UPHEAVALS OF THOUGHT

Philosophising involves the emotions at various levels. Philosophical questioning presupposes flexibility of thought, openness to new ideas, a cultivation of 'non-attachment', and a realisation of one's own ignorance (Griswold, 1986:125, 126). This can create emotional upheaval: feeling stupid, inadequate, or out of control. The answers to philosophical questions cannot be spoon-fed, nor can the methods of answering such questions be taught or prescribed. Each of us has to do our own thinking and has to be 'open' to the ambiguity philosophical ideas present.

Philosophical thinking also includes what Israel Scheffler calls the 'rational passions': the lust for truth, contempt of lying, and desire for accuracy in observation and inference. Without inspiration, curiosity, and excitement over intriguing problems, there could be no philosophical enquiry (Scheffler, 1983:18). A wide variety of emotions are on 'full alert' when engaged in a philosophical dialogue: excitement, anger, frustration, delight, etc. Classroom philosophers need courage to develop and express their own thinking and to be 'open' enough to have their own thoughts influenced and challenged by others. The resilience required for philosophical enquiry is highlighted in what the late philosopher of education Victor Quinn calls the 'social, intellectual virtues' (Quinn, 1997:83–93).

In this chapter we have moved beyond an individualised conception of emotions and argued that they do not simply happen to bodies, but that they are forms of knowledge—'subjects *do* their emotions' (Zembylas, 2007:297). Human bodies normally exist in groups and in social interaction, not in isolation, and this shapes how we experience our emotions and 'the mechanisms with which emotions are 'disciplined' and certain norms are imposed and internalised as 'normal' ' (Zembylas, 2007:299, 300). In philosophical enquiries these bodies can be playful, imaginative, fantastic, pertinent to current events, or concerned with the immediate and the everyday. One's whole being is affected in the critical self-reflection and self-correction that comes with being a member of a community of enquiry that investigates experiences critically, creatively, caringly, and collaboratively.

Questions raised in philosophical enquiry can be wide-ranging and do not have to be sensitive or controversial to provoke emotional dissonance or disturbance. Philosophy with children is not a detached intellectual exercise. Philosophising entails a passionate commitment to rigorous and reflective thinking. Children and teachers experience perplexity, curiosity, and wonder. If all goes well, members of a community of enquiry experience the pleasure of agreement and the frustration and challenge of disagreement. They may experience confusion, struggle and disenchantment, excitement, disappointment, elation, and embarrassment. Making judgements involves emotions such as doubt, uncertainty, and confidence (see e.g. Schleiffer, 2006:42). All of these emotions are characteristic of the process of thinking and philosophical enquiry.

In P4C there is a shift in responsibility for the lesson away from the teacher and towards the classroom community. Teachers may experience confusion, surprise, or unease when they realise the democratic nature of the practice in which children help to direct both the content and shape of a lesson. The link that learners make between a narrative and their own experiences is an essential part of the practice and significantly contributes to the anxiety teachers experience when working philosophically with picturebook narratives.

These emotions are not just 'props' or 'supports' for intelligence, but they are the essential elements of human intelligence. Nussbaum (after Proust) refers to them as 'upheavals of thought'. Like geological upheavals, they are part of the same landscape of cognition, and as 'thoughts about value and importance they make the 'mind project outward like a mountain range' (Nussbaum, 2001:1, 3). We suggest that the multi-layered, complex mix of emotions involved in exploring picturebooks philosophically informs insights gained in the pursuit of meaning and truth in communities of enquiry, rather than detracting or distorting them,.

Making sense of a picturebook such as *Frog in Love* is an aesthetic experience in the Deweyan sense; it lingers on in our minds as 'an experience'. For philosopher John Dewey, experience involves both receptive undergoing and productive doing: an interaction with, and a reconstruction and transformation of, our environment and self. Aesthetic quality clarifies and concentrates meanings which are diffused and scattered in ordinary experience (De Haan, 1995; Dewey, 1991). In our interaction with the story, 'concentrated' meaning emerges, like a stock cube. What is normally dispersed in everyday experience now stands out and will be remembered. Value, and therefore emotion, is attached to the experience.

It is often assumed that the relationship between reader and picturebook is a *causal* one: the *effect* on the reader is *induced* by the text and pictures, which in turn is the *effect* of the artist's intentions and emotions. This is sometimes referred to as the *expression theory of art* and professed by R. G. Collingwood (Warburton, 2003:37–65). This aesthetic theory assumes a lack of choice by the reader about the intensity or nature of the effect a work of art has. In this view, a young child reading *Frog in Love* may unwillingly and passively absorb the emotions and intentions of the artist. Understanding emotions as *cognitive appraisals* or constitutive judgements helps to form a different standpoint which is relevant for our exploration of censoring certain picturebooks. Art appeals to and expresses emotions, and at the very same time it includes significant cognitive elements:

> aesthetic appreciation is already riddled with judgments, including judgments about the medium, about the subject matter, about the artist, and about the art as art (Solomon, 1993:134).

The aesthetic appreciation of a picturebook involves a process that draws on body and mind, emotion and cognition.

COMPLEX JUDGEMENTS

In this chapter we have problematised contemporary popular psychological understanding of emotion by focusing on one book in particular, Nussbaum's *Love's Knowledge*. With the help of the picturebook *Frog in Love* we have disentangled some of her complex arguments about 'love', what it means, and how literature can provide insight. We have argued against a behaviourist approach to emotions, and through a detailed exploration of 'love' in the context of *Frog in Love* we have suggested an alternative, philosophical approach to emotions that regards them as neither fixed entities nor feelings 'inside' our 'selves' that need to be managed or controlled, but as complex *judgements*.

There is an intricate link between the role emotions play in literature and the engagement thinkers experience in a community of philosophical enquiry. Authors' artistic ability creates narrative contexts that enable the reader to care about the events and characters. It is the unexpectedness of the 'twists and turns' in literature that surprises and compels the reader. Emotions are not used as 'hooks' to 'catch' children's attention and commitment to the construction of new ideas, but it is the emotional dimension of a narrative that provides insight into its meanings—insights that are as ambiguous as life itself: finite and full of events outside our control. In contrast, specially written resources for the teaching of philosophy are sometimes devoid of emotions. The narrative is seen as an instrument to focus minds on the deliberately inserted philosophical issues that can be 'lifted' from the story. The quality of the writing (or illustrations) is not seen as relevant for the depth of philosophical engagement and understanding.

In picturebooks the 'gaps' between words and pictures require imagination and *empathetic understanding*, offering a distinct kind of (emotional) knowledge. Reading *Frog in Love* requires much 'gap-filling'—a continuous creation of affective connections between various parts of the story, the characters, the pictures, and our own everyday experiences. In the next chapter, we explore the ambiguous nature of high quality contemporary picturebooks in the context of dominant approaches to teaching literacy and the perspectives of some literary critics.

6 Literary and Philosophical Responses to Picturebooks

PIGEON-HOLING PICTUREBOOKS

This chapter explains what is innovative about philosophical responses to picturebooks in a field dominated by aesthetic, literary, and psychological approaches. With the help of a detailed critique of examples of classroom dialogues with children, interspersed with examples from our own work, we claim that the indeterminate and ambiguous nature of contemporary picturebooks demands a pedagogy in which teachers do not control what counts as truth and meaning. We draw out the implications for what and who children's literature is for. This first part of the book concludes with an overview of characteristics that we look out for when we select picturebooks for philosophical enquiry.

The boredom children can suffer when faced with specially created instructional resources disappears when teachers introduce books that do not moralise or patronise, but offer rich, complex, and ambiguous narratives that communicate to young readers that they are taken seriously as thinkers. This includes giving learners the freedom and support to make sense of narratives themselves by drawing on their own strategies, values, and life experiences.

In Chapter 3 we referred to the quiet revolution that has taken place in the production of good quality, contemporary picturebooks (Arizpe & Styles, 2003). Serious study and appreciation of this new cultural form has typically lagged behind its initial appearance (Lewis, 2001), so it is not surprising that picturebooks have escaped the notice of philosophers and educators. Many educators still pigeon-hole picturebooks as resources for teaching literacy to young readers, rather than being recognised as aesthetic objects that can provoke deep *philosophical* responses from people of all ages.

Philosophy with picturebooks is new in a field that is dominated by aesthetic (e.g. Doonan), literary, and psychological approaches (e.g. Arizpe & Styles; Baddeley & Eddershaw; Hunt; Lewis; Nodelman; Sipe & Pantaleo; Styles & Bearne & Watson; Wallen). There is much talk about the mutually dependent narratives of picturebooks that make them postmodern texts but little about the consequences of postmodernism on teaching and learning practices. The dominant influence of traditional developmental psychology on (visual) literacy and language learning (Arizpe & Styles, 2003:30) may explain this lack of philosophical coherence. Our search for the coherence between educational theory and practice is an ongoing concern in our work.

Even in the highly scholarly and well-researched field of oracy and (visual) literacy, teachers are seen as remaining firmly in control of what counts as truth and meaning in contemporary picturebooks. In *Not So Simple Picturebooks*, for example, the authors explain that:

> The best picturebooks are open to interpretation because they leave so much unsaid. Coming to terms with the subtext demands from children a high level of thinking, but *with sensitive teacher intervention* they can gain considerable insight into what lies beneath the apparently simple surface of a book (Baddeley & Eddershaw, 1996:1; our emphasis).

Their developmental assumptions are also made clear:

> the older the child the greater their insight will be into *the* meaning . . . [and] . . . the response of the older children was excitingly *mature* and that the books were preparing them for coping with the complexities of more demanding texts at later stages of their development as readers (Baddeley & Eddershaw, 1996:1; our emphasis).

In other words, 'sensitive teacher intervention' is the instrument to grasp 'the' meaning of the book and helps to bridge the transition from books with simple texts (but complex meanings) to more difficult texts, although they do not regard picturebooks as 'a stage to be passed through and left behind' (Baddeley & Eddershaw, 1996:75).

Geoff Fox values ways in which picturebooks can teach readers to read 'between' and even 'beyond' the lines. 'Juggling with inferences', for him, is part of the art of reading of any piece of fiction. 'Gaps' deliberately left by the author need to be 'filled' by the reader. Significantly, there seems to be a right way of doing this 'gap-filling' (Fox, 1996:160–162) which qualifies learners as 'mature' readers (see quote above). Gaps are filled and surfaces smoothed over through *symbolic* readings. What constitutes 'mature' or sophisticated reading are the inferences made through metaphors. The experienced adult is regarded as the expert who initiates and guides the novice reader in this practice.

Whilst we believe there is a place for learning about the lives and interests of authors and illustrators, as well as their distinctive styles of writing and creating images, the metaphor of a 'smooth surface' with all the 'gaps filled' highlights the false promise of a certain and secure meaning capable of being established with the help of expert adults. Even in an otherwise excellent introduction to what they call 'visual literacy', Evelyn Arizpe and Morag Styles purport to offer open-ended approaches to literacy learning, but the techniques described in their book *Children Reading Pictures* (2003) involve teachers who are firmly in control of the questions that are asked in class. Their pre-prepared questions are carefully constructed for learners to arrive at the 'right' answers, despite the authors' claim that risk-taking and normalising fallibility is essential for inclusion in literacy, and that learners are involved in a 'modest community of inquiry' (Arizpe & Styles, 2003:161).

MISSING THE POINT

At first sight, the 'community of enquiry' method has a strong appeal to educators interested in oracy and literacy. This is because of the surface similarities with other discussion type classroom activities. But it is misleading to use the phrase when it is only the *teachers*, rather than the *learners*, who ask the questions. We illustrate our claim that in much (visual) literacy and oracy *practice* there is an implicit and sometimes explicit desire by adults to remain in control of constructing meaning, despite the rich theoretical offerings of the contemporary writing in those academic fields. We will focus in detail on some transcripts of dialogues with children and the authors' evaluations of children's contributions. The examples have been taken from the above mentioned book by Arizpe and Styles (2003) which reflects the findings of a two-year study of children's responses to a handful of contemporary picturebooks. A closer look at some examples in the book serves to illustrate the difference between the more common literacy approach and our own philosophical approach to the very same picturebooks.

Some readings are more '*mature*', '. . . *some of the children missed the point* . . .', and '*Joe* . . . *came closest*' (Arizpe & Styles, 2003:90,106,127) in formulating the 'correct' answer that dividing a page with a gorilla's head in quadrants in Anthony Browne's *Zoo* (1993) signifies crucifixion (see Figure 6.1).

Such answers are arrived at by mediations such as: '*Look at this shape. Does it remind you of anything else? We've said windows; we've said bars of cages. Is there anything else this shape reminds you of?*' (Arizpe & Styles, 2003:90). Adults here, as '*more experienced readers*' (Arizpe & Styles, 2003:56), carefully construct their questions to lead to what is seen by the adult as the correct interpretation.

As such, the readers' explorations stay 'within' the book[1], and although this process involves sophisticated translation and interpretation of the narrative, no deliberate room has been made for the *community of readers* to explore the questions and ideas the narrative provokes for *them*. The dialogue initiated by teachers' questions is goal orientated

Figure 6.1   Image from *Zoo* by Anthony Browne.

and serves the teaching of visual literacy, language, and literacy learning. The educational activity is still very much driven by adults' agendas within an epistemological framework that assumes objective and static knowledge and truth. An example shows that, despite their well-intentioned efforts, the dialogues are not a 'dialogue between a child and his *future*', as they claim, but 'between the child and an adult's *past*' (Arizpe & Styles, 2003:153). Ten year olds, presented with the disturbing image of an orangutan in the same picture book *Zoo* (see Figure 6.2), respond as follows:

Sue: Because he is sort of similar to a human, he should be treated like a human.

Lara: Because he looks like he's got hair coming down . . . it has got really long hair.

Sue: And it has got hairy ears.

Tony: And it has got grey hairs like an old person.

Sue: He looks like he's got his hair in a bun at the top and like . . .

I: How do you know he is sad? . . .

(Arizpe & Styles, 2003:84, 85)

Figure 6.2   Second image from *Zoo* by Anthony Browne.

The teacher's question seems pre-planned and is unrelated to what the children are saying. Other dialogues with younger children about the same picture show the teacher's similar preoccupation with the question of how we can know or tell that the orangutan is sad (Arizpe & Styles, 2003:85). Her questions invite the young readers to find evidence for the answer to a question that she finds important—a typical teacher move.

Teaching philosophy in communities of enquiry gives space to take a direction *away* from the book, even where that would involve children's *own* experiences and may contradict adults' perceptions. This could be put in motion by asking questions that follow on from children's contributions and at the same time problematise the meaning of the central concepts they use. Matthew Lipman explains in an interview that 'Philosophy begins when we can discuss the language we use to discuss the world' (Naji, 2005:26). Philosophical questions encourage reflection on our everyday language (e.g. categorisations) and experiences and connect with what preoccupies the children. See Table 6.1 for some possible philosophical questions.

The questions problematise the meaning of the central concepts 'sad', 'happy', 'emotions', 'human', 'animals', and 'right treatment' and question the assumption that we can always tell whether a creature is sad. Also, the belief that animal emotions are like human emotions is problematised. Philosophical questions make *everyone* think, including the

Table 6.1   Literary and Philosophical Responses to *Zoo*

Literacy	Philosophy
How can you tell the orangutan is sad?	What is it about the way the orangutan looks that suggests sadness?
	Do you think the orangutan's sadness has anything to do with where it is or how it is being treated in the story?
	In what way is the orangutan 'sort of similar to a human'?
	What does it mean to 'be treated like a human'?
	What is the difference between animals and humans?
	What does it mean to be sad?
	Can we ever be certain someone is sad?
	Can you be happy and sad at the same time?
	Do animals have emotions like we do?

teacher. After all, as Ludwig Wittgenstein poignantly observed, 'A philosophical problem has the form 'I don't know my way about' ' (Wittgenstein, 1958). The 'my', significantly, includes both learners *and* teachers. We recognise a philosophical problem when we do not even know where to look for the solution. This is often accompanied by a bodily sensation indicating excitement and confusion. The complexity of philosophical questions makes it difficult even to *start* to answer the questions raised. No methodology is prescribed by the subject itself. This feature of philosophical enquiry, and the unexpected direction given to the enquiry by the community, can cause anxiety with teachers as facilitators.

Many contemporary picturebooks offer an additional advantage to young or struggling readers. The gaps between words and pictures, and the ambiguity of meaning, create a space in which readers bring their own experiences and knowledge to the reading process. Children often pick up more visual cues than older adults, who, on the whole, are more word orientated. These factors help to establish a genuine and collaborative relationship between adult and child in the complex process of meaning-making. At the same time, a more equal relationship in which both adult and child learn from each other as part of the reading experience can cause resistance among some teachers, as it challenges their status as the one who knows better or more or best. The associated decrease of power can provoke avoidance (*'there is no time for philosophy in an overcrowded curriculum'*) or censorial reactions, often projections of teachers' own fears (*'this will upset the children'*, *'children need certain answers'*).

We include the following examples from our classroom practice to illustrate a philosophical approach. Ten year olds were puzzled about the gender of the orangutan in *Zoo* (Figure 6.2): '*It must be a woman, and she is sad, coz' she misses her family, her children*'. The egg on the floor of the cage was his cue for the hypothesis. A girl disagreed: '*Look at the grey hairs, she must be old*' [therefore she couldn't still have children]. With the help of one of us as the facilitator, the community of learners subsequently enquired into a whole range of issues lasting many months (sessions of one hour a week). Here are some of the questions we explored: How old can/should you be to be a mum? Do mums miss their children when they have left home? Can you be happy living on your own? Can a zoo be a home (the children thought there was a fireplace in the cage: '*it is like a lounge*') and what makes a home a home? Could a human live in a cage? Is a house a cage of some sort? Is a school like a cage? Is there another orangutan higher up ('*it looks like a bit of hair at the top*')? Where do animals belong? Where do humans belong? Is 'belonging' the same as 'feeling at home'?

Until teachers are prepared to enter unknown territories of (often interdisciplinary) enquiries, referring to facilitation as 'focussed yet open-ended' (Arizpe & Styles, 2003:93) is misleading and can cause cynicism and misunderstandings. We have often been challenged by individuals and groups who are suspicious of the genuineness of the philosophical space we have helped to create in the classroom.

When teachers ask open-ended questions they usually focus on how people feel ('*What would you feel like if you were the orangutan?*') preventing *reasoned* responses. After all, we cannot disagree about each other's feelings as they are by definition private. Even worse, a question such as '*What do you think Anthony Browne wants us as readers of the book to feel?*' (Arizpe & Styles, 2003:93) is frustrating as this closed question (Browne probably knows the answer) can never be answered (unless we ask him). It communicates to children that they have to guess the 'right' answer, and it assumes that authors are in the best position to give the final word about 'the' meaning of their art. As we have seen in Chapters 2 and 3 in particular, artists often draw on their own unconscious childhood memories and 'deepest selves' and therefore may not even know themselves what their narrative 'is about'.

Apart from focusing on emotional identification by asking psychological questions, we have found that teachers often use questions as instruments to bring about good behaviour; they have to be seen to give the 'right' messages, as, for example, in: '*Do you think [the rubbish] says anything about the way people treat the planet?*' (Arizpe & Styles, 2003:160). An alternative learning objective we propose is the development of good judgement based on reasoning (e.g. initiating enquiries provoked by a question such as 'What counts as 'rubbish'?). Children may be judged to be 'missing the point', but *whose* 'point' is it in the first place? Knowledge acquisition and construction has political and moral dimensions we explore later in this book.

FROM MONOLOGUE TO DIALOGUE

In Chapter 3 we proposed that the modelling of a dialogical community of enquiry in action in philosophical novels is one of the main advantages of the Philosophy for Children (P4C) program. We have noticed in our own practice that the picturebooks that work particularly well for philosophical enquiries are those that contain plenty of exploratory open-ended dialogue. As a model for the kind of interaction developed in communities of enquiry such dialogues can take place between children and adults, between children and their peers, between children and their soft toys, or even between animals or fantasy characters, such as monsters.

For example, in *Sam's Worries* (1990), a delightful picturebook written by Maryann MacDonald and illustrated by Judith Riches, the central character Sam tells his Mum about the fears that keep him awake at night. He is worried that there might be a volcano under his house, cobras in his garage, or an earthquake while he is at school. He is also worried that the dinner lady is a witch, that he might lose his library books, or that vampires, monsters, and bogeyman really do exist. On top of all of that, he is worried—something he (importantly) does not tell his mum—that he may have jeopardised his place in heaven. There surely is no place in paradise for boys who steal biscuits from the biscuit tin!

He struggles to accept his mother's caring attempts to reassure him. She argues that there never has been a volcano or an earthquake here and cobras live in India, and although the dinner lady may look a bit 'creepy', she is not a witch. The library books will not be forgotten because they have been stacked up on the piano. With the 'biscuit problem', of course, Mum cannot help as she hasn't been told. She tucks him in bed, kisses him goodnight, and leaves.

Unusual in a book written for young children, this is not the end of the story. Instead of taking Mum's word for it and dropping off to sleep effortlessly—something parents certainly would hope for and often assume—the book continues to question Mum's wisdom by allowing both Sam and his teddy bear to put forward some persuasive counter arguments. Sam initiates a further dialogue with his bear. He whispers that although there never has been a volcano or an earthquake, 'there is always a first time'. Bear agrees and adds that 'cobras might swim here from India'. Sam is not convinced the dinner lady is not a witch either. After all she 'might just be pretending to be a nice lady'. Bear listens carefully and offers a good reason for this: the dinner lady may do this 'to fool mothers'. Also, Bear points out: just because your library books are on the piano there is no guarantee that you will not forget them. Sam adds another complexity: you 'could lose one on the way to the library'. They are now on a roll, and Bear argues that 'if vampires and monsters and bogeymen don't exist, why are so many people afraid of them?' Sam concludes that 'Mothers don't know everything'. Bear agrees and admits that he knows how Sam feels about the biscuits because he is a biscuit thief himself.

This is a crucial moment in the story. The text reads: 'Sam felt better. His bear understood'. Bear empathises and sympathises with Sam: he also steals biscuits from the biscuit tin. They are in the same boat, and their closeness helps Sam to resolve his anxieties at a deeper level than his conversations with Mum make possible. Under the sheet they take up a secret private place—removed from unnecessary adult intervention (see also Chapter 8). Their closeness and the equality of their relationship are also signified in the pictures. Their faces and facial expressions are very similar (see Figure 6.3).

Sam's Worries is respectful of children's own ability and desire to solve their own problems through reasoning and on their own terms. The depth of Sam's worries merits careful scrutiny of the arguments involved, but also an acknowledgement that, as is the case with many of our fears, reasoning alone does not dissolve his worries completely. Together they come up with

Figure 6.3   Image from *Sam's Worries* by Maryann MacDonald and Judith Riches.

an ingenious solution that works for both: Bear does the worrying when Sam is asleep at night, and Sam takes over during the day to enable Bear to catch up with lost sleep.

This picturebook is so suitable for philosophical enquiry because of its subtle combination of various factors. The illustrations are magnificent. Pastel colours and the thoughtful use of light create a soothing, dreamlike atmosphere. The main characters are not just very thoughtful, but also constructively critical in exposing the adult's limits in entering Sam's world. As adults we need to be humble and cautious when interpreting how children make sense of experiences. Sam and Bear create their own independent world under the quilt—a secret world where sins can be safely expressed. The 'biscuit problem' has great appeal to readers of all ages as it easily translates into moral wrongdoing of any kind. Though not always out of moral concerns, during philosophical enquiries children have expressed their worries that they may be 'too fat' to fly up to heaven, or perhaps heaven may 'be full', or perhaps they are not allowed 'in' because they are 'special needs' and are 'sometimes naughty'.

When using this picturebook for philosophical enquiry, children have questioned the concept 'heaven' and speculated about the 'mechanics' of going to heaven. This came as no surprise. We have found that 'heaven' is among the popular topics for philosophical questioning. Here are some samples: Are you 'alive' in heaven and do you sleep on a bed or on the floor? Are teddy bears or other toys dead? Do they come alive when adults are not looking?[2] Do teddy bears go to heaven? *Sam's Worries* also gives excellent opportunities to explore epistemological questions, such as, 'Who knows best, Mum or Bear?', 'If something has never happened, does it mean it will never happen?', 'How do we know our beliefs are true?', 'What is knowledge?', and 'What is truth?' The dialogical structure of this picturebook is helpful as a model for a community of enquiry. Such a dialogue can be textual or pictorial. Or it can be provoked by the relationship between the text and illustrations. Words and pictures are so interdependent that reading the words without the pictures would be like '. . . giving a performance of a concerto without an orchestra' (Graham, 1990:17). The picturebooks we work with are truly works of art.

PICTUREBOOKS AS WORKS OF ART

Author Maurice Sendak[3] compares the picturebook artist with a 'composer who thinks music while reading poetry'. And that a 'true picturebook is a visual poem'. He insists that it is the job of the illustrator to 'interpret the text as a musical conductor interprets a score' (Sendak quoted in Lanes, 1980:110). For him, children respond best to illustrations that suggest: 'a beat—a heartbeat, a musical beat, the beginning of a dance' and that there must be a 'breathing of life, a surging swing into action' (Sendak quoted in Lanes, 1980:110).

The late Max Velthuijs reports on his habitual beating the 'fear of the empty canvas' by making rough sketches, subsequently followed by lengthy periods of inaction. In an interview he explains: 'Ideas are carried along with you until they are ripe' (De Rijke & Hollands, 2006:190). He describes that the pictures would always come first—a process that could take him many months. He considered himself to be foremost a painter. Only later the words would come, which he believes is easy and then 'they go together, become one'. Monique Hagen describes him as neither a writer nor an illustrator, but 'a painter who tells stories while painting' (De Rijke & Hollands, 2006:192). Velthuijs's own favourite story is *Frog in Winter* (1992), described by a couple of literary critics as:

> a beautifully orchestrated piece, full of energy and contrast. A bold rhythmic pattern in the use of colour . . . from the icy blue and grey

of the harsh wintry landscape to warm terracotta and vermilion of the cosy Dutch interior. In Frog in Winter, Max discovered the possibilities of Frog's mouth line. Max uses gouache, a technique used to paint many layers of watercolour, which is how depth is created (De Rijke & Hollands, 2006:191).

Joanna Carey describes Frog's mouth as a 'sensitive line that registers every flicker of emotion' (Carey, 2004)[4]. Velthuijs explains that 'Colours evoke feelings. You can't calculate that, you can only recognise it' (Velthuijs in interview in De Rijke & Hollands, 2006:191).

Jane Doonan, who deals explicitly with the aesthetic quality of the pictures in picturebooks, explores the idea of how pictorial art communicates. She points at the expressive powers of pictures, which enables the book to function as an art object: 'Something which gives form to ideas and to which we can attach our ideas' (Doonan, 1993:7). Doonan argues that:

> By playing with the ideas provoked by a work of art, we create something of our own from it. And in that play we have had to deal with abstract concepts logically, intuitively and imaginatively (Doonan, 1993:7).

It is impossible to contemplate pictures *passively*. Doonan compares it with reading a poem by gazing at the printed page without reading it. Making sense of pictures requires an attitude that is 'dynamic, restless, searching, testing, less attitude than action: creation and recreation' (Doonan, 1993:77). Graham stipulates that the addition of the illustrations gives access 'to deeper levels of meaning making' (Graham, 1990: 21). Through high quality illustrations, much can be inferred about the characters in a book, such as the line of Frog's mouth in the Frog Stories. Constructing meaning in certain picturebooks is not a process of finding out what pictures denote or literally represent, but that the pictures 'express and metaphorically display what cannot be pictured directly—ideas, moods, abstract notions and qualities . . . we are interpreting all the time' (Doonan, 1993:8).

Sometimes images and words deliberately contradict each other. In Jenny Wagner and Ron Brooks' *John Brown, Rose, and the Midnight Cat* (1977), the envious English sheepdog John Brown says on one page that 'You don't need a cat' and on the opposite page, just above the words 'You've got me', we see live mice under the table (Figure 6.4).

This contradiction requires sophisticated inference to bring together what is said and what is unsaid (Arizpe & Styles, 2003:79). That children appreciate irony in picturebooks is widely documented (see e.g. Arizpe & Styles, 2003; Doonan, 1993; Hunt, 2001; Lewis, 2001; Nikolajeva, 2008; Nodelman, 1988). Importantly, the 'gaps' between text and image may be experienced differently as we grow older, as we bring our established habits of thought to the reading of the narrative. Judith Graham warns

'You don't need a cat,' he said.

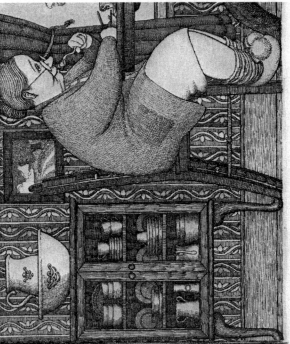

'You've got me.'

Figure 6.4   Second image from *John Brown, Rose, and the Midnight Cat* by Jenny Wagner.

that it is not the teacher's role to do the 'gap-filling' for children. Teachers should not *tell* children what the story is about (Graham, 1990:114–115). Meanings will grow if, and only if, we give children plenty of time and take their views seriously. Graham (1990:115) states that, 'All the taped and videoed evidence is that teachers intervene too much and do not allow literature to do its own work'. Targeting the 'right age' for a particular resource can result in missed opportunities for philosophical play as it fails to do justice to children's ability to appreciate art philosophically and on their own terms.

EXPERIENCE RATHER THAN AGE

Making sense of the relationship between images and words in picturebooks opens up endless possibilities for interpretation—a process children are 'absorbed' by, as well as finding it intellectually challenging (Arizpe & Styles, 2003:79, 80). This absorption has to do with being transported into the unknown where 'new worlds will be opened' (Bettelheim & Zelan, 1981:139). Bettelheim and Zelan propose that much of this engagement in mind-travel through literature is unconscious and mediated by emotions. Children are fascinated by imaginary events, by magic power, and by entering the secret languages of adults. Picturebook artists often draw on unconscious and childhood memories. Illustrator Satoshi Kitamura is critical of academics who 'analyse as if everything is done consciously'. He says: 'we don't do that often' (Kitamura quoted in Watson, 1996:238)[5].

Emotional and personal engagement is a necessary condition for philosophical enquiries to be meaningful, as they are rooted in childhood and other experiences. A drawing from the work of a learner illustrates this point. The drawing was made by Hans van Heerden who attends a school in Johannesburg, South Africa. He and his classmates were exploring the picturebook *Tusk Tusk* (1978), written and illustrated by David McKee[6]. The story is often chosen for its themes of tolerance of difference and conflict resolution. In the story, black and white elephants kill each other by turning their trunks into weapons until they are all dead. A small group of 'peace-loving' elephants, however, manages to escape the massacre and disappears into a maze. The reader is not privy to what happens in this maze, but years later grey elephants appear. At first they live in harmony until the elephants with the big ears and the small ears start to give each other strange looks. The story ends with uncertainty about the future of the remaining elephants. Unsurprisingly, the learners connected imaginatively and emotionally with the story as they are situated with their conscious and unconscious minds and bodies in post-*apartheid* South Africa, with all its uncertainties, including crime and violence across cultures, gender, religions, and races, exacerbated by socio-economic disempowerment and poverty. One of the learner's drawings shows an elephant armed to the trunks (Figure 6.5).

Figure 6.5 Drawing inspired by *Tusk Tusk* (David McKee) made by Hans van Heerden (aged 8).

We have noticed that it is not so much *age* but *experience* that seems to be the significant factor in the co-construction of philosophical meanings when exploring picturebooks. It is relevant that experiences cannot be quantified as *some children* will have had experiences *some adults* will not have had. The argument that children have *less* experience than adults is a peculiar and invalid argument against child participation (see Murris, 2000a; Haynes, 2008).

The picturebook *Tusk Tusk* is 'real literature', if we mean by literature 'texts which engage, change, and provoke intense responses in readers' (Hunt, 1999:1). So how has the rich potential of picturebooks for philosophy gone by largely unnoticed or identified as appropriate for younger children only? Peter Hunt observes that, despite their educational and commercial importance, children's books have been marginalised. He explains:

> Childhood is, after all, a state we grow away from; children's books—from writing to publication to interaction with children—are the province of that culturally marginalized species, the female (Hunt, 1999:1).

Adults' responses to children's literature are contradictory. On the one hand, picturebooks are important enough to evoke censorship, as children's vulnerability requires protection, but on the other hand, their importance for 'real' reading and philosophical reflection is denied. As Hunt summarises: 'Children's literature is important—and yet it is not' (Hunt, 1999:2).

WHAT IS CHILDREN'S LITERATURE FOR, AND FOR WHOM?

Children's literature is in itself a curious phenomenon. There is a problem in defining exactly what counts as *children's* literature simply by looking at its target audience[7], who it is written by[8], or what it is about[9] (Brann, 1993:289). Moreover, there are significant cultural and historical differences. For example, fairytales with their (originally) often violent and sexually charged content used to be part of adult culture, but their highly sanitised versions are now an intricate part of children's literature (Hunt, 1992:10). Their role in inculcating moral and social values may explain their position in children's literature. We have found that books that are considered 'good' for giving the right moral message are not 'good' at all for philosophy. In order to decide what could be a 'good' story for philosophy it is helpful to distinguish between children's literature and narratives written for didactic purposes (see e.g. Lesnik-Oberstein, 1999:21).

Children's books are often not primarily regarded as works of art, but adults' main interest is in what they are *for*. Literature can affect us at a deep level and invites us to appreciate what it means to be human: to experience beauty and awe and to laugh for its own sake. Good narratives tempt us to daydream, to imagine what could be possible, and to ask questions without necessarily knowing the 'right' answers. What makes a narrative philosophical is that it is an investigation into 'existence'; it illuminates humans' concrete being (Ende, 1993:282).

A 'good' book in the aesthetic sense can affect you physically—make you sigh, calm, or excited. It can create disturbance, anger, or joy. The quality of words and pictures (and their interdependency in the case of picturebooks) influence the power a story has and with it the depth of thought and feelings it provokes in philosophical enquiry. The reasons for constructing special literature for children may be instrumental because adults have a moral axe to grind, but many children will inevitably switch off. After all, *who* is children's literature for? Velthuijs reminds us poignantly that:

> Children are people. They are a bit smaller than we are, but we share the same emotions: sorrow, pain, loneliness, but also happiness and joy. So, why should we be difficult and produce something specially for children? We are children ourselves (Linders & Velthuijs, 2003; our translation).

For author Michael Ende it has been a serious Western mistake to divide literature into two classes: one for grownups and one for children. Such a division, he says, is non-sensical:

there is no topic within human experience, the basic idea of which would not be interesting or understandable for children. It depends, however, on the way in which one speaks about it, from the heart—or just from the mind (Ende, 1993:282).

In other countries, the relationships between story and storyteller, adult and child can be radically different from those in the West (Hunt, 1999: 4, 5). Japanese picturebook author and illustrator Satoshi Kitumara, who lives in England, resists the cultural assumptions about picturebooks in the West; he does not regard them as a kind of special provision for children. After all, there are as many differences of taste among children as there are differences between adults and children (Watson, 1996:236). Apart from being a gross simplification, identification of *the* child as reader is bound up with adult values and constructions of childhood. Children's books are just as much a part of a culture's ideology. The question '*who* is children's literature for?' is a profoundly political one. Answers to this question are bound to shed some light on how we view children, their ability to think for themselves, and their place in society. This is necessarily tied up with our judgements about the didactic nature of books written for children. Should children, as Perry Nodelman asks, 'act like the animals they naturally are or the civilised social beings adults want them to be' (Nodelman, 1999:76)?

Nodelman problematises the notion of didactic books even further. Narratives are didactic not only when they encourage children to behave like sensible adults, but also when they invite children to indulge in what (in essence?) comes naturally to children. The ideology of the first is that children should stop being like children. Books of the latter category are didactic in a more subtle manner: they teach children *how* to be childlike. Jacqueline Rose and Perry Nodelman call this process 'colonialisation'. Nodelman explains: 'adults write books for children to persuade them of conceptions of themselves as children that suit adult needs and purposes'— characteristics of 'a child' such as 'intractable', 'anti-social', and 'self-indulgent' (Nodelman, 1999:77). In our work in schools, we often hear children described as 'ego-centric', 'immature', and 'naïve'. Why do adults do this? Nodelman offers a clue:

> It affirms the inevitability and desirability of a sort of animal-likeness—and child-likeness—that both allows adults to indulge in nostalgia for the not-yet-civilised and keeps children other than, less sensible than, and therefore deserving of less power than adults (Nodelman, 1999:77).

Picturebooks are a part of the intricate ideological web that makes our culture: a culture that systematically keeps children at a distance from adults. They embody what adults hold dear and what they hold to be 'the' nature of children. The interdependency between words and pictures in picture-books, or what Nodelman calls 'intersecting sign systems' and Lewis 'a kind of miniature ecosystem'[10], requires sophisticated reading with endless possible interpretations from a wide variety of disciplines. Each field will 'see' different meanings and construct its own importance to a picturebook based on the specific instruments and knowledge available in a particular field of human enquiry. Various disciplines assist in the deconstruction of picturebooks' implicit ideologies (see also Chapter 2). Familiarity with the history of art helps to understand how certain shapes, choice of colour, and style construct moods and meanings. A Freudian or Jungian psycho-analyst would find plenty of material for analysis in picturebooks through the unconscious meanings of visual images (Nodelman, 1999:78). Literary criticism brings its own rich understandings to yet another way of looking and thinking.

What we have set out to show is how philosophy adds yet another distinct and novel perspective to existing interpretations and uses of picture-books. Philosophical enquiry interrogates picturebooks *philosophically*[11]. Knowledge of the history of Western ideas helps to identify some of the cultural and historical assumptions within the narratives. Such understanding informs the open-ended questions asked, initially, by the adult and also guides other interventions.

We are aware of the cultural specificity of the claims we make about the interface between children, philosophy, and literature in education. Many of the moral dilemmas teachers face on a daily basis are related to two core-values: *autonomy* and *protection*[12]. They pull teachers in opposite directions, for example, when deciding on the appropriateness of certain books and topics for enquiry, or when encouraging a child to speak in public. These difficult judgements are informed by our beliefs about childhood and what it means to respect children as persons—a rich field of enquiry to which we will turn in Part II.

CONCLUSION PART I:
PICTUREBOOKS FOR PHILOSOPHICAL ENQUIRY

We are now in a position to summarise the educational and philosophical elements explored in this part of the book and that are significant for us when selecting the picturebooks we care about and use in our philosophical work with children and adults[13]. The picturebooks we choose share certain characteristics, although none of them is in itself a necessary condition or jointly sufficient. They are united in the way members of a family share certain resemblances: one's nose that is like that of one's father, the toes that are like those of one's sister. Here is a list of criteria we look out for, although not one picturebook ever features all of them.

EPISTEMOLOGICAL

- Ambiguity and complexity (uncertain meanings).
- A play with 'reality'—opening up other possible worlds and other ways of doing things.
- Life-like, but different enough to highlight certain aspects of 'reality'. The familiar is made to seem strange, so that we look at it again in a different light.
- Humour and playfulness.
- Rootedness in the bodily, the concrete, and the everyday.
- Featuring abstract concepts and topics that are investigations into human existence and that provoke questions or problems that cannot be settled easily by observation, calculation, or reference to established fact.
- Engaging the emotions and imagination.
- Contradictory emotions and behaviour in text, images, and the 'gaps' in between that set up a dialectical relationship with the reader.

ETHICAL AND POLITICAL

- Implicit or explicit questioning of the power relationship between adult and child with child characters who interrogate the normal subject positions created for children.
- Uncondescending attitude towards children.
- No 'otherising' of adults by presenting them as caricatures (as e.g. in Roald Dahl's work), but critical and self-critical by holding up a 'mirror' to the adult reader.
- Playful opposition to authority, seriousness, and conformity (with stretched, broken, or abandoned rules).
- Blurring of boundaries between social or anti-social behaviour.
- Offering opportunities to imaginatively immerse in other characters, places, and times.
- Invitations to critically reflect on own values and experiences.

AESTHETIC

- Open-ended exploratory dialogues between human characters or fantasy characters such as talking animals, monsters, witches, robots, or teddy bears.
- Representing a wide variety of aesthetic styles and diversity of cultures.
- Containing ambiguity in words and/or pictures or containing contradictions between the two ('pregnant pictures').

- Interdependency between words and pictures ('intersecting sign systems' or 'miniature ecosystems').
- High quality artwork (written and visual).
- Inviting emotional, imaginative, and cognitive responses.
- Featuring narrative characters that mediate between 'the extremes of reality' (as explained and argued for in Part II, Chapter 7).

Part II
Being Child

Part II considers ideas of child and childhood, particularly from philosophical perspectives. We investigate the problems of responding authentically to children's claims to knowledge, particularly when ideas are expressed through playful and imaginative dialogues in the context of a flexible and creative philosophical space. This includes a look at ways in which children's engagement with philosophy challenges our understanding of what philosophy is.

7   Slippage Between Realms

> The human brain is chock-full of ideas, but how and why these grow into a story is difficult to say. The only condition is that you give yourself space to allow your thoughts and feelings to come out. All that matters is that in your own work you dare to be yourself. To be yourself is the greatest achievement; there is no recipe for it. As for me, I'm lucky to be a frog (Max Velthuijs in interview, from De Rijke & Hollands, 2006:195).

TRUTH AND FICTION

This chapter explores the complex relationship between art and reality. It starts by enquiring into the notion of empathy and what motivates and engages readers of picturebooks. The central question is how our metaphysical beliefs—decisions about what is real or not—influence our emotional engagement with stories, and what role the imagination plays in philosophical thinking. Traditional semantics of the natural sciences is still paradigmatic in decisions about the suitability of books for young children, as illustrated through some examples of censorship by Montessori teachers. This leads us into a re-conceptualisation of the role of the imagination in reasoning, exemplified through our own classroom practice. Illustrated by the Frog character in Velthuijs' picturebooks, we engage with the seemingly irrational idea that although fictional characters are not real, they still provoke real emotions. We argue that fiction helps to engage the imagination and to orient our emotions, and is therefore never innocent, and that this explains educators' urges to censor certain fiction. Drawing on the work of Kieran Egan, we argue that the use of fantasy characters helps to mediate abstract thinking and to make sense of everyday experiences, and that neither should be looked down on or sentimentalised.

We have argued in Part I that contemporary picturebooks challenge the Platonic underpinnings of our modern educational system. They have moved away from 'clear-cut narrative structures, a chronological order of events, an unambiguous narrative voice and, not least, clearly delineated and fixed borders between fantasy and reality' (Arizpe & Styles, 2003:22). Art's ability to interrogate reality and truth is only gradually dawning on educators.

The blurring of reality and fantasy in contemporary picturebooks allows children to feel at ease with the playful and intellectual juggling of ideas that artwork provokes. The quality of, for example, Anthony Browne's visual art in his picturebook *Zoo* (1993) (Figure 7.1) and the interdependence between words and image ('Do you think animals have dreams?') provoke complex philosophical questions about the way in which we treat animals, including *human* animals (do *we* live in cages?).

That night I had a very strange dream.

Do you think animals have dreams?

Figure 7.1   Third image from *Zoo* by Anthony Browne.

The artistic quality is not coincidental. Without it, we arguably would not emotionally *and* cognitively commit ourselves to the enquiry. Art demands a response; the 'gap' it leaves for the enquirer is of profound significance. Similarly, life itself is not 'clearly delineated' with 'fixed borders between fantasy and reality', but is a mystery—a mystery some contemporary picturebooks express beautifully. They invite epistemological speculation of a kind that does justice to the fact that our knowledge about the world is limited and always open to question.

When using the picturebook *Zoo* to introduce philosophy with children (P4C) in a school in North Wales, a class had begun their enquiry with the question of whether animals are real, when a contribution by a ten year old—'I don't think animals are real'—was met by a roar of disrespectful laughter. For the others the proposition that animals *are* real was an obvious truth. They explained that we can see them, feel them, and smell them (which resulted in more laugher). The facilitator's intervention started by taking his contribution seriously, and an invitation to expand on his idea lead to a fascinating and complex one hour long dialogue about the question, 'How *do* we know that what we experience here and now is real'? Could sitting here, talking to each other all be a dream? Like French philosopher Descartes[1], they soon rejected the idea that you could find out by pinching yourself. After all, you could be dreaming you were pinching yourself! Significantly, the teacher was not only just as much puzzled about the question as the children, but she had no ready-made answers either. Each and every person had to think for themselves. The difficulty in establishing what is true or not can cause profound emotional and cognitive conflict.

Knowledge about truth and reality constitutes self-identity. As we have seen in Chapter 4, narrativity is an essential part of knowledge construction. Stories become part of us. We *are* our stories, and it is in this sense that we create ourselves and the world we live in through stories. In listening to stories and in 'reading' narratives we actively construct meaning, and in doing so we construct ourselves. Narratives do not formulate meanings themselves, but invite the reader to 'communicate' with the narrative which involves participation in the production and the comprehension of a text (Bruner, 1986:24, 25). The meaning of the text has to be constructed by the reader out of a variety of possible meanings. They can be persuasive through *internal coherence*, based on a widely-shared understanding of human behaviour. When, for example, reasons for actions are given in a narrative, the reader understands and accepts them as reasons on the basis of the narrative context, which gives the narrative its full meaning. Reasons are accepted or rejected on the basis of a sufficient acceptance of the narrative context (Cowley, 2006:8, 9). Factual inaccuracies are often irrelevant. In both Ungerer's and Sendak's work, for example, impossible lunar shifts are portrayed[2]. Sendak explains this artistic license:

I love full moons. It was my old friend Tomi Ungerer who pointed out to me that my books are full of discrepancies. Full moons go to three-quarters and even halves without reason. But the moon appears in my books for graphic, not astronomical, reasons—I simply must have that shape on the page (Sendak quoted in Lanes, 1980:93).

Animal characters are a well-known substitute for human characters in picturebooks (Clark, 1993:20), although Margaret Clark identifies the limits to this substitution:

The animal character only works if it retains some of its natural habits as well as assuming human feelings. In retelling Aesop's fables, it seems permissible to give the tortoise a more lively personality than that of the natural plodder, but the point of the story is lost if the tortoise starts to run . . . before your animal character opens his mouth to say good morning, you must know quite a lot about him. . . . None of this need to be spelt out in the text, but you must know it before you can make him convincing (Clark, 1993:20).

So without losing credibility *Frog* in the Velthuijs' *Frog Stories* can wear swimming trunks—unlike real frogs—but retaining his natural habitat of living near water is crucial (see e.g. Figure 4.4 in Chapter 4).

A story's ending may not follow logically from prior events. Nevertheless understanding a story involves knowing how and why the various elements of it lead to its particular ending. Without such a coherence of the whole the reader will not be persuaded by its parts. Although a narrative is open to a variety of interpretations and viewpoints, some narratives are more plausible and truthful than others, and so are our opinions about them. We cannot say whatever we like about a narrative, despite the fact that there is not one single correct narrative account.

BEING FROG

Literature allows us to question established habits of thought philosophically. Scientific categorisations are interrogated: rats can be strangers (*Frog and the Stranger*), frogs can be homesick (*Frog and the Wide World*), and birds can be buried and possibly come alive again (*Frog and the Birdsong*). Frogs can love ducks, frogs become friends with rats (*Frog Finds a Friend*), and they can swim faster than ducks (*Frog Is a Hero*). Philosophical questions almost leap off the page. Characters such as Velthuijs' *Frog* tug on our heartstrings. He is difficult to be indifferent about. We get to know him better and better as we read more *Frog* stories. He is vulnerable and 'human'. He does his best but inevitably makes mistakes; it is his fallibility that is so easy to identify with.

However, there is something puzzling about our analysis of engagement with the *Frog* stories. What *is* it that makes us empathise with Frog? After all, he has never existed and never will exist as a *real* creature. He is a fictional character, and readers, *including* young children, seem well aware of that. Nevertheless our emotional responses resemble those of real situations. Characters and events in literature can make us *really* weep and laugh and grieve. In real life, though, knowing something is *not* real will change the emotional response to it—for example, discovering that the noise you heard on the floorboards is *not* caused by rats but by your cat.

Could it therefore be claimed that our responses to fiction are *inconsistent* and *irrational* (Radford, 2002:239–249)? And does such a claim have implications for the suitability of children's literature for philosophy teaching? After all, philosophy is often equated with a *rational* pursuit of *truth*. Finding an answer to these complex questions is urgent for a deeper understanding of adult's inclination to censor stories. How do our metaphysical beliefs—our theories about what is real—influence our emotional engagement with stories, and what is the role of imagination in philosophical thinking?

Traditional semantics would claim that the mind makes objective, rational judgements about, for example, the story *Frog Is a Hero* (1995) by 'mirroring' its characters, events, etc. with 'real' life or the world 'as it is'. Judgements about the truth value of a story are the result of comparing its characters and events with the world as we perceive it.

American philosopher Richard Rorty in his influential book *Philosophy and the Mirror of Nature* (1980) has critiqued this so-called 'correspondence theory of truth'. The mind, he argues, is not like a *mirror*; words do not *represent* objects. The word 'frog' does not have meaning for language users merely *because* it represents an independently existing real creature, but because it is a useful *tool* for us humans to have. It helps us, for example, to distinguish frogs from toads or to know what we are ordering when 'frog legs' are on the menu. It does not follow that frogs do not exist; their real existence is just not relevant for deciding whether statements containing the word 'frog' are true or not. The idea of 'representation' misleads people into thinking that stories can be more or less true depending on how well a narrative 'grasps' or corresponds to independent facts. Rorty claims that beliefs are true when they are useful and people are able to agree on them (the notion of 'justified true beliefs').

When Frog, in his desire to rescue his friends, claims that he is the best swimmer of all (even better than Duck) the truth of this statement does not depend on examining scientific facts about real frogs and ducks, but on reaching agreement that perhaps *this* Frog is a better swimmer than *this* Duck in *this* particular story. For example, a class of eight and nine year olds were puzzled about the illogicality in *Frog Is a Hero*: '*Why didn't duck go and save the others, she can even have food on her back!'* It was also argued that ducks can fly (another advantage over frog). Then a boy said *'all birds are stupid'*, provoking an astonished *'Ohhh'* from several peers—as if they half-heartedly admired his courage to say something so politically incorrect. The dialogue then moved into an exploration of what 'stupid' means.

In a fictional narrative the reader needs to adopt a certain perspective, one that involves *seeing things from another's point of view* (Neill, 2002:253). Empathetic understanding is not irrational, involves imagination, and generates real emotions—we really do feel sad (and delighted in the end) for Frog. Works of art demand an imaginative attitude towards the characters, and the success of an author hinges on her ability to understand the fictional world from a variety of perspectives (Neill, 2002:253). Knowing the character Frog well through engagement with the other Frog stories could make a difference in the process of negotiating narrative understanding. Frog's desire to help his friends may have given him so much courage and energy that a community of thinkers could indeed agree that he is the better swimmer of the two. For example, in another class, the idea that physical strength is directly related to the size and shape of one's body was challenged by a ten year old who thought that the sheer courageous determination to save someone's life can make you much stronger than anyone ever thought possible, so *'the story could be true'*. The idea that emotions can do extraordinary things to the body is also found in David McKee's *The Monster and the Teddy Bear* (1989), in which a teddy bear is so angry that he expands on the page and becomes so large that he is able to throw the monster out of the house.

The factual inaccuracies in fiction playfully open up unexpected pathways of thought and (ironically) encourage truth-seeking. When narrative accounts 'grate' with reality (e.g. a boy swapping his dad for something more interesting, that is, a goldfish![3]) learners are provoked to find out what might be true and possible in the account by comparing the narrative with their own life experiences, values, and knowledge.

SCIENCE AND THE MAN IN THE MOON

Censorship of picturebooks is often justified by out-dated Enlightenment semantics, within which even fiction is supposed to represent the world as understood by the natural sciences[4]. When invited to address a large audience of Montessori (mainly) nursery teachers, careful prescriptive guidance for this conference presentation had been given to ensure our 'correct' selection of stories. Characters in the stories, it was argued, had to be *real*, that is, accurately reflect creatures as found in the natural world on the assumption that children cannot distinguish between fiction and reality. The caterpillar in Eric Carle's *The Very Hungry Caterpillar* (1969) would meet this criterion, we were told. When choosing appropriate stories, the Montessori nursery teachers compared characters in a narrative with what is available to the human eye (as a means to decide what is real). As we don't see frogs sitting on chairs talking to hares, the Frog stories were judged to be inappropriate. In our discussions with the audience, it became clear that for Maria Montessori, children's imagination needs to be fed by careful and exact observation of their natural environment. The imagination should be based on the findings of scientific research as a means to creatively transform the world as it is.

Montessori distinguished sharply between fantasy and imagination. She argued that nothing real can be created through fantasy. Myths, legends, and fairytales were dismissed as being merely speculative and therefore not appropriate classroom material for young minds. She almost certainly would have thoroughly disapproved of Tomi Ungerer's picturebook *Moon Man* (1966)[5], as we know through space travel that there is no such creature as a man 'curled up in his shimmering seat in space' that can travel to earth hanging on to 'the fiery tail of a comet'. The idea that the Moon Man could escape from prison in his first quarter (because he is thin enough) would indeed be a cardinal sin as it gives the wrong scientific message that the moon itself becomes smaller, rather than how it appears to us here on earth. In her view, such tales read to children at the age of four could do 'serious and even permanent injury' (Standing, 1957:316). Their experiences are so limited, she claims, they do not need such stories as the 'commonest sights and sounds' are already full of 'mystery and wonder'. Life itself is already interesting enough, and the young child is already busy piecing together 'this funny old jigsaw puzzle of a universe'. Introducing characters that do not exist may expose children to physical and mental dangers as children 'at this stage . . . accept all these things as objective realities' (Montessori quoted in Standing, 1957:317). Fairytales such as *Peter Pan* and *Goldilocks* have caused young children to jump out of their bedroom windows, and it is claimed that imaginary creatures such as dragons, witches, fairies, and monsters can trigger long-term traumas. Montessori writes:

> It is a common belief that the young child is characterized by a vivid imagination, and therefore a special education should be adopted to cultivate this gift of nature. His mentality differs from ours: he escapes from our strongly-marked and restricted limits to wander in the fascinating worlds of unreality, a tendency which is also characteristic of savage peoples. There are other forms of imperfect development in the child which have their parallel in the savage; but we do not deliberately encourage these—such as for instance poverty of

expression in language, the existence of concrete terms, and gener-
alization of words by means of which a single word is used to indi-
cate several purposes or objects: the absence of inflections causing
the child to use only the infinitive is another example (Montessori
quoted in Standing, 1957:318).

Montessori's analogy between child and 'savage' is significant for her
claims of how and when fiction should be gradually introduced in a child's
life. The implicit 'develop-mentality' and 'otherising' of child and childhood, critiqued throughout Part I, will be further explored in subsequent
chapters. In this section we focus on her assumptions about imagination.
She mistakenly assumes that imagination is the creation of images that
first and foremost are derived from the external world as if this is—and
she assumes it is—a straightforward and non-contentious process. It is as
if our perceptions give us 'direct', 'uncontaminated' access to the world
as-it-is without being influenced by the linguistic concepts we have at our
disposal. Yet we 'see' frogs and toads around a pond *because* we have
learned the concepts 'frog' and 'toad'. Meaning-making is always 'situated' and depends on the linguistic concepts we bring to observations and
the interpretation of information. Constitutive to this process is personal
history and experiences, gender, and other political, social, and cultural
factors. Perception and reasoning are profoundly influenced by who we
are as people. This subjective nature of rationality is inescapable, and
epistemological scepticism does not need to follow. Engagement with the
Frog narratives involves reasoning, and some reasons are simply better
than others as they prove more justifiable in dialogue. We cannot just say
whatever we like about Frog.

The imagination[6] is central in our reasoning about Frog—imagination
as the capacity to flexibly rehearse possible situations, and to combine
knowledge in unusual ways as, for example, in thought experiments. The
relationship between imagination and reality is complex. It may be easier to
imagine being a character in a fictional story than imagining the existence
of seven billion people.

LONELY MONSTERS

Monsters are popular narrative characters. In Chris Wormell's *The Big
Ugly Monster and the Little Stone Rabbit* (2004)[7] the main character is a
monster that is so ugly that all animals flee when they catch sight of him
(Figure 7.2).

Flowers drop their petals and trees shed their leaves. Even the grass with-
ers and dies. Blue skies turn grey, and when he touches water it instantly
dries up with a hiss. Surrounded by no living things, the lonely monster

Figure 7.2 Image from *The Big Ugly Monster and the Little Stone Rabbit* by Chris Wormell.

carves animal statues out of rock for he desires someone to talk to. But even they crack and disintegrate when he smiles at them. The exception is one little stone rabbit (for no apparent reason). The monster talks and sings to him, dances and juggles, and plays draughts with him. Years go by, and the monster is happy. Sometimes the monster and the rabbit just sit and watch the ominous weather. The stone rabbit never changes, but the monster gets

But one day the monster never came out
of his cave and the stone rabbit sat alone.

Figure 7.3   Second image from *The Big Ugly Monster and the Little Stone Rabbit*
by Chris Wormell.

older and older, uglier and uglier. His hair turns grey and his teeth fall out.
Then one day the monster doesn't come out of his cave, and the rabbit sits
alone (Figure 7.3)

Children's responses to this picturebook narrative have been (typically) unexpected. When reading the story is stopped at this point and
the young learners (on this occasion aged between 4 and 8) are asked to
make sense of this particular picture, they speculate that the monster is
'ill', 'asleep', or is 'so ugly that he never wants to come out again'. The
drawings of five year olds portrayed a wide variety of creative interpretations: one drew a map of the cave, and one boy thought that the
monster didn't come out of his cave because he was watching football
on television (Figure 7.4).

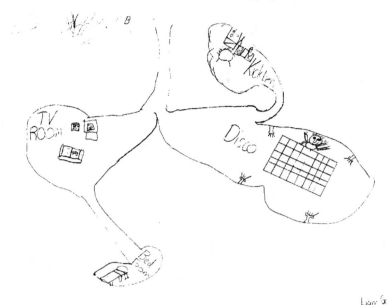

Figure 7.4 Drawing inspired by *The Big Ugly Monster and the Little Stone Rabbit* (Chris Wormell) made by Liam Geschwindt (aged 5).

In a London school, a reception class speculated that:

'the monster cracked himself, coz he was so ugly'
'the monster is having breakfast'
'he bumped his head'
'drunk too much'
'he is ill, in hospital' (offered by a boy suffering from leukaemia)
'he is asleep, too tired'
'making more animals'
'it's too cold for him to come out'
'he doesn't want to come out, coz there is no one to play with'

When acting out what the cave looked like from the inside, one boy held an imaginary torch! Their answers showed a capacity to put themselves in the position of the monster (e.g. '*he bumped his head*', and he might be too 'tired', 'cold', or hungry).

Such responses are no less rational than the expected adult answer that he is dead (although young children do offer this as a possibility). The hypothesis of death is only more rational in the real world of creatures that are born and die. But in the world of monsters it is not irrational at all to believe they may never die. In a sense, the thinking has to be more creative and be generated by individuals themselves when the more obvious explanations are either ignored or 'missed' altogether. More obvious explanations often involve an inauthentic 'guessing-type thinking'—guessing what the teacher (and the curriculum) finds important or what the author may have intended. There is not much ownership in such thinking and little authenticity in such teaching. It denies children the possibility of taking responsibility for their own thoughts and the freedom to think for themselves. It puts children in our adult frame of mind in which, as Michael Bonnett puts it:

> we hear things and just pass them on down the line, without really making them our own by testing their validity in terms of our own unique existence (Bonnett, 1994:103).

Philosophical enquiry encourages participants to ask themselves the question: 'What does this really mean for *me*?' As the answer depends on the situational embeddedness of each individual, answers will be different. It is disturbing to hear some teachers say that 'my children don't think', 'they need to be spoon-fed', or 'they are still so immature'. They are reflections of an educational system that teaches thinking through solving (adult) problems; 'accelerating' adult, less imaginative, modes of thinking; and undervaluing children's personal experiences.

The imagination is not restricted within the boundaries of the 'real', and therefore needs to be regarded as an enemy of truth and rationality. Imagination and rationality are not opposites. Sarah Meadows identifies the contradictory set of meanings given to imagination in education and psychology:

> on the one hand irrational, merely fanciful, a pale shadow of reality, deceiving, trivial, useless, something children do but should be educated out of; and on the other hand it is seen as free and poetic, as in the Romantic vision of the child born 'trailing clouds of glory' but all too soon subjected to the shades of the educational prison house (Meadows, 2006:440).

Assumptions about the role of imagination in reasoning influence the value adults attach to children's contributions in enquiries. Imaginative rationality is intuitive, creative, flexible, passionate, and metaphorical.

REALITY AND ENGAGEMENT

The educational philosophy of Maria Montessori exemplifies a particular take on the link between reality, fantasy, and imagination, which influences censorial actions when working and living with children: characters such as monsters should not feature in books for young children. In this chapter we have raised questions about the link between reality, rationality, and emotions. Are our responses to fictional characters indeed irrational? How is it possible that we get upset or frightened by certain events or happenings? After all, a fictional character such as the Big Ugly Monster is not real, and yet his predicament can still move readers. Could it be possible that fiction arouses emotions in a 'purer' form than real situations?

Like Nussbaum[8], philosopher Roger Scruton argues that the reader is not 'contaminated' by self-interest. According to Scruton, 'sympathetic emotions' are more easily released in us by fiction than reality (Scruton, 2002:120). In fiction there is a 'safe distance': fictional characters pose no threat to us, as opposed to real situations when our own interests are at stake. He writes that in fiction

> we are free from the normal cost of sympathy, which is the active need to intervene. In entering a fictional world, we are exercising our feelings, but not acting from them (Scruton, 2002:121).

He believes that sympathetic emotion is more than feeling. He sees it as

> an active assessment of the world, as a place in which my concerns are engaged. Through the free play of sympathy in fiction our emotions can be educated, and also corrupted. And that is one reason why art matters (Scruton, 2002:121).

Because art matters it can pose a threat to the more vulnerable among us. In *The Republic* Plato famously banned art to prevent corruption of the young (Plato, 1987:129–133). Although his pupil Aristotle was less keen on censorship, they both share a theory of art as *representation*: art mimics, imitates the world, and evokes emotions in the recipient of the work of art. Plato regarded the emotional effect of art as bad: emotions need to be controlled for the sake of rationality[9]. In contrast, Aristotle maintained that art could be a source of knowledge (in his *Poetics*) and catharsis: a purging of emotions, which enhances rationality (Feary, 2005:96, 97). Nowadays, art is more construed as a playing with signs, signs that do not necessarily refer to anything in reality; on the contrary, they shape reality. Art does not imitate life but helps shape and construct it. Characters or events in a story can start to live a life of their own in their readers' mind and actions. We have noticed this on many occasions. For example, after reading David McKee's story *Not Now, Bernard* (1980) features of the story have become part of everyday life when children (often playfully) start using the phrase 'Not, now . . .' (by filling in their own name) to highlight adults' pre-occupation with their own concerns and the lack of attention they pay to the children around them.

Literature offers other possible worlds that put the actual world in a new light. Because of this active role in meaning-making Jerome Bruner calls fiction 'the end of innocence' (Bruner, 2002:10). He explains that stories 'always have a message, most often so well concealed that even the teller knows not what the axe is he may be grinding' (Bruner, 2002:5, 6). Great fiction, Bruner contends, is subversive in spirit, not didactic (Bruner, 2002:11).

The aesthetic quality of a work of fiction, the emotions it generates, and the thoughts it provokes are all interconnected. Quality picturebooks provoke strong responses *because* they are works of art. We do not subscribe to the now popular notion of aesthetic relativism or subjectivism: the idea that taste depends only on the preferences of a particular group or individual and that it is impossible to make claims about better or worse art, good or bad works of fiction. A similar sentiment is expressed in the mistaken belief that beauty is merely in the eye of the beholder[10]. For most of the picturebooks we work with, it is possible to put strong reasons forward to support the claim that they are works of art (despite their young readership) and, more importantly, their suitability for philosophy teaching often depends on their aesthetic quality.

RAINDROPS *AND* ALIENS

The aesthetic quality of the narratives used for P4C has received little attention. On the contrary, it has been argued that it distracts from the necessary *philosophical* focus[11]. We focus in this chapter on another important feature of these specially written philosophical novels. It will help clarify the reasons for our picturebooks alternative. For our analysis we have taken the following paragraph from Catherine McCall's novel *Laura and Paul* (2006). Its style and format is similar to the P4C program and starts as follows:

> Something was moving. Slowly. It was shiny and sort of round but long. Laura tried to make her eyes look harder. A raindrop? For a minute she wondered where it was. 'Silly, it must be where you are' she said to herself. 'But where am I?' (McCall, 2006:1).

McCall's choice of focusing on the everyday and the familiar is typical of current educational resources for subject teaching. Modern education uses knowledge of local environments and familiar experiences as the starting point for learning (Egan, 1992:72). For example, when teaching geography, teachers are encouraged to start with the most concrete, a child's immediate experiences, her bedroom, her home, her garden, her village, etc., gradually working 'outwards'. Such an approach to curriculum construction is what Kieran Egan calls the 'expanding horizons' curriculum (Egan, 1995:119). Learning is organised from 'the concrete to the abstract, from the known to the unknown, from active manipulation to symbolic conceptualization, from perception dominated thinking to conceptual freedom' (Egan, 1989:2, 4).

Starting a story with raindrops exemplifies the 'expanding horizon cur-riculum' in that it begins with the familiar. After all, raindrops are part of most children's everyday experience. The narrative moves from wondering about the existence of raindrops to an enquiry into one's own existence. On the whole, specially written P4C novels follow this methodological structure[12]. Their starting point for philosophical reflection is familiar everyday experiences, and the narrative characters are humans, not dressed up animals for example. Such a design has been influenced by American pragmatist John Dewey who observed that education should start with the experience children already have (Dewey, 1978). In turn, Dewey was influ-enced by Herbert Spencer who argued that teaching should proceed from 'the simple to the complex . . . from the definite to the indefinite . . . from the particular to the general . . . from the concrete to the abstract . . . from the empirical to the rational' (Egan & Ling, 2002:94). This may be how our bodies develop biologically, Egan observes, but the theory falls short of explaining children's intellectual development (Egan & Ling, 2002:94).

Egan critiques the idea that learners' *imagination* is best engaged by such an approach to teaching and learning. Without introducing a dichot-omy between reason and imagination he argues that narratives set up a dialectical activity between the familiar and the everyday by featuring the extremes of reality and the limits of experience (Egan, 1992:73). The more distant and strange a narrative is, the more engaged a learner will be and motivated to bring new understandings to the everyday and the familiar. Egan explains:

> Students are interested in limits and extremes because such exotica provide the context within which their daily lives and experience are meaningful. By establishing the limits, we can get a proportionate sense of the local and everyday; we learn where the familiar fits, what its meaning is (Egan, 1992:73).

Although Egan is primarily concerned to make his observations character-istic of a particular age group (eight to fifteen year olds), we have found in practice that people of all ages are absorbed and fully immersed in class-room material that features unusual characters (e.g. humans covered in body hair, aliens), extreme concepts (e.g. immortality, the size of the uni-verse), and obscure thought experiments (e.g. what if you had to choose between being sat on by a rhinoceros, swallowed by a fish, squeezed by a snake, or eaten by a crocodile?[13]). In our philosophical practice we encour-age people to wonder and to be in awe about the world as-it-is, but Egan would argue that it is not achieved easily through wondering about rain-drops alone, but more readily through 'those features of the world and of experience that are, or can be, thought of as strange and exotic'. This explains the attraction to 'the spooky, the scary, the spine-tingling films or books that suggest a quite different reality lurks just behind or below the surface of the everyday world' (Egan, 1992:79). With its archetypes, heroes, powerful emotions, and extreme and other-worldly themes, literature is a limitless educational resource for philosophising. Literature offers readings that are life-like, but which, at the same time, are different in order to highlight aspects of 'reality'. Anne Wilson argues that this difference 'is part of the point: the familiar is made to seem strange, so that we see it again' (Wilson, 1983:21).

Our picturebooks often have strange, distant, and magical settings. The stories are built on binary opposites, such as big/little, bad/good, hairy/bald, dirty/clean, love/hate, human/animal, and brave/cowardly, and the creatures they feature mediate between these opposites: frogs in swimming trunks, robbers that are both good and bad, ugly or wild monsters, or the man on the moon. It has been the work of Kieran Egan that has helped us understand why these binary features of fantasy characters are so crucial in our philosophical work. Children might not use abstract concepts explicitly, but they constantly use abstractions in their thinking: 'concrete elements are tied to some affective abstraction' and the body[14] (Egan & Ling, 2002:97). In order to understand stories, Egan explains:

> children must in some sense be familiar with security/danger, courage/cowardice, hope/despair, and so on. Children need not, of course, be able to articulate or define such terms to be able to deploy them (Egan, 1995:117).

We have noticed how learners powerfully engage emotionally and cognitively with creatures such as ghosts (mediating between life and death), talking teddy bears (mediating between nature and culture), and monsters (mediating between human beings and animals). Paradoxically, these narratives are *unlike* our everyday experiences, but are still meaningful, and make us question what it means to *identify* with a narrative character (an oft heard criterion for the suitability of a story).

Unlike the more familiar 'expanding curriculum' design, our own starting points for lessons (also at university) are often ambiguous, mysterious, fantastical, and imaginative. Egan would approve. He argues that (always) starting with the familiar in curriculum design is a misinterpretation of Dewey. His use of the concept 'experience' has been misinterpreted as the 'everyday practical world of children's lives' but then as *seen by the adult*. Egan proposes that educators should focus on the world as the *child* sees it—as 'transfigured by fantasy'. Otherwise we ignore the imaginative side of children's thinking processes (Egan, 1988:19, 20; 1986; 1992:163, 164; 1997). So, paradoxically, by focusing on the extremes and limits of experience, and the bizarre and the strange, the familiar world around us seems to become more meaningful (Egan, 1992:78).

Egan's theory of imagination helps us value characters such as talking teddy bears, frogs in swimming trunks, and other humanised animals, featured so frequently in picturebooks, and often referred to pejoratively by adults. It helps us understand why their non-particularity (they are not creatures in the world as we know it) frees the reader up to respond to narratives philosophically and in a non-instrumental way.

In this chapter more arguments have been put forward for the use of picturebook narratives for teaching philosophy. The process of growing up brings certain intellectual gains, but there may also be an important loss. Humans' ability to recognise and generate metaphors reaches its peak by the age of five, followed by a gradual decline, and culminates in 'arteriosclerosis of the imagination in adulthood' (Egan & Ling, 2002:94). Egan and Ling put forward the thesis that young children's intellectual life is characterised by 'the imaginative skills attached to metaphor and image generation, and to narrative and affective understanding' (Egan & Ling, 2002:95). The implications are profound for curricular design and the evaluation and assessment of young children's thinking when interpreting transcripts of classroom dialogues. This will be the topic of the next chapter.

8   Talking Dogs and Moving Bears
The Realm of Meaning

Censorship in the classroom takes different forms: restricting access to certain texts, constraining the teaching space in which they are viewed, failing to validate children's questions and responses, or interpreting their ideas within limiting perspectives on children's thinking. This chapter explores teachers' responses to open-ended discussion with children, noting the need to interrogate the ethical standpoint and beliefs about knowledge that underpin them. Our experience is that younger children's responses to picturebooks often evoke sentimental reactions from adults. Such sentimentality leads adults to distance themselves from child (hood) and to miss opportunities presented for philosophical exploration.

The chapter includes examples of conversations with young children stemming from picturebooks, where themes of magic, imagination, fantasy, and reality come to the fore. These areas of enquiry open doors to philosophical questioning but appear to present greater challenges for many adults. To illustrate this point we refer briefly to examples of related conversations with teachers and student teachers. Each of these episodes has prompted deep reflection, and they are among the rich examples to which we return time and again, as powerful illustrations of a curious struggle in encounters between 'adult' and 'child'. They raise questions about ways of knowing and facilitation of philosophical enquiry with children. They illustrate the complex ethics of teaching and learning situations: how easy it might be to slip into emotional indulgence or distancing rationalism.

The examples help draw attention to differences between literal and metaphorical lines of enquiry. Philosophy thrives on the capacity to re-describe, to imagine the possibility of things being otherwise. Creative and imaginative thinking are associated with the ability to think freely, without the constraints of given theory about explanations for events, as well as the ability to construct 'other worlds', all strengths when it comes to philosophising. The possibility of 'imaginative philosophising' seems to hinge on whether adults have the confidence, knowledge, and resourcefulness to respond creatively and playfully, rather than work exclusively to promote children's so-called skills in the 'performance' of thinking or philosophical enquiry. We believe that it is essential to work with these and other similar examples to build capacity to move beyond current pedagogical limitations. In this chapter we illuminate our sense of the 'knowing space' created by philosophical questioning of picturebook narratives, and we seek to understand the claims to knowledge that the children are making. This leads to consideration of what Gaita (2004) terms the 'realm of meaning' in philosophical dialogues. Notions of 'feeling for the philosophical' and 'opening up the philosophical space' are at the heart of our work. A philosophical space is one in which we are both provoked and pushed into thinking and at liberty to explore our thoughts with one another.

TALKING DOGS

The Narrative Context

John Brown, Rose, and the Midnight Cat (Wagner, 1977) is a popular picturebook (see Figures 3.1 and 6.4). The central human character, Rose, is a widow who lives with her dog, John Brown. They are shown in close mutual companionship. All seems well until Rose spots a handsome black cat in the garden and wants to let it indoors. John Brown refuses, telling the 'midnight cat' to keep away. In front of Rose, he won't acknowledge the existence of the cat. Rose secretly gives the cat milk. While she is not looking, the dog tips the milk out of the bowl. This continues until Rose goes to bed one evening and does not get up the next day. She indicates she is going to stay there forever. John Brown spends the day downstairs, Rose's slipper close to him. Eventually he returns to Rose, asking if the cat will make her better. She says yes, and he lets the cat in. The cat sits on the arm of the chair in which, earlier in the story, the dog has sat. Rose and the cat gaze at each other. The dog lies on the rug in front of the fire.

It's Strange That the Dog Could Talk

After listening to the story, children in an early years class (ages four to seven) volunteer questions about why the dog is sitting on a chair, why he does not appear hungry when Rose takes to her bed, and why the cat makes Rose feel better. Amy says, 'I thought it was strange that the dog could talk'. Several other children agree that this is puzzling. Amy explains, 'Well because normally dogs don't talk, but that one did, that puzzled me.' Another child adds, 'No dogs talk and that dog did'.

In the discussion that follows, children talk about dogs barking, and one child suggests that you can teach dogs to talk. In contradiction to what she has said earlier about dogs not normally talking, Amy says, 'Benj can speak' (Benj is the name of her dog). Amy informs the class that he can say, 'Good morning everybody'. A challenge to Amy's statement comes from another child asking, 'Why doesn't he say it to us?' Amy explains that the dog is too embarrassed when he comes to the school gates, and he doesn't speak in front of other people. Amy continues:

Amy	And he can say 'hello Sheila', 'oh be quiet', mummy says.
T	Mummy has to tell him to be quiet?
Amy	Yes, and Benj goes up and says 'oh you little poop'.
T	What to your mum and . . .
Amy	Benj goes up and says 'nincompoop', and mummy just goes upstairs again.
T	So she doesn't hear, she doesn't hear him calling her a nincompoop?

Other children's reports seem to be of a different order: 'When dogs wag their tails they are saying hello' and 'When my dog waggles her tail that means people are here and that our dog is happy'. Mark says that his dog talks in his (the dog's) dreams. When the teacher asks the children to explain how the dog in the story could speak, their explanations include 'magic' and 'fairies'. Mark adds, 'Well . . . you can talk to the dog and then they can make you better, can't they, sometimes?' This group of children were able to use the relationship between John Brown (the dog) and Rose (the widow) to explore what having a dog in the household might mean: the comfort, familiarity, and intimacy of living with a dog; the mystery of animals; the nature of communication; wider family dynamics of power, game playing; projection and control. By and large their conversation hovers between the world of the story, where magic is likely, and reports based on observation of their pet dogs. The story of Benj creates a bridge between these two worlds.

Amy's account captivates most of the class. It is striking that she begins with the claim that 'normally dogs don't talk' and is later able to use the opportunity to express something else about her experience of family life, through the medium of their dog Benj. Amy shows the ability to entertain both of these lines of enquiry and to manage the contradictions they entail. Her story expresses tension between the various characters in the tale and between the narrator and the characters. It includes the surprise of imaginary/symbolic events of the dog using words and humorously engages our emotions. It conveys meaning, but it is not obvious what this might be. It creates openings in which other possible worlds can be explored. But what kind of truth is revealed here and what part does the adult play in such conversations?

Different traditions of thinking can be brought to bear on the analysis of classroom interaction to provide 'readings', for example of language use, group dynamics, behaviour, and development. These disciplinary traditions need to be made explicit if there is to be any potential for listening afresh. One reading might be that children create stories that reflect linguistic and cultural patterns they come across in children's literature or television.

Artistic and cultural expression makes extensive use of fantasy in general and anthropomorphism in particular. Another reading might be that children are expressing a feature of psychological development identified in the literature as 'magical thinking'[1] (Woolley, 1997). Woolley reports that research suggests that 'children live in a world in which fantasy and reality are more intertwined than they are for adults' (Woolley, 1997:992). She concludes that differences between adults and children are both cultural context and domain specific. She argues that explanations of the world in terms of magic, science, and religion can co-exist in the minds of children and adults alike. This human capacity to creatively manage the co-existence of these different 'domains' of thinking, 'rational' and 'imaginary', is central to the argument of this book.

In terms of our concern with children's 'voice' in philosophical enquiry, different 'readings' of interaction can be more or less benign in their impact. Whether or not the voices of the children are heard is linked to the extent to which the 'reading' ties what individuals say to generalities, particularly age-related stages that hearken to biological or social constructs of maturation, imitation, learning, formation, or behaviour. Each interpretation expresses distance or proximity between adults and children. Each reflects an epistemological position[2]. Some appear much closer to concern with the expression of children's voices, highlighting the interrelationship of ethics and epistemology.

We are interested in 'readings' of interaction with children that penetrate what Gaita (2004) refers to as 'the realm of meaning'. These draw on psycho-analytic and socio-philosophical traditions. We want to recognise the 'novel perspectives' (Corradi Fiumara, 1995:10) children offer and to enhance the ability of adults to tactfully take these up. We might for example draw on memories of childhood and other types of sources (literary or artistic perhaps) to explore the possibilities for experiences of thinking created in the dialogues. It is particularly fruitful to move from a position of asking 'what is a child?' to the question 'what does it mean to be child?'

'FANTASY VERSUS REALITY': RELATED CONVERSATION WITH TEACHERS

In the story of *The Tunnel* (Browne, 1997; see Figure 1.4), a young boy who has ventured through a tunnel into the forest beyond is depicted as a statue, frozen in mid-movement, and described as 'a figure, still as stone'. His sister, although afraid, follows her brother through the tunnel out of concern for him. When she finds him she hugs his frozen figure, and he gradually returns to 'living' colour and movement: a transformative moment.

This story was read in the course of working with a group of teachers who began to explore the theme of magical transformation until one teacher asked: 'But can children tell the difference between fantasy and reality?' This kind of question soon puts a stop to a group's philosophical engagement, something we interpret as an unconscious strategy of avoidance. It may have something to do with the risk-taking and uncertainty involved in philosophy. Perhaps being playful or 'childlike' creates disturbance for some adults. Perhaps the distancing creates a place of safety. The teacher's question about children's development is a rationalising intervention, enabling her to sidestep involvement with the enquiry about transformation. While some teachers appear liberated by the provisional nature of philosophical reasoning, others are threatened. A teacher's own deep sense of security may be a precondition for the adoption of the kind of playful and exploratory disposition tending to imaginative philosophising (Corradi Fiumara, 1995:109).

Whilst engaged in inset[3] on philosophy with children (P4C), we have also noticed that some children's comments prompt laughter and an exchange of looks, as if the adults assume a common view: a shared joke, a stance of 'endearment' (Haynes & Murris, 2009a). This appeal to adult sentiment also makes it possible to create distance from the views that are being expressed by the children: of course dogs can't really talk, boys cannot turn back to flesh from stone, and the children's views are naïve. The narrative here is that adults are living in the real and rational world while children are fundamentally 'other' in their thinking[4]. Such distancing infects the characterisation of everything that young children say and results in their being disregarded as charming perhaps but generally unreliable.

The point at which children stop making claims ('telling tales'), through accounts of the kind Amy and others give in the example reported, is regarded as the point when children are capable of distinguishing fantasy from reality: the emergence of a more rational approach to the world, closer to that of adults. However, many people continue to engage in imaginative play well into their early adolescence and beyond. In the rational adult world of professional education, the imagination is given its proper place, and older children are expected to know the truth, to the point where they would be reprimanded for lying. Younger children's tales are not called lies but stories or fibs (Van Manen & Levering, 1996). Adults who persist in the kind of 'story' that Amy is telling might be perceived as deluded, of low intelligence, or mad.

In the context of P4C enquiry, where the emphasis is on reasoning, there is a need to establish where contributions of this kind belong, in the philosophical realm. This has implications for teachers' dispositions and lines of questioning. Instead of dismissing comments such as Amy's as naïve, we could consider how her ability to articulate something in this imaginative way enriches the philosophical discussion. This leads to alternative narratives of child.

Freud identified the period of early childhood as a particularly creative one. Writers such as Bettelheim (1991) and Egan (1991, 1999) have theorised about the significance of the imaginative world during this time. Winnicott (1971/1991) has described this period as 'transitional' and characterised by the adoption of all kinds of objects and activities that reflect the child's journey of separation from the mother, as well as a journey from subjectivity to objectivity. Benj is able to say the 'naughty' things that Amy herself does not 'voice' and to call her mum a 'nincompoop'. In Amy's account of events, her mum does not even have to hear what Benj says. It is satisfying enough for it to be voiced. Benj appears as Amy's secret accomplice. When we include the possibility that the children in this dialogue are making oblique references to an inner self, we might be better prepared to explore the possible meanings it may contain. This is one possible line of analysis: one that does not apply exclusively to the experience of childhood but to flutterings of the self throughout the human lifespan. We could call this 'being child'.

Winnicott (1971/1991) argues that the task of reality-acceptance is life-long and that all human beings carry the strain of relating inner and outer realities. He suggests that provision of an intermediate area of experience, in which the nature of reality is left unquestioned, provides relief from this strain. It is his view that transitional phenomena are permitted to the young child when parental figures intuitively recognise the strain in objective perception. He writes:

> Should an adult make claims on us for our acceptance of the objectivity of his subjective phenomena we discern or diagnose madness. If, however, the adult can manage to enjoy the personal intermediate area without making claims, then we can acknowledge our own corresponding intermediate areas, and are pleased to find a degree of overlapping, that is to say common experience between members of a group in art or religion or philosophy (Winnicott, 1971/1991:16).

He sees this realm of illusion as being retained throughout life. It appears again in the intense experiencing that belongs to imaginative work, the arts, religion, and creative activity in any subject: the space of enquiry (Kennedy, 1999). Transitional phenomena do not belong exclusively to a stage of early childhood, but are a recurring aspect of human experience, bound up with creativity and meaning-making. Winnicott writes:

> It is creative apperception more than anything else that makes the individual feel that life is worth living. Contrasted with this is a relationship to external reality which is one of compliance, the world and its details being recognized but only as something to be fitted in with or demanding adaptation. Compliance carries with it a sense of futility for the individual and is associated with the idea that nothing matters and that life is not worth living (Winnicott, 1971/1991:76).

If we recognise his account of the human relationship with reality, and the connections between the realm of illusion/playfulness and creative experience, this will have a strong bearing on all our interactions, as teachers/adults with children. The intense experiencing we associate with creative apperception, in the case here exploring stories and pictures, needs to be managed in the classroom with what Van Manen (1991) calls pedagogical tact. We want to suggest that this pedagogical tact includes a kind of listening that is philosophical (CorradiFiumara, 1990) because it is able to stay with the 'intermediate' and to reach beyond the given, to thinking otherwise.

THE ROLE OF METAPHOR IN PHILOSOPHICAL THINKING

Reference to the part played by the creative domain, in 'managing reality', links with work on embodied thinking and the significance of metaphor in the reasoning process itself (Corradi Fiumara, 1995; Johnson, 2008; Lakoff & Johnson, 1980, 1999). Lakoff and Johnson argue that reasoning itself is largely metaphorical and imaginative. They suggest that metaphorical thought is the main tool that makes philosophical insight possible and simultaneously constrains the forms that philosophy can take (Lakoff & Johnson, 1999:7).

Egan (1991) views children's capacity for the metaphorical as an asset to be cultivated as a vital feature of intellectual development. He argues:

> It is not something to be replaced by logico-mathematical, more rational, more realistic forms of thinking. These forms grow out of it and ideally grow along with it; it is what gives rationality life, color and meaning (Egan, 1991:86; original emphasis).

Corradi Fiumara (1995) explores metaphor as interaction between language and life, a process that bridges the segregated classes of body and mind and the accustomed distinctions of rational versus instinctual. Corradi Fiumara suggests:

> Through a metaphoric appreciation of language, knowledge is seen not so much as the task of 'getting reality right' but rather as the enterprise of developing linguistic habits for coping with whatever reality-in-the-making we may have to confront (Corradi Fiumara, 1995:72).

Following these arguments, Amy's story about her dog Benj can be interpreted as a poetic contribution to philosophical dialogue. Anthropomorphism features prominently in many stories, especially for children. Such stories form a major part of the literary and oral heritage of many different cultures, particularly myths, legends, and folk tales. Animals are used, for example, to reveal consequences of actions and to bear moral messages as in Aesop's Fables, cartoons, and Walt Disney films. It is also found in literature for adults, as illustrated in the next section.

STORIES AND THE REALM OF MEANING

John Berger's novel King (2000) is about the homeless and dispossessed and is narrated by the dog that 'minds' two of the main characters. The dog is autonomous and sophisticated. In the passage below King is shouted at, stoned, and told to scram by a man in the park. King describes what happens next:

> I'm watching his eyes. He makes as if to run for it along the path, so I snap at his heels. He jumps, standing up, on to a bench, eyes vacant. I settle on the path to keep him there. He stands on the bench, indecisive.
> Good dog, he says, you're a good dog, aren't you?
> I behave as if my ears, which are standing up, are deaf.
> Where do you live? He asks sweetly. Have you got a home?
> I growl.
> We'll be friends won't we?
> He doesn't know I can talk, yet in this situation he'd like me to reply.
> I do not make a sound.
> Do you know, he says, slowly, as if talking to a child, I still have a lot to do today?
> You're lucky! I suddenly reply.
> He is so surprised, so taken aback, that he slips his mobile into his jacket pocket and stands there, hands hiding his crotch.
> Christ! he whispers
> (Berger, 2000:94–95).

There are parallels between Amy's story and Berger's story. Berger's is more elaborate, carrying the hallmarks of the sophisticated writer. They both include dialogues in which the secret of the dog's ability to talk is essential to the action. In both accounts, the dog is subversive, surprising. We can't help but celebrate their getting away with it. These dogs are the heroic champions of the powerless, the unheard.

Anthropomorphism is endemic in many cultures, expressing human relationships with nature and with reality. As a literary technique, it considerably extends our ability to use language to create meanings that we would struggle to express more literally and directly, as discussed in Chapter 7.

The British comic actor Peter Bayliss is described by Peter Barnes as an original and an eccentric:

> There was a time when he went everywhere with an invisible dog. He could throw his voice slightly and his barking was uncannily accurate. Legend has it he took the 'dog' with him to Fortnum and Mason's tea room to negotiate a contract with Cameron Mackintosh. . . . He asked the waitress for a saucer of water for his dog, and included the canine in

negotiations. Every time Mackintosh suggested a salary the dog would bark. Bayliss would say: 'My dog doesn't think that's enough'. He came away with a lucrative contract (Barnes, 2002:18).

The dialogue that is possible because of the presence of Bayliss' invisible dog seems to create at least two planes for philosophical thinking. Firstly, it reveals the ambiguity of the power positions between the actor and the agent. Secondly, the invention motivates us as spectators. It stimulates the curiosity that might be absent if the parties were to negotiate more conventionally. It helps us to question the appearance of things.

Gaita (2004) draws on his contemplation of the relationship between humans and animals to explore what it means to be fully human and to track the foundations of ethical thought. He argues that this understanding is often shaped by stories and that it is an error to assume that the cognitive content of such stories has to be extracted from its story-telling form, as science and philosophy are wont to do, in order to arrive at its factual or conceptual value. The literary or artistic forms of such stories are critical to the sphere of human meaning to which they relate. Gaita suggests almost everything important in human life occurs in the realm of meaning. He reminds readers:

> Think how often literature and art more generally give us reason to say that we have come to see meaning where we had not before, or deeper meaning than we had thought possible, or even sometimes sense where we had not seen it. These are ways of seeing that are characteristic of the realm of meaning (Gaita, 2004:105).

Gaita suggests that the realm of meaning is of human origin and a 'gift of culture' (Gaita, 2004:197). Gaita's many reflections on his own and other stories of dogs and other animals draw out distinctions between the psychological and moral dimensions, between what is necessary and what is possible, in human relationships with animals. He argues that it is in this realm of meaning, rather than in the nature of things or in the fabric of the universe, that our ethical thought is embedded. His work exemplifies the kind of thinking and conversation that is possible when story, experience, and philosophising are creatively interwoven.

BEARS MOVING

The Narrative Context

Corduroy (Freeman, 1976) is a story in which a girl and her mother visit the toy section of a department store. The girl sees a teddy bear and asks her mother if she can have it. Her mother suggests the bear is less than perfect, with a button missing from his dungarees. During the night, the bear goes around the store in search of a button. He gets into all kinds of difficulties. The next morning the girl arrives to buy the longed for bear. The film version is not an animation, but a film with live actors and a 'moving' toy bear[5].

Toy Bears Don't Move Do They?

In the early part of a discussion about this film several children comment on the bear moving. Kerry says, 'I found it strange when the girl was hugging the bear he moved his head', and Liam adds, 'Why did the bear get off the shelf and walk?' Others ask similar questions. For a few moments it seems there is unanimity: they have rejected the possibility of a toy bear moving. Once again it is Amy who decides to depart from the prevailing line of discussion when she says, 'I disagree . . . because teddy bears, when you go out of your room, they can move'. Amy adds, 'I think it's quite puzzling because they don't move when you're in the room' the reason being: 'because they don't want you to know that they can move'. Molly supports her saying, 'I agree with Amy because every time I go out of my room and come back in to play something has always moved'. Liam informs us that his bears talk to him in the night. Three other children recount experiences of their bears or other toys moving during the night.

A lively discussion follows in which children report on their experiences of their toys turning up in places other than those they have left them. They explore the possibility that it is their mums and dads that move them, but some children in the group are not entirely convinced by this explanation. Kora becomes interested in the idea of the bears moving when they are not being watched: 'Um they could be moving right now while we're at school . . . because all this talking of teddies moving in the night, they could be moving in the day'. Amy reports that she looks through her keyhole to see her teddies moving, 'They keep coming out of my wardrobe and I keep coming in they go like that and they shouldn't'. Meanwhile Dean and others argue that the story is 'only' a film and it is not real.

In terms of the type of sustained conceptual enquiry that distinguishes philosophical dialogue from other kinds of conversations (Gardner, 1996), the early points made by Amy (teddies do move) and Dean (it's only a film) contained promising seeds to be cultivated. Their questions create the potential for discussion about the nature of experience and perceptions of reality. So how might the teacher respond? Quite apart from acknowledging the children's experiences as genuine (considering the tidying up that parents are apt to do in children's bedrooms) it might have been productive to link Dean's contribution ('it's not real') to Natalie's ('you don't know if teddies move or not') by asking something like, 'How do we know whether something is real?' But what if she had taken a different tack altogether, perhaps asking, 'What if teddies <u>did</u> move, what would that be like?' This is a critical decision by the adult.

When Amy's account of the moving bears was related to a group of student teachers it created considerable disturbance about the role of the teacher. One student expressed strong concern about whether it was right for an adult to allow Amy's claims about the bears moving to be left unresolved. She said she was a scientist. She could not contemplate a situation in which she would not want to ensure that children learned the truth of things. She said that children have to be told what is real, and teddies do not move in reality.

Natalie makes the same claim as Amy about seeing her teddies move through a keyhole. Does the keyhole provide a clue? A keyhole is so small it will only allow one person to look at a time, with one eye. There can be no other witnesses to support or challenge the claims being made by the onlooker, unless of course another 'keyhole' can be found. The absence of other spectators leaves open the possibility that teddies can 'come to life'. It's a powerful argument, and we have to decide how to respond to Amy and Natalie's claims. We have to ask what the stories can mean, how they might inform our understanding of the concept of reality.

DWELLING ON THE EPISODES OF ENQUIRY

Connections between the dogs talking and the bears moving are striking. The covert nature of the dogs' and the teddies' actions seems significant, both in the original narratives and in the subsequent contributions to dialogue. The secrecy is revealing. In Amy's contribution, the action in question occurs in Amy's bedroom and involves the wardrobe. Pieces of furniture that open and close—wardrobes, chests of drawers, desks, and boxes—are often associated with secrecy. Other children's accounts refer to intimate spaces such as their beds or rooms: personal, familiar places where toys are kept and private play occurs. The bedroom refers to the time when anxieties are faced, the place where the dark hours and the dreaming hours are spent. The bedroom space provides sanctity to entertain pleasurable and magical fantasies, to face imagined or dreamed terrors or the fear of being alone. In their discussion of hiding places and secret spaces, Van Manen and Levering speculate about the connections between the sense of the secret place and the meeting with one's own secret self, suggesting:

> This sphere presents an opportunity to experiment with possibilities of being, of daydreaming, of feeling, of wondering, of sensing. It is precisely when some part of the house assumes the indeterminate quality of secrecy that the child is permitted the experience of creative peace and quiet intimacy of his or her own familiar and yet secret self (Van Manen & Levering,1996:25).

The dwelling place itself contains and structures our personal life, the point from which we depart and to which we return. It is home to the unconscious. Bachelard proposes that the main benefit of the house is that it shelters daydreaming and protects the dreamer (Bachelard, 1958/1994). As such it offers a mooring, whether temporary or permanent, perilous or calm. It provides a feeding ground for the inner self.

Amy is willing to bring her private world to the group, and in doing so she reveals something about her life. What are we to make of this disclosure and what is noteworthy about such a move? In the supervised and adult led world of school these other worlds bear all the mysteries and uncertainties associated with the discovery of foreign places. Amy and Molly and several of the other children let us in on their private worlds, their dream like experiences, and their poetic fantasies. We can choose whether or not to acknowledge truth in the things of which they speak. The discussion of Corduroy the bear is operating in the borders, at the boundaries of private and public, of playing and reality, of solitary and social, of risk and safety. It is this metaphorical location of our dialogue that lends it a philosophical quality. It is arousing and sensual in its exploration of being-in-the-world.

Philosopher Gaston Bachelard (1960/1971) has described 'reverie' as a state of dreaming solitude. By definition, we are talking here of misty, elusive phenomena that we find hard to grasp with hard analytic tools. We must rely on whether what is being described resonates with our experience. Echoing Winnicott's discussion of transitional phenomena in the context of managing the strain inherent in coming to terms with reality, Bachelard sees reverie as liberating us from what he calls the reality function:

> From the moment it is considered in all its simplicity, it is perfectly evident that reverie bears witness to a normal, useful irreality function which keeps the human psyche on the fringe of all the brutality of a hostile and foreign non-self (Bachelard, 1960/1971:13).

Bachelard wants to distinguish between life in society and life in the world, between the mind and the soul and between concepts and images, between reason and imagination. He wants to stress the binding rather than the escape value of reverie, popular with psychologists as an explanation of the function of daydreams and fantasies. He wants to avoid precise and stable scientific language, a positioning that pins down and holds constant. It is the poetic that conducts this being in reverie, and we must reach beyond the meanings of the words themselves. For Bachelard, cosmic reverie is a state of the soul. We associate this propensity for reverie with childhood itself and with memories of childhood. But Bachelard suggests that the state of childhood has a durable character and is a theme that lasts throughout life. It is not something we leave behind.

We can interpret the discussion of the bears moving as a kind of shared reverie, brought into being through the reports of hidden worlds beyond the reach of rational daylight explanation, protected by the shadows of solitary experiences. In dialogues such as these, we can note those that choose to enter the shared reverie, those that appear to remain outside it, and those that hover at the edges.

Bachelard argues that dreaming reveries and thinking thoughts are two disciplines, difficult to reconcile. He seems to be saying that reverie is a distinctive aspect of consciousness, a 'consciousness of well-being' (Bachelard, 1960/1971:177). Reverie is not akin to penetration but to contemplation:

> the philosopher who gives himself enough solitude to enter the region of shadows, bathes in an atmosphere without obstacles where no being says no (Bachelard, 1960/1971:167).

By solitude we understand the courage to be alone with oneself and with the world, not a literal isolation from others. Bachelard offers a philosophy that accepts the need for that provided by the contemplative and the mere gazing.

RECIPROCAL PEDAGOGY

Philosophical enquiry engages with searches for meaning and truth. In the critical episodes reported in this chapter we have been interested in the ways that disciplinary perspectives shape teachers' responses to children's talk. We have chosen to draw on psycho-analytic, literary, and philosophical sources in our interpretations of these episodes, and we claim that such readings are more conducive to listening to children's voices in classrooms. Drawing on ideas offered by Winnicott, Bachelard, and Egan, amongst others, our readings explore transitional and intermediate domains of experience, expressed through metaphor and narrative, in philosophical reasoning with children. We have considered forms of thinking and dialogue that offer access to what Gaita has termed 'the realm of meaning'.

We are deeply concerned with the kinds of intellectual and emotional resources required to engage imaginatively and playfully with children, when philosophical questions of reality, fantasy, and magic are being explored. This chapter has suggested that an absence of such resources limits philosophical enquiry, and this is illustrated through the example of distancing moves made by teachers, such as the claim that children are incapable of distinguishing fantasy and reality. We suggest that examples, such as talking dogs and moving bears, are valuable for working with teachers to interrogate ideas about both philosophy and child. They allow us to reflect on the constraints of exclusively literal and logical philosophical discourse and to explore outlooks, beliefs, and skills associated with the creative philosophising to which many children seem particularly well disposed. These investigations are part of the re-examination of the automatic authority adults have often assumed in more traditional pedagogy, and which is incompatible with the reciprocal pedagogy of the community of enquiry. In the next chapter we take this discussion forward by critically examining constructs of child and childhood.

9 Philosophy, Adult and Child

In the previous chapter, we examined the idea that readings of children's contributions to classroom conversations are tied to political and philosophical perspectives on child, knowing, and knowledge. As shown in the many examples from literature explored in Part I, these beliefs frame adults' expressions of authority in ways that can be more or less acknowledging or dismissive of children's experiences. In many parts of the world there have been positive signs of social policy development regarding the care and treatment of children, but deeper questions of children's voices and participation in everyday life have really only just *begun* to be explored, particularly in the context of schools.

The implications of listening to children's voices in classrooms are profound, suggesting major shifts in classroom practice and the education of teachers. We argue that philosophy with children (P4C) can be *transformative*, providing a key to more inclusive and meaningful experiences of learning, via communities of enquiry. This chapter considers ethical arguments associated with inclusive, participatory pedagogy through P4C, bringing together philosophy and child. Such a co-incidence incorporates political discourses of rights, power, rationality, knowledge and competence, and cultural perspectives on autonomy, community, and relationship. These topics have been written about in depth by authors in the field of P4C and in childhood studies, and the aim here is to summarise and highlight key ideas connected to our topic, leaving each one open to further questioning.

Education is a moral activity, and epistemology and ethics are intertwined. Beliefs about children's interests and abilities frame their education; some constructs of philosophy and child constrain, rather than expand, educative conversations. As shown in the previous chapter, in order to listen to children's 'voices' in philosophical or other educational interactions, it is necessary to question the pigeon-holing of their thinking: as naïve or as merely replicating a given developmental pattern. We cannot seriously engage with children in authentic searches for understanding if we have already determined that they lack the authority to speak from their experience or the competence to make choices about which questions to pursue. If we expect such searches to follow a given trajectory it results in over directive or over protective teaching. There is a need to pay careful attention to child and pedagogy.

People agree that children should become more knowledgeable through schooling. However, variation in children's experiences of *being* and *Being* at school has to do with the ethical stance of adults, their beliefs about learning, their attitudes to young minds, and their conduct of relationships. This variation reflects ways in which overt or subtle forms of adult power can deny children freedom to explore their ideas *and* simultaneously restrict the value of interaction, both at school and at home. In a domestic context, David McKee's classic *Not Now, Bernard* (1980) humorously illustrates parental power (Figure 4.1). The boy Bernard is eaten by a monster who then moves into the house and tries hard to get noticed by Bernard's mum and dad, to no avail. The monster is subdued into obedience by this systematic lack of attention. The narrative of so many picturebooks rests on the absence of adults from children's imaginative worlds, a feature that makes them a powerful stimulus to philosophical enquiry. The teachers in Bradman and Ross' picturebook *Michael* (1990) call him the worst boy in the school, they say 'we give up' and tell the other children to 'come away'. In our work this has prompted much discussion about listening, learning, and the experience of being at school.

Adults can *choose* how to be with children, and this has a profound effect on a child's ability to work with others, to develop a confident and grounded voice, and, above all, to flourish and learn. Burman puts it this way:

> As adults in positions of relative power, we have responsibilities to explicate (rather than eschew) our commitments; and we also have power to negotiate and consult with, and to provide opportunities for those for whom we speak to make their views known (Burman, 2008b:174).

The everyday exercise of this choice by adults grows from their moral standpoint, their experiences beyond the classroom, being alongside children, their personal sense of child, and from a distinctive understanding of critical and reflexive[1] pedagogy. Van Manen suggests:

> when living side by side with adults, children soon prompt increasingly reflective questions . . . as soon as we gain a lived sense of the pedagogic quality of parenting and teaching, we start to question and doubt ourselves. Pedagogy is this questioning, this doubting (Van Manen, 1991:150).

Let's consider some of the subtleties and practicalities of this questioning, doubting pedagogy. This is a pedagogy that thrives on diversity, rather than presuming conformity. Non-conformity is also beautifully illustrated in the aforementioned story of *Michael* (see Figure 9.1) whose teachers ignore him whilst he designs, builds, and successfully takes off in a rocket, prompting questions from one group of children about whether he is 'naughty' in his single-minded pre-occupation with rockets and lack of interest in any lessons (Bradman & Ross, 1990).

All Michael said was, "Ten, nine, eight, seven, six…

Figure 9.1 Image from *Michael* by Tony Bradman and Tony Ross.

CHILDREN'S PHILOSOPHISING: ADULTS' OBSERVATIONS

In a community of enquiry that aims to be democratic and self-critical, processes need to be in place if 'community' and 'enquiry' are to be more than mere words. Our approach is to consider good *conditions* for critical and responsive enquiry and dialogue, based on contextualised experiences, rather than proposing universal approaches to P4C. Wider experience suggests that deep, exploratory conversations are more likely to occur within relations and contexts of giving and taking. Certain kinds of journeys shared by adults and children are a good example. The motion of travel induces contemplative thinking and reflective talk, attributable to being on the move; looking out at the passing world; venturing into unfamiliar landscapes and places; the containment of a journey: its rhythms and disruptions. Perhaps adults are more available to children at these times, captive and less likely to be distracted by work or domestic chores. Many journeys are memorable and take on significance as enduring narratives. The metaphor of the journey is also fitting for the kind of exploration into the unfamiliar and unknown that characterises philosophical picturebooks and the imaginative conversations that they prompt. The journey does not have to take us very far. A ladder from a toy fire engine begins a fantastic journey *In the Attic* for a young boy whose mother tells him they don't have an attic in the house. He concludes that she has not found the ladder (Oram & Kitamura, 2004). Through P4C many have experienced the fascination of such adventures with young children.

As a father in conversations with his young children, philosopher Gareth Matthews noticed his six year old daughter's capacity for philosophical thinking and that some of the bedtime stories he read to his three year old son raised philosophical issues that he was discussing with students in his university philosophy classes. Becoming more aware of the philosophical nature of some children's literature, he used these stories with his university classes to convince them of his view that philosophy is a natural, spontaneous, and universal human activity. Such observations have been made not only in some family or social settings but in some early childhood settings too (Paley, 1987, 2005). Several accounts and analyses of young children asking philosophical questions and engaging with philosophy in educational contexts have been published (for example Daniel, 2005; Haynes, 2008; Murris 1993, 1994, 1997, 1999; Murris & Haynes, 2002). Murris' work on picturebooks (1992) underlines the value of narrative framing for such explorations developed in Chapter 4. Murris has articulated a distinctive case for children's ability to philosophise (Murris, 1997, 1999, 2000a).

Matthews has written extensively on the subject of children's philosophical development (Matthews, 1980, 1984, 1994). British philosopher Stephen Law endorses the view that children can think philosophically (Law, 2006:39). He, like many others, are persuaded by growing evidence that shows that when learners are offered opportunities to engage regularly in deep thinking it can have a measurable impact on their academic achievement, self-esteem, and linguistic and social skills. The evidence of the impact of P4C on children's lives and learning is substantial (for example SAPERE, 2006; Trickey & Topping 2004, 2007). *Performance* in education is one thing, but it is another step to recognise what it is about philosophical thinking that enables human flourishing and to acknowledge the wider educational and social implications.

Writing about child and childhood in P4C comes close to naturalism at times, stressing children's capacity to question and come as 'strangers to the world' and with special imaginative strength to bring to philosophical thinking. Is philosophy a 'natural' activity for children? Burman guards against any return to ideas of what is natural in children (Burman,

2008a:87). There are risks associated with casting philosophising as an essential characteristic of children. However, with the best of intentions, many teachers are drawn to P4C out of a desire to capitalise on a quality associated with 'being child' and to re-create this philosophical dimension in the classroom. Burman whispers in our ears again, asking whether the appeal of such qualities lies in an ideal of childhood as a 'projective slate on to which our phantasies of escape and thwarted desires are written' (Burman, 2008b:148). We walk a tightrope.

Lived experience tells us that there is *something* about the questions that some children ask in P4C that takes us away from repetition and towards discovery, as well as giving a sense of connection with wider human searches for knowledge. Catalan philosopher and educator Eulalia Bosch writes:

> The magic of this situation is that educators—teachers, parents or others interested in education—are, in fact, situated on this threshold that connects the most spontaneous comments of kids with the deepest of philosophical issues. The only difficulty is in recognising this space and learning how to move in it (Bosch, 2005:13).

This idea of a philosophical 'space' conjures up the powerful physical, emotional, and intellectual draw of genuine puzzlement and searching and associated with deep learning. We are interested in creating conditions in which this dynamic 'space' might become possible in diverse classrooms: the structural changes, the shifts in thinking, and the moves teachers make to confidently enter this 'space' with children, however transiently. This 'space' alludes to broader discourses of critical pedagogy and presupposes our willingness to radically open our ideas of child, adult, philosophy, and schooling. We return to other contributions on these related ideas from the diverse field of P4C debate later in the chapter.

ADULT AUTHORITY: PANDORA'S BOX?

If we are committed to the broader aims of P4C, we need to look beneath the surface novelty of some children's refreshing use of language and philosophical questions or the idea of P4C as a reliable means to other educational ends. Our moral convictions about the possibility of a different education need to stand up to the challenges of introducing communities of enquiry to the school setting. As illustrated throughout this book, this participatory way of working throws up some demanding questions about the authority claims of adults, particularly in the light of the moral foundations of disciplinary traditions in many schools.

The education of children has been at the forefront of public debate for decades. The 'war for children's minds', as Stephen Law (2006) calls it, is a profoundly political one. Law is among some contemporary thinkers advocating the currency of Enlightenment values and arguing that the liberal tradition in education is not responsible for laissez-faire moral relativism (Law, 2006:91–107). Educational settings offer particular opportunities for the exercise of children's moral thinking and action in a public space (Warnock, 1996). Law argues convincingly against authoritarian forms of teaching in the realm of moral education. In terms of freedom of thought, Law makes a useful distinction between *A*uthoritarians, who emphasise more or less deference to external *A*uthority, rather than independent critical thought, and *a*uthoritarians. He suggests an authoritarian mother, for example, may insist on table manners and regular bedtimes but still encourages her children to think independently (Law, 2006:17). Frank Furedi argues that 'telling' children things is somehow out of vogue. This unwelcome trend, he claims, results in many parents and teachers being afraid to simply *impart* knowledge or to impose this kind of everyday rules-based authority as adults: this is why he believes education has lost its way (Furedi, 2009). In this discussion of adult authority in education there are clearly some important subtleties to consider.

Psychological studies carried out in the late 1960s, categorising parenting approaches, articulated differences between 'authoritarian' and 'authoritative' adult behaviour with children (Baumrind, 1967). Follow up studies claimed that the latter was more likely to result in secure, happy, and successful individuals (Maccoby, 1992). Whist these studies took place in a North American cultural setting, and should not be overly generalised, it is worth noting the distinctions made. It is not a case of abandoning all rules, neglecting moral education and adult responsibility in the 'raising' of children, but of understanding why it is so vital, *and* in the common interest, for people to learn to think for themselves and approach moral judgements critically and meaningfully. In Law's view, this is mainly a matter of learning to reason *and* encouraging certain habits and dispositions. Law endorses philosophy in schools, although he does not make any reference to its origins in the work of Matthew Lipman and other key figures in the P4C 'movement'.

P4C goes a step further: the cultivation of good judgement is at the heart of Lipman's educational philosophy (1991) and involves learning to reason *with* others, combining critical thinking with the discipline and practice of deliberation. This is one interpretation of *authoritative* teaching perhaps, with some in-built safeguards, provided teachers remain reflexive and critical (Haynes, 2007a). Authority resides not with individuals but with the process of reflective dialogue[2]. The community of enquiry is central to the idea of moral education in P4C and opens pathways beyond customary dichotomies associated with permissiveness versus authoritarianism, and with individualism versus collectivism.

Within and beyond the school setting we constantly bump into the fact that child/hood is deeply contested ground. Many of the picturebooks, identified as 'troublesome', present difficulties precisely because they draw attention to this contestability—for example, the girl Tiffany's confident stance with the robbers in Ungerer's work (1961), Ida's ambivalence regarding her baby brother in Sendak's *Outside Over There* (1981, see Figure 0.6), the depressed and mournful child in Tan's *The Red Tree* (2001). Stereotypes of child and childhood should be questioned. Given the current focus on measurable educational gains, there is the risk that other values, such as the creation of inclusive communities involving children's independent participation and exercise of agency, could be lost. Critical P4C goes well beyond the idea of a series of lessons in which children ask questions and explore possible answers. It suggests radical changes to the running of schools and in adults' and children's everyday lives.

TRACKING BACK: CHILD, PHILOSOPHY AND EDUCATION

We can only touch briefly on ideas about childhood to highlight some of the dominant themes connected to the practice of P4C[3]. Historically, the most abiding essentialist images of child are rooted in the ideas of John Locke (1632–1704) and Jean Jacques Rousseau (1712–1778). Locke argued that human knowledge originates in sense perception so at birth the mind is a clean slate, a *tabula rasa*, on which the data of experience are impressed. Rousseau believed that the development of human character should follow nature. His account of the child 'Emile' emphasises readiness as a criterion for selecting learning activities through a sequence of natural stages of childhood. Rousseau's view contrasted sharply with the dominant one in Europe at the time, influenced by John Calvin, who saw childhood as a necessary evil to be passed through as quickly as possible, with minimum time spent on 'childlike' activities such as play. The traditional view showed a good child to be as adult like as possible, whereas for Rousseau, the child was a primitive innocent. For him, childhood constitutes our later self, and we do not leave childhood behind when we become adults.

What Is a Child?

Whilst we have already hinted that there are difficulties inherent in the formulation of this question, Marie Louise Friquegnon (1997) offers a précis of the two main traditions. On the one hand the 'deficit model' of child portrays children as inadequate adults whose childishness needs extinguishing. It takes an apprenticeship model as a guide to child rearing, where children imitate, follow, and obey without question. Friquegnon argues that this model fails to make use of qualities such as playfulness, trust, enthusiasm, and openness. On the other hand the 'romantic/progressive model' of child emphasises the innocence of children and the need to allow childish qualities to flourish. Romantic/progressives want to allow the child freedom to choose which of its manifold potentialities to realise and to refrain from intervening. Friquegnon argues that the latter model fails to develop a sense of social responsibility.

Friquegnon suggests that everyday use of the terms 'childlike' and 'childish' betray the mistaken view that the desirable intrinsic qualities of childhood are incompatible with adult responsibility. She argues that both models are inadequate. Human nature and society are not fixed once and for all. Child and childhood can only be partially defined. Just like other developmental concepts (e.g. maturity, youth, adolescence, knowledge, and progress), they are value laden and culturally variant. However, basic features of the *process* to adulthood are not invariant. These are broadly common physical and psychological needs, the satisfaction of which enables human potentialities to be realised. However, cultures disagree on which qualities and potentialities should be emphasised.

Developmentalism

During the twentieth century, ideas about children's learning drawn from the field of developmental psychology, and supported by empirical work seeking to establish universal accounts of the maturation process, tended to be in the ascendancy. These have been thoroughly critiqued (Burman, 2008a, 2008b; Walkerdine, 1984). Essentialist perspectives on childhood still have a strong presence in education, challenged by writers that argue for recognition of diversity of children's lives and experiences and who emphasise the relevance of place and culture to children's position and capabilities. Within developmental perspectives, as Burman argues:

> Development is typically portrayed as an isolated activity, as an epic odyssey or journey, a trajectory that seems to speak of the specific child, but is in fact a methodological abstraction, a statistical fictional 'individual' synthesised through analysis of multiple patterns of populations in the course of which she has been stripped of all that tied her to her time, place and position, but which retains traces of a very particular set of cultural values (Burman, 2008b:167).

The issue of culture is critical, particularly when it comes to arguments about a child's freedom and autonomy, for example. Culture includes reference to social class or group, to place, to language, to ethnicity, to religion. Some of the most passionate debates in contemporary society concern the rights of parents to be involved in their children's decision-making and education. The parent–child relationship is one that can help to illuminate the wider question of community and inter-dependency versus freedom and autonomy of the individual (Archard, 2004). The rights discourse is discussed later in this chapter.

Children are routinely described and treated as other. One expression of this difference, appearing benign, is the sentimentality often associated with imagery of children and referred to in several places in this book. Burman characterises this as a 'distancing move', re-inscribing power relations between adult and child, a move which, in repudiating identification, gives way to the expression of separation and aggression (Burman, 2008b:149). The question 'What is a child?' focuses on common behavioural indicators of maturation and seems to require an emphasis on establishing *differences* between children and adults.

Education has often sought to fix this question of what a child is, rather than leaving it open. Within the Continental philosophical tradition, we might be more likely to find a question like, 'What does it mean to *be* a child?' which is more concerned with ways in which so-called childlike qualities inform *all* human experience and understanding. In phenomenology, it is lived experience that informs our understanding: our daily lives, what we read, see, hear, touch, and feel, through bodily presence. Our bodies also carry the memories of our lived experience, so our childhoods are never completely closed chapters, as Gaston Bachelard puts it 'like a forgotten fire, a childhood can always flare up again within us' (Bachelard, 1960/1971). As demonstrated in the previous chapter we can look to works of literature that talk about childhood, or psycho-analytic accounts, such as those of Winnicott, who writes of the connections between the realms of illusion and playfulness and the realm of creative experience, highlighting the *continuity* of childlikeness in human experience (Winnicott, 1971/1991).

Being Child

A recent discussion between Kennedy and Kohan (2008) focuses on the ontology of childhood through the lenses of temporality, power, and language. Kohan cites pre-Socratic thinker Heraclitus: 'Time is a child childing, its realm is one of a child' as a prelude to exploring complexities in the concept of time itself. Chronologically, child is at the beginning of the life period: time as counted duration. But the time of childhood is another way of living time: a childlike way of being. Childhood is not a period of time but an intense and forceful experience of time. Kohan adds: 'childhood is not [. . .] an absence of power but a singular mode of practising power' (Kennedy & Kohan, 2008:8). Kennedy refers to childhood as an elusive condition of psychological immediacy, similar to other forms of aesthetic experience such as enjoyment of art or intimacy. We are all artists, all philosophers, and all childlike. Kennedy suggests 'as much as the philosopher carries a childlike way of questioning into adulthood, the artist carries a childlike way of acting on the world into adulthood, and both of these act to transform the world' (Kennedy & Kohan, 2008:11). The playful and imaginative works of many of the picturebook authors and illustrators featured in this book are examples of such a capacity to carry a childlike way of acting on the world into adult work. Kohan and Kennedy ask what forms of schooling can be imagined when childhood is understood in these ways. Kohan suggests that we cannot talk about philosophical questions; it is the *relationship* to the question that counts, the putting of something into movement. This contrasts with the skills based view that certain criteria for philosophical questions can be taught and applied. The relative degree of emphasis on 'shared lived experience' or 'developing skills' is a marker of the distinction between the 'with children' and the 'for children' in the debate about philosophising in classrooms.

Does Age Matter?

The territory of childhood involves arguments about the onset of rationality, abstract thinking, and judgement. At what age should we start philosophising with children in school? Judith Hughes (1995) argues that young people do not suddenly become capable of dealing with abstract ideas at a particular age or stage but rather that this is an evolving capability. The philosophical capacities and inclinations of the under sevens have been the subject of intense debate. It is with the very youngest age group that adults seem to struggle the most to agree about what should and shouldn't be done in educational terms. Some of the key arguments are articulated in a pair of short articles by Karin Murris (2001)[4] and Richard Fox (2001) published in the British journal *Teaching Thinking*.

Fox argues that P4C generally underestimates the difficulties children have with philosophy. He suggests that children do not make systematic progress in philosophical thinking until much later, typically from fifteen to sixteen years. He says that young children are made for action, and they struggle with the patience and empathy required for extended discussion. Using hypothetical examples, he proposes that the conceptual exploration characteristic of philosophy is not 'typical' of young children. However, Murris argues that young children can engage with philosophy when it is meaningful for them and suggests that the adult's ability to draw on children's concrete experience within an enquiry is the key to this participation. Through examples from practice she illustrates ways in which some young children have used abstract concepts in the context of their life world. Murris brings the argument back to the central question of 'what is philosophy?', arguing that it is more than the construction of argument typified by much academic philosophy, that it is a way of being in the world: as Wittgenstein called it, 'a form of life'.

The debate between Murris and Fox hinges quite centrally on different perspectives on rationality and the future of thinking. Put simpy, Position A is that P4C could offer children 'training' in philosophical thinking that will enable them to reason and argue in the ways that reasonable adults do. Adults will bring rigour to this process through explicit teaching of reasoning skills in age appropriate ways. Moreover, this will help children to learn, to get on well with others, to solve differences, and to empower them to participate fully in a democratic society.

Position B is that philosophy is constantly reinventing itself, and that the inclusion of children brings both a challenge and an opportunity to look afresh at philosophy itself. In this view, children bring something quite unique to the project of philosophy, based on their concrete position in the world. Moreover, proponents of this view argue that Position A fails to take sufficient account of the dynamics of power in society, in which children occupy the position of a historically disempowered political minority. Walter Kohan (1998) argues that one of the functions of philosophy is to question dominant forms of discourse and their interpretation. It is a form of social critique and creativity to propose alternatives. We propose that picturebooks act as alternative philosophical texts.

Vansieleghem (2005) argues that the instrumental approach of Position A does not constitute an experience of freedom for children: the emphasis on autonomy and critical thinking is a repetition of a pre-existing discourse, not the creation of a new and inclusive one. Kohan further suggests:

> Children will build their own philosophies, in their own manner. We will not correct the exclusion of children's philosophical voices by showing that they can think like adults; on the contrary, that would be yet another way of silencing them. (Kohan, 1998:7).

It is not the intention to make an absolute dichotomy of these two positions, but to show how they highlight different features of the P4C project and help to keep the philosophical dialogue open.

The Teacher in the Dialogue with Children

Pragmatist philosopher John Dewey's (1859–1952) educational thought is foundational to the pedagogy of P4C. His account of pedagogy attends to process. Dewey regards children as active, rational, and collaborative participants in knowledge making, and he sees schools as integral to the community. In *My Pedagogic Creed* he states:

> I believe that much of present education fails because it neglects this fundamental principle of the school as a form of community life. It conceives the school as a place where certain information is to be given, where certain lessons are to be learned, or where certain habits are to be formed. The value of these is conceived as lying largely in the remote future; the child must do these things for the sake of something else he is to do; they are mere preparation. As a result they do not become a part of the life experience of the child and so are not truly educative (Dewey, 1897).

Such socially orientated views on education are reflected in the learning theories of Bruner and Vygotsky and exemplified in Neil Mercer's studies, emphasising the significance of purposeful classroom interaction and children's position as co-constructors of knowledge (Mercer 1995, 2000; Mercer & Littleton, 2007). In the wider world and in the spheres of teaching children, training teachers, and childhood studies, the last thirty years have been all about the realisation that children are far more competent than usually given credit for and that they are able to contribute actively to everyday life when asked or permitted to do so.

HUMAN RIGHTS AND CHILDREN'S RIGHTS

Reflecting these trends, the literature on P4C makes a number of claims about children's capacity to reason and to make moral choices (Lipman, 1993a; Sprod, 2001). It is in keeping with wider debate about the extent to which children should enjoy the same rights as adults, given democratic visions of a just society and the role of education within it (Letwin, 1993; Curley, 1993; Friquegnon, 1993). Views of the child as a more autonomous individual are in keeping with the growing movement for children to enjoy human rights and begin to be reflected through characters in contemporary picturebooks such as those in Gaiman and McKean's *The Day I Swapped My Dad for Two Goldfish* (1998) and *The Wolves in the Walls* (2003), where adults do not have all the power and children ask questions, solve problems, and play a more equal part in decision-making.

If supporters of P4C are right, and children, including the youngest pupils in nurseries and schools, are capable of philosophising, then a number of principles are implied:

- Implications for the law resulting from the child's right and ability to reason
- Implications for ethics and moral education from the child's right and ability to engage in ethical enquiry
- Implications for politics and social life (running of schools) from the child's right and ability to participate in communities of enquiry
- To affirm children's right to think philosophically is to assume an education into rationality, responsibility, and personhood (Lipman, 1993a:143).

In constructing the interface between adults and children, some prefer the emphasis to be on adult accountability, on their responsibilities and duties vis-à-vis children, rather than on the idea of rights for children as such (Archard, 2004). However individualistic an idea, human rights affirming the dignity and worth of the human person, and the promotion of better standards of life and greater freedom, have become fundamental markers of political thinking and action. Whilst interpretation is always culturally laden, few argue with the relationship between basic human dignity and worth and human flourishing. But statements concerning human rights do not, in themselves, change the experiences of those at whom they are aimed.

The Declaration of the Rights of the Child states that: 'the child, by reason of his physical and mental immaturity, needs special safeguards and care' (United Nations Children's Fund, 1995:3). One of the stickier issues facing adults who seek to respect children's human rights is their reading of, and response to, this 'special-ness' and how it is reflected in the maturation process, however it is constructed. Archard points out that one of the immediate problems is:

> how to dovetail a psychological account of human development, or an epistemological account of the acquisition of knowledge, with the establishment of criteria whose possession guarantees a certain moral, political and juridical status. The particular difficulty is that maturation appears to be gradual, whilst the granting of rights tends to be all-or-nothing. For the purposes of becoming a reasoner, or knowledgeable, the passage from childhood is continuous and cumulative; for the purposes of acquiring citizenship the same passage is discontinuous and abrupt (Archard, 1993:10–11).

As well as laying down Articles for the protection and care of children, the Convention of the Rights of the Child (United Nations Children's Fund, 1995) recognizes the child's rights to autonomy, in accordance with her/his stage of development. This implies the goal of maintaining an 'open future' for the child, the awareness of choice, and the means to make decisions. The Convention endorses children's rights to express their thoughts, views, and feelings and to have these listened to and taken into account in decisions affecting them.

In working with children and seeking to enable their freedom to participate, a balance has to be struck between encouragement for the expressiveness of the independent selves of children on the one hand, and supporting the maintenance of a sense of identity and belonging within a web of relationships in families and communities on the other hand. According to Sprod, some postmodernists and feminists have attacked the goal of autonomy as a notion that fails to sufficiently acknowledge human connectedness and culture (Sprod, 2001). Sprod argues that we cannot account for moral agency without a concept like autonomy, and that, rather than ditch the idea altogether, we need to develop a notion of autonomy that 'far from denying dependence and development, writes them centrally into the concept' (Sprod, 1998:37). Burman (2008b:215–216) recognises conflicts in the child rights discourse arising from the evaluation of children within their cultural contexts alongside the desire to treat them as equal subjects transcending cultural practice. She suggests that not only do rights rest on inescapably normative content but that the rights discourse often leads to a counter-position of rights, for example those of women and children, or parents and children. In our experience educational work on children's rights is very limited in classrooms. Discussion of rights comes from many directions. In 1990 Derrida published *Du droit a la Philosophie* arguing for the right of all to philosophy (Cahen, 2001), and there are many people in P4C networks who would like to see philosophical enquiry built into the official curricula of schools as an entitlement for all children.

THE CHOICES FACING ADULTS IN P4C

The choices made by the educator are critical in shaping children's experiences in the classroom. As there are often so many factors to take into account, published policies and guidelines will not do: personal and professional judgement must be called on. Much current literature informing this ethical decision-making process assumes forms of communicative autonomy, with the onus being on the responsible adults to engage with forms of communication that can maximise children's autonomy. In the interests of making such finely tuned ethical judgements and recognising the need for educators (and others) to act, Burman proposes the formulation of genuinely inter-personal and inter-subjective approaches to both development and education (Burman, 2008b:175). Adopting a Foucauldian perspective, Burman explains that regulation and resistance operate in relation to one another: recognising the monolithic power of developmentalism without overstating its intransigence *enables* the activation of change (Burman, 2008b:230). Our experience is that reflexive communities of enquiry can work with this dialectic and act as catalysts for transformation of school relationships.

Kennedy argues that the oral nature of philosophical enquiry is crucial to its radical role. He claims that the historic devaluation of children's ability to reason is part and parcel of their assigned status as a politically inferior and dis-empowered group. Like other groups of people in society, such as women, ethnic minorities, and the poor, children have traditionally been marginalised. Their claims to knowledge and their ways of expressing their thinking are devalued through a process that identifies them as *outsiders*. Paradoxically, from such a position, children have a great deal to contribute to the work of deconstruction and reconstruction that typifies philosophical thinking and enquiry (Kennedy, 1999; Haynes, 2008). The critical practice of P4C illustrated in this book reflects this dynamic ethical position.

The discussion throughout this book has shown that the classroom community of enquiry is much more than an organisational form to be managed within a given paradigm of school and curriculum. It is a concrete and unique coming together of persons, situated in place and time, with an agenda of philosophical questions that emerge from, and whose answers are shaped by, experiences of the participants, whilst at the same time being connected to the wider philosophical project. The concrete experiences of children in each community of enquiry are a critical component of searches for truth and the creation of knowledge and understanding.

Our approach entails a certain view of the community of enquiry itself, as a lived opportunity to shape the detail of democratic practice and to modify it in the light of experience, in response to the observations and suggestions of those involved. In practice this means looking out for every chance to hold back as a teacher and giving as many decisions as possible to the group, even when they are sticky or involve a degree of risk. The concept of *philosophical listening* is central. This is elaborated in the final part of this book.

The making of decisions in these areas of relative risk is what marks out the territory of teaching as a moral activity. Teachers' decisions reflect an ethical and political stance because they involve the rights, interests, and wishes of others and themselves. The key areas in which these choices are made are when teachers:

- mediate between children's participation and protection;
- make judgements concerning the competence and autonomy of children as thinkers;
- express particular views of philosophy and the construction of knowledge;
- mediate between self-regulatory forms of moral education and more traditional means of social control in school;
- seek to shift the imbalance of power in school and to redistribute it more fairly;
- acknowledge the ways in which children are socially constructed as 'Other' and recognise that this is a process that marginalises them.

In the next chapter we consider important qualities of philosophical conversations, such as authenticity, courage, and trust in the processes of enquiry and dialogue.

10 Authentic Ownership of Knowledge and Understanding

There is an urgent need to move beyond talk of strategies, skills, and techniques applied *to* children in classrooms. We concluded the previous chapter by highlighting the critical-ethical decisions to be made by teachers who really want to engage students in philosophical enquiry and who recognise its transformative potential. We suggest that such professionals will be committed to seeking authentic relationships with children, to a fallible stance, and to the understanding that children require genuine dialogue to experience independence of thought and to practise scepticism. This chapter considers the idea of authenticity in philosophical dialogue. In considering concerns about risk and danger in open-ended enquiry, we draw a distinction between intellectual uncertainty and emotional insecurity. We talk about trusting the process and the children involved in it, as well as the courage that is called for, in creating the philosophical space.

SEEKING AUTHENTICITY

The best conditions for independent thinking and self-criticality arrive as teachers loosen the reigns and share responsibility with the class for the form and content of enquiry. These conditions take time to establish and to be self-sustaining. Philosophical thinking that includes learners' voices and participation is bound to be uncomfortable because of the ambiguity of not knowing—neither knowing the direction an enquiry will take, nor the meaning of the concepts into which the community is enquiring. Whilst care is taken to build a safe environment for open-ended dialogue, our concern is that too much care results in suffocation of disagreement and voicing of ideas, with students too keen to stay within prescribed boundaries and to present teachers with what they want to hear.

When teachers smile knowingly to one another or laugh as children express novel ways of understanding the world, this endearment allows them to avoid any re-examination of their own beliefs and assumptions. Endearment seems to presuppose vulnerability *and* inequality, the kind we feel when watching a lioness licking her cubs, but only when they are safely behind bars or on television (Kuier, 1981). A documentary film showing some children arguing for the need for 'some bad in the world', because a peaceful world would imply drinking endless cups of coffee and always being nice to each other (SAPERE DVD, no date), is usually shown on courses on philosophy with children (P4C) and often prompts adult laughter. Their wondering does not seem to touch teachers' belief that peacefulness is a goal towards which we should naturally strive. Similarly, adults are often amused when young children vividly express their ideas about concepts of mind and thinking, in Socrates for Six Year Olds (The Transformers, 1990), saying things like, 'Sometimes I have no thoughts left' or 'you could be thinking with your heart'. This laughter is an example of adult distancing from child. Children's speculations are seen as unusual, sweet, perhaps foolish, but harmless.

How do we begin to break down this distancing from children's ideas? The possibility of authenticity and reciprocity in meaning-making is at odds with the dominant construct of the child at school and the construct of teaching thinking as skill building (Bonnett, 1995). This distancing is a form of marginalization that undermines children's involvement in authentic dialogue, and we need to challenge such limits to freedom and the scope of enquiry.

We often find that children test the genuineness of the philosophical space opened up for them, for example, by asking controversial questions. This should not come as a surprise as it is an unusual space in schools. It is a bit like junior footballers in their first season of getting used to a full-size pitch, unsure how to make best use of the larger space. Children get bored and give up when this space is neither genuine, nor used appropriately. Or they learn to conform to what is expected by teachers, as this makes for an easier life at school on the whole.

It is telling that the principle of 'academic freedom' is not used in the context of young children's education. Kelly makes the point that such freedom is not a privilege reserved for academics, but that 'openness in the face of knowledge' is 'essential to the development both of knowledge itself and of democracy' (Kelly, 1995:128, 129), therefore, essential for schools. The freedom to ask pertinent questions and to speak one's mind sits uncomfortably with blind political correctness, which can inhibit thinking in schools. Putting people in politically correct strait-jackets seems to be a current response to fears of moral relativism. It is all too tempting to follow the crowd, to routinely do what 'one does' without ever being able to make this 'one' specific or traceable.

If we give children the freedom, in the existentialist sense (Bonnett & Cuypers, 2003:328), to be responsible in the situations in which they find themselves, we make it possible for children to be authentic in class. Bonnett and Cuypers identify the anxiety provoked by this burden to be authentic and the temptation to evade such personal responsibility. Philosophical questioning and dialogue makes us all the more aware of this responsibility and pushes us to the edge of what is comfortable and acceptable in class. The voice of authority for the security of children provides an exit from the burden of this responsibility, enabling adults to retain the role of gatekeepers of knowledge. It is much 'safer' to use plausible excuses not to tackle difficult questions, such as the risk of causing upset, the timetable, curriculum, the parents, or the school's senior management.

WEARING THE CLOAK OF SCEPTICISM AND FALLIBILITY

A related locus for teachers' anxiety is the nature of philosophical questioning, an art that cultivates what Kelly calls 'habits of scepticism' (Kelly, 1995). It presupposes flexibility of thought, openness to new ideas, and detachment. Philosophical dialogue cannot be considered as such unless it is radically open and room is made for uncertainty and the periodic sense of being at a loss, for everyone concerned, including the teacher. Tubbs (2005) has argued that the speculative experience of philosophy requires a home, a culture, a *concrete* aporia (from Greek, literally meaning 'without passage' or 'impassable'). These are pre-conditions for the development of an embedded discourse of reasonableness, for philosophical dialogue in a particular place and time.

Authentic philosophical questioning can push teachers to the edge of what is comfortable and acceptable in class. The bewilderment that accompanies philosophical questions, characterised by a Wittgensteinian 'I don't know my way about', induces anxiety in some teachers as it might be associated with a lack of authority. Buckreis (2005) asks whether authority, for some teachers, might be a substitute for security.

In addition to a willingness to manage uncertainty, reasonableness presupposes the freedom to articulate experience and opinion. It assumes persons being taken seriously as thinkers and being listened to with genuine respect and openness. Giving serious room to consideration of the merits of various and diverse perspectives links clearly to Burbules' (1995) conception of objectivity and is the practical side of engendering reasonableness in interaction, constituted in time and in space. The 'reasonableness' of discourses between adults and children has to be re-negotiated if it is to be inclusive, be expansive and escape its present confines.

The dialogical cultivation of reasonableness, as articulated by Benhabib (1992) and by Burbules (1995), Greene (1995), Kohli (1995), and Robertson (1995), among others, is at the core of this project. Burbules' exploration occurs within the broad paradigm of communicative ethics. This paradigm offers an historically situated, dialogical, radical counter weight to the individualistic, normative, universalising, and linear enlightenment account of rationality: what Greene terms 'the weight of dead authorities' (Greene, 1995:7).

Burbules describes four aspects of thinking and behaviour as essential to the possibility of reasonableness which he views as describing a relationship with others, rather than as adherence to sets of rules and procedures. It is primarily within relationships and communities that he suggests the virtues and flexible aspects of character needed to be reasonable can develop. These comments about the embedded conditions in which reasonableness grows reflect the feminist critique of rationality that has argued against the privileging of rational forms of discourse, at the expense of emotional, sensual, corporeal, and imaginative dimensions of human experience, in pursuit of truth and the good. Throughout this book we have shown how such dimensions of experience can be drawn on in philosophical enquiry, particularly when narrative forms come into play.

According to Burbules, reasonableness includes: striving for objectivity, accepting fallibilism, maintaining a pragmatic attitude, and being judicious. He regards objectivity not as an individual achievement but a quality that grows through engagement with others. We have to care enough to make the effort to hear what others are saying, argues Burbules, and the real sign of objectivity is the capacity to recognise the merits of each view. He suggests that 'values of tolerance and pluralism are methodological as well as moral' (Burbules, 1995:91).

This intertwining of the methodological and the moral is particularly important when considering how adults might attempt to cultivate objectivity in the context of a classroom community, since children are among those who have been excluded historically when certain standards of rationality have been adopted (Vansieleghem 2005). Benhabib (1992) has also argued the importance of the processes of communicative discourse being 'radically open' to ensure the inclusion of those whose social position has silenced them or resulted in their not being heard. Kohli gives her view of some conditions of this radical openness:

> Any notion of dialogical or communicative reason must take into account the differences between and among people. Without attending to the particular, situated experiences of different groups of people, different subjectivities, different identity positions, concepts such as freedom, democracy and equality ring hollow (Kohli, 1995:108).

Burbules' conception of fallibilism implies risk, reflection, and the capacity to admit to being wrong (Burbules, 1995). Biesta and Burbules (2003) explain fallibilism as a major tenet of the pragmatist perspective on education developed by Dewey, a founding influence on P4C, as reported in the previous chapter.

The capacity for change implies affect as well as intellect. In the context of adults' traditional role in school, the call to fallibilism exerts a contrary pressure to the expectations that adults in charge should exemplify absolute clarity, certainty, assurance, authority, and the final word. When it comes to teaching very young children, we have come across practitioners who argue that doubt and uncertainty are developmentally inappropriate: first and foremost adults should be providing definite answers and a sense of security. Such a perspective associates all forms of cognitive doubt with damaging emotional insecurity. Curiosity and wonder depend on the opening made by doubt, on the postponement of final resolution. If met with only definite answers, they will soon abate (Haynes, 2005b). We return to this theme of uncertainty versus insecurity later in the chapter.

For Burbules, the pragmatic attitude that comes with reasonableness is fostered within a commitment to conversational forms of management and decision-making and an atmosphere in which failure and frustration are viewed as normal and useful contributors to growth and learning. Picturebooks are full of failure, confusion, and uncertainty. *Igor the bird who couldn't sing* presses on with his quest to sing regardless of repeated rejection (Kitamura, 2006). Joseph Kaye notices unsettling things around his home and doesn't understand what is going on in *Changes* (Browne, 1997). Fish tries to imagine the animals and people outside his pond and lies dying when he jumps out of water to 'see' the world beyond, literally a fish out of water (Lionni, 1974).

In spite of rhetoric to the contrary the 'culture of success' currently regarded as desirable in schools leaves very little room for untidiness or errors and failure tends to be inextricably associated with underperformance. Burbules also argues that judiciousness is a feature of reasonableness that allows us to build in awareness of the limitations of reason and acceptance of fallibilism and imperfection. This reference to judiciousness hints at the essential value of forms of expression and interaction found in the arts, discourses of human survival, passion, belonging and meaning, on which the discourse of reason feeds and depends. Reasonableness is not disconnected from or elevated above everyday life (Burbules, 1995).

Robertson (1995) agrees with the need to re-create reason as an educational aim, if it is to be dynamic and compelling. Adding to Burbules' version of communicative relations, and acknowledging Kohli's discussion of the relationship between emotion and reason, she argues that reason is both immanent and transcendent. Reason does not only exist within locatable and actual relations and experiences, she suggests, but it also exists as an ideal. There is always a meta-dialogue concerning the reasonableness of discourses of reason. Human beings are interested in understanding whether some ways of forming beliefs and deciding how to act are more likely to succeed than others. We always use one set of criteria or another to evaluate our progress (Robertson, 1995).

So much talk about teaching seems to rest on the metaphor of 'grasping' knowledge. Classroom interaction raises profound questions about the *ownership* of knowledge, teaching, and learning. Drawing on Stanley Cavell's work, Standish reflects on the pathological and existential dimensions of scepticism and wonders what a 'non-consumptive' relation to knowledge could be like (Standish, 2005). Standish reminds us of the connection between control and knowledge. In Dutch, the word for concept is *begrijpen*. The verb *grijpen* highlights the invasive, almost aggressive 'grabbing' nature of conceptual knowledge. We grab a child when we are angry or when we have little time to spare to save him/her from danger. Significantly, it is a fear-based response.

RISK AND DANGER

When the *content* of thinking in classrooms reflects questions and topics that are sensitive or controversial, perhaps pertaining directly to the lives of people in the school community and beyond, how do we weigh up the risks and the benefits of thinking about the things that matter the most to us? Wittgenstein suggests, 'You could attach prices to thoughts. Some cost a little, some cost a lot. And how does one pay for thoughts? The answer, I think, is with courage' (Wittgenstein, 1988). If we adopt Wittgenstein's metaphor of thoughts having 'prices', what kind of courage might be needed to 'pay' for them in classrooms?

We suggest that approaches to teaching that encourage criticality and creativity *should* cause a stir at times since they trade on processes of justification, involving dis/agreements, distinctions and location of common ground, alternatives, departures, and novelty in thinking. If they don't sometimes generate passionate debate then we challenge their claim to teach thinking. Teaching thinking has to be demanding. Philosophy with children has certain characteristics built into the design of the community of enquiry. These dynamic characteristics exist to open up the ground of thinking and listening, to encourage student participation, to provide some structure for the processes of reasoning, and to nourish the dialogue. These features include:

- A dedicated time and space, a starting point that *provokes* questioning, and an agenda created by pupils' questions, faithfully presented
- The teacher holds back on her/his views and works to ensure that ideas get a fair hearing and alternative points of view are explored
- The mainly oral medium of enquiry, removing barriers to thinking and participation for many students
- Encouragement to risk taking, trying out ideas and playfulness in thinking, freedom to change one's mind, and disagreement normalised
- Searches for meanings, as well as for truths, and provisional answers based on more rigorous *or* persuasive arguments and examples.

Children who do philosophy frequently comment on the pleasure of being listened to with respect (Haynes, 2008). Schools such as Tuckswood Community Primary School in Norwich, England, adopted P4C throughout the school as part of a wider commitment to extending and strengthening children's participation in *all* aspects of school life from the very start. At a

SAPERE[1] conference in London in November 2004, students from a large English secondary school confidently reported that experience of philosophical enquiry had widened the range of issues that students could safely explore and discuss, including those that would stir the strongest feelings, such as political questions, religion, and sexuality.

So what is the *cost* of this kind of open-ended enquiry? In the lived experience of the communities in which we teach, we need to carefully consider the relationship between those who are taking part in the dialogue and the questions that are being discussed. We need to be alert to the possibility that enthusiasm for critical thinking and reasoning can mask our awareness of the political and cultural outlook that such teaching advocates and that we embody through our authority as teachers within the educational system. Is questioning and critical thinking always a good thing? Are there some things we should not question in classrooms? In answering this question, noting the issues that cause us to hesitate might help us to respond to the demands and dilemmas of this kind of teaching.

While welcoming methods such as the community of enquiry, teachers might find they want to limit or to mediate the process in practice because to follow it completely appears to present dangers. Certain questions fill teachers with anxiety because they touch on deeply held beliefs or personal sensitivities or allude to moral panics, for example concerning risks to children's safety. Teachers patrol boundaries of privacy and confidentiality.

Educators do impose limits on opinions that can be freely expressed. They (we include ourselves) can be constrained in the toleration of pupil dissent or protest, for example, if opinion is translated into action, such as the time when some young people in the UK made the decision to take part in demonstrations against the invasion of Iraq during school hours. In this instance some adults expressed doubt as to the reliability or integrity of the young people's opinions, while others were caught up in whether they should be reprimanded for non-attendance at school. No matter how clear the ground rules, as teachers we will certainly find ourselves in the position of having to respond to unanticipated questions and issues. What lies at the heart of the sense of 'danger' in respect of some questions and how legitimate are moves to limit discussion? How can we ensure that the reasoning that informs our judgements as teachers is robust?

As reported in the introduction, some of the picturebooks we recommend for P4C cause some teachers to feel very uneasy because they mention strangers or might lead to discussion of topics like death, differences, religion, politics, or sex. The topic of strangers is the reason some teachers refuse to work with Ungerer's *The Three Robbers* (1961), in which a small orphan girl cheerfully accompanies three strange thieves to their castle, in preference to going to stay with her wicked aunt (see Figure 0.5 in the Introduction). Teachers argue that this book gives the wrong message to children about dangerous strangers. Strangers and secrets are closely associated.

There is discomfort when questions like 'Why do people have secrets?' is raised. In the current climate of childhood the topic of secrets is taboo, a result of its association with the *possibility* of child abuse. The very word 'secrets' has come to be infused with ideas of adults using the appeal of a shared secret to conceal illegal maltreatment and to maintain adult power and access to the child. Van Manen and Levering (1996:138) suggest that our understanding of childhood itself is intertwined with the concept of secrecy as prohibition. Within this understanding, the child has many faces, but one of the most compelling is of the image of the child as vulnerable and therefore requiring special love, care, and security. Linked to this is the idea that the child is a person not yet formed, needing to be educated and trained to come into her own. The child is also seen as dependent, and this dependency provides the adult with his/her sense of responsibility. Van Manen and Levering argue that these beliefs lead to irresolvable debates about what is good or bad for children. Childhood becomes *defined* in terms of what must be hidden from children, and the leaving of childhood is about gradual or brutal initiation into secrets of the adult world (Van Manen & Levering, 1996:139–140). It is the danger of secrets that seems to overshadow all other discussion about secrecy.

Public insecurity and mistrust result in a preference for teaching from a script and holding on firmly to the certainty of the position of teacher as all-knowing subject. Todd (2003) refers to the adoption of such a stance as the 'sanitisation' of teaching, where teachers simply avoid *any* possibility of ambiguity. In primary education at least, this sanitisation is partly facilitated through the presentation of teacher-as-maternal-figure. In the construction of the teacher as mother, love and passion are enveloped within an image of safety as opposed to risk. Walkerdine (2001) suggests that the pre-occupation with safe spaces for children reflects anxieties about a postmodern landscape in which the protection of children is beyond the control of adults, both in private and public domains.

While on the one hand there is an avoidance of controversial topics, on the other hand children's personal experiences may be elicited in certain areas of the curriculum, through the arts, literature, personal, and social education. Davis cites a number of typical examples from the classroom that raise more general questions about children being expected or required to discuss what he characterises as personal information, such as their family, friendship, religious beliefs, and deep responses to stories or works of art as an ordinary part of everyday learning (Davis, 2001:247). Davis argues that such expectations compromise the privacy rights of children and their families.

Ormell (2005) argues that schools do not exist to solve deep problems of society, and education should avoid stirring up emotions, tackling instead 'what can be understood' in order to build young people's intellectual confidence. This echoes the view that teachers should present an authoritative certainty, preserving doubt and questioning for adults. Ormell suggests that teachers should not pursue topics simply because they 'get children talking' but should aim for a quieter type of stimulation, enhancing curiosity and imagination. He is uneasy about classroom conversations that lack closure. We agree that teachers should not court controversy simply as a covert means of engaging pupils' attention, but we do not share Ormell's vision of a dispassionate curriculum, devoid of exploration of values and beliefs, including those of students. It is impossible to conceive of social or moral education, for example (let alone subjects such literature, art, and history) that do not involve interpretation and evaluation of beliefs and actions (Foreman-Peck, 2005; Haynes, 2005b).

In the public domain of the school, anxiety and evasiveness when controversial topics come up reflect the range of influences on relationships between teachers and pupils. Teachers are public servants accountable beyond the classroom and bound by public policies. Teachers do not operate in isolation but as part of a profession, an educational system, a school institution, a team of staff. They are figures of authority and deliverers of results. Legally, teachers are 'in loco parentis', expected to be guardians of students' safety and well-being. Arguably, the safe-guarding role puts teachers in a position of surveillance. Considerations of age and/or maturity of the child nearly always surface strongly among these voices of concern and restraint.

Politics and religion are often regarded as particularly sensitive. Teachers may be very wary about any suggestion that they are using their position of power to influence young people's political views or encouraging students to question school policy or break school rules. Among practitioners of philosophy with children there has been much discussion lately, as elsewhere, on religious beliefs and faith. In an article published in the SAPERE newsletter Darren Chetty articulates important concerns about possible conflicts of interests originating from his experience of P4C in schools (in Chetty &Splitter, 2005). He asks whether the enquiry process encourages children to question their religious and cultural upbringing, highlighting tension between individual autonomy and identity and belonging. He suggests that religious belief can be an important part of a child's sense of place in the world, adding that family beliefs and customs:

> will most likely be contested by the child as an adolescent. It is likely that reason and faith will play a part in informing the child's decisions as to which customs to embrace and which to reject. P4C's emphasis on justifying our opinions may pre-empt this possibly more organic process (Chetty & Splitter, 2005:3).

Hannam and Echeverria have also written about the doubt often associated with identity development during adolescence (Hannam & Echeverria, 2009:21–22, 26–28). Wary of developmental abstractions that close avenues of thinking, we would prefer to leave open the question of whether or not such adolescent doubting is an 'organic process'. However, we recognise the tensions and share the concern about whether exploring the basis of religious beliefs could unwittingly make children more vulnerable and further accentuate the gap between home and school. However, is it not the duty of educators to open up possibilities for thinking otherwise? Chetty points out that while P4C is a democratic methodology, schools are far from being democratic institutions. The balance of power favours teachers and the dominant curriculum. So Chetty's question is not whether the basis of religious faith should be questioned at all, but when, where, and how, given other inequalities between groups of people in society. He wants us to consider the age and maturity of learners. He wants to draw attention to the ways we use our authority as teachers, which may serve to reinforce inequalities.

The responsibility of this authority is expressed by teachers in different ways, such as resorting to control or evasion. Teachers want to minimise disruption and disturbance in the classroom, they are worried about making children afraid or insecure. They don't want to upset pupils or their parents, expose or deepen social or cultural differences in the school community. It may have to do with a lack of familiarity with using moral terms and arguments when making professional judgements. It can be uncomfortable not having 'the answer', and this is alleviated perhaps through political correctness or asserting the desire for inclusiveness in school policy and ethos. As discussed in Chapter 5 with reference to the work of Martha Nussbaum, we argue that emotions are often indicators of moral concerns. Avoidance does not educate, and policy (even that which refers to children's rights) does not always serve as a guide to action for teachers seeking to mediate competing influences. Each case needs careful thinking through with clear reference to moral principles.

CLASSROOM EXPERIENCE

In discussion of these issues with a group of colleagues on a P4C course for teachers, Lisa Naylor related an episode from one of her classroom enquiries, when she felt the uncertainty and concern about the way she should exercise her responsibilities as the teacher. Lisa was teaching ten and eleven year olds at Gallions Primary School, opened in 2000 to serve a new area of housing in East London, England. The class in question had been doing philosophy for about two years. A number of children in the class had arrived from other countries during the academic year. About a third of the class was Muslim, about another third Christian, and the remainder included Buddhists, Atheists, and Agnostics, and one child who was Pagan. In the account below, she described the classroom episode and what went through her mind:

The stimulus for the enquiry was a poster of everyday objects and a number of questions came up as usual. We started talking about whether life was a dream and how we knew whether it was or it wasn't. M argued that life wasn't a dream because 'dreams don't have boundaries but life does'. Several children argued that we don't know if it is a dream or not and will only find out when we 'wake up'.

The enquiry moved on to religion and J, who is a pagan, asked the class how they knew that there was a god (this is a theme that comes up repeatedly in our P4C sessions). He said: 'What proof do you have that God exists?' Several of the children replied that they didn't need 'proof' and that they just 'know' that he exists.

J asked them how they could spend so much of their life 'believing and praying' to something or someone that they are not absolutely sure exists. He was clearly struggling to understand how people can be so sure of something that they have no concrete proof of. J shows great respect and maturity in his questioning and always precedes his questions with 'I completely respect your religion and am just trying to understand more about your belief'.

After pursing this line of questioning for some time, J said 'Actually, I don't want an answer to my question because I don't believe there is one'. On talking to him later on, after the enquiry, he said that we can never know the answer to his question. It didn't seem to be a problem for him that there was no answer; in fact, he seemed more intrigued than ever by the issues raised.

To conclude an enquiry, we often have a round of final words. J, a devout Muslim girl in the class, said 'this enquiry has really made me think about my own religion and now I'm wondering whether Allah actually exists'. J didn't appear distressed or concerned about this. She was very matter-of-fact. When questioned later, she just said that the boy J had really made her think about things and on questioning she realised that she didn't actually have any proof that Allah exists.

As a teacher, I felt quite uneasy about her statement and as soon as the enquiry was over, we discussed how it is good to ask questions and challenge ideas but that philosophy does not intend to undermine or attack anyone's belief or religion. I was worried that J's parents and other members of the community or Mosque school that the children attend on the estate, would complain to the school about what had happened in the enquiry. I wondered whether I could justify the questions that were asked. Belief does not just concern religion, but culture, tradition and identity.

I wondered what right I had to be allowing (and by allowing, clearly encouraging) J to question and challenge others' beliefs. I was quite concerned about the enquiry and spoke to the Head teacher about what was said. I also emailed a couple of experienced P4C facilitators for advice.

Despite all of my concerns, I was extremely interested in J's line of enquiry and the children's responses to him (he was actually being a fantastic facilitator!). In a strange way, I felt that J was asking questions that as a (white, non-religious) teacher, it would be completely politically incorrect for me to ask.

HOW DO WE WEIGH UP PARTICIPATION AND PROTECTION?

Lisa's generous making public of her doubts has certainly sharpened and enriched many discussions about the judgements teachers have to make, particularly in this role of dialogue facilitator. Whether we are talking about older or younger children the tension seems to be between the right, or ability, of children and young people to make decisions and judgements for themselves and the right or authority of adults to make some of those choices on behalf of children. Our discussion also seems to hinge on ideas about the desirability of uncertainty and its place in teaching thinking. As indicated earlier, that answers are 'provisional' is a non-negotiable part of the practice of philosophy.

We cannot treat all controversial issues in the same way since their sensitivities arise from different sources. However, whether discussion might touch on the judgements we make about strangers, what happens when we die, or the existence of God, the hesitation about the suitability of these topics for children carries the underlying assumption that children need to be protected in some way. This protection might be associated with (lack of) awareness of wider social and political inequalities, and the pervasiveness of discriminatory discourses, such as whiteness, for example, as pointed out by Chetty in his research on P4C and anti-racism (Chetty, 2008).

We often find the judgement aligned to the view that children are not capable of deciding for themselves *what* they should discuss and of managing the associated uncertainty. The reliability of their views and decisions are open to question. Their autonomy is understood to be limited by their dependence and inexperience. If this view is adopted, adults feel that they should assume authority in these decisions. This desire to protect stems from a view of the child as vulnerable: parents and carers have a special role to play, and family relationships need to be safeguarded to help build the child's sense of place, belonging, and resilience.

We argue that it is usually possible to find a way to involve children in the decision-making, and that efforts should always be made to do so. When it comes to trying to make difficult judgements on behalf of children about their needs, it might be useful to make a distinction between security and certainty. Few people will argue with the importance of secure emotional attachments for healthy development, or the value of a sense of personal safety and protection from abuse, either at home or at school, in making it possible for a child to be 'free' to explore and learn. Uncertainty is different. Uncertainty is part of curiosity about the world and about others, and it motivates us to go beyond what we already know. It is the ground of uncertainty that makes it possible to think about the views of others.

It is the ability to listen that will serve as the best guide to action for teachers in making judgements about how to pursue thinking and discussion of sensitive issues. Our experience is that groups that work together frequently, as Lisa's class does, develop the ability to be *self-regulating*, particularly when encouraged to pay attention to the needs and concerns of others. The active involvement of parents helps to provide checks and balances on our perceptions and understanding of children's experience of school. Openness and consultation in respect of the agenda for discussion helps to provide support and protection for participants. If we are serious about participation we need to question the everyday authority we assume as adults, let alone as teachers. Part of the skill of listening is making room for thoughtful silence, or dwelling[2]. Part of the skill of listening is taking into account the inequalities of power, including those between adults and children. Part of the skill of listening is recognising the significance of identity, the narratives of individuals, and the meanings attached to deeply held values and beliefs.

Jonathon Glover argues that, if things go well in a dialogue about beliefs, *all* participants will hold their beliefs more tentatively, aware of the precarious nature of the foundations of all beliefs (Glover, 2005). We can hope that the boy J, like the doubting Muslim girl in the account of the dialogue in Lisa's class, will continue to thoughtfully examine the basis of his beliefs. Such reflectiveness does not have to undermine any sense of belonging; it serves as an antidote to intolerance and creates the common space where differences can be explored, curiosity can be expressed, and new ideas can be taken on board. Children are naturally exposed to each other's values in a school community. Philosophical enquiry provides a space for measured exploration of such values that can be educative for all.

AN ORGANIC APPROACH TO DEMOCRATIC EDUCATION?

Gregory (2008:53–54) presents five responses to the concern about children coming to disagree with their parents' key beliefs. He argues that the evidence over thirty years is that mostly children do not fundamentally change their beliefs but learn to base them on sound reasons. He suggests most parents see this as a good thing. Gregory argues that, in the interests of democracy, judgements should be informed by critical evaluation of alternative views and children discuss questions of religion and politics whether or not they are tackled in the classroom. He suggests we should have faith in young people's integrity by trusting their ability to discuss even the most sensitive of topics.

One way to address this problem could be to educate learners and teachers in ethical decision-making, so that all are more sensitive to the moral dimensions of the decisions made on their behalf. Through such a process teachers tend to become more aware of their 'emotional labour' (Winograd, 2003) when negotiating between the core values of autonomy and protection.

There is no guidebook or insurance policy to cover the new and unfamiliar territory that we enter by encouraging children to think independently, to question, and to engage in dialogue. When difficult issues arise, we do need the courage to ask ourselves whether it is not just an old anxiety that makes it a problem. Such decisions can be made with greater confidence where there are good channels of communication between all concerned. Intimacy characterises the development of a more organic democratic perspective in a genuine and reflexive community of enquiry.

In the enthusiasm for critical thinking, we need to be alert to the power we have as educators and look for ways to give greater control to students over the content and direction of enquiry. We need the courage to trust that, when given the opportunities to be self-regulating and the security of knowing that teachers will be respectful and support their choices, children can determine for themselves what they should think about and question. We find Tiffany's (2008) idea of the classroom as a democratic laboratory a useful one. Here there is less emphasis on individual autonomy and more recognition of the diversity of the community and a variety of stakeholders.

The final part of the book examines problems of listening at school and the qualities of listening implied when children are respected and trusted and that enable dialogue to become philosophical.

Part III

Philosophical Listening

This final part of the book returns to the ethical and political dimensions of philosophical enquiry with children using picturebooks and explores problems and current challenges for those who would seek to listen more attentively to children in classrooms and schools. It investigates the idea and role of hospitality in the context of school life. It examines the notion of philosophical listening and the contribution that it might make to educational practices that allow for deeper and more meaningful participation by the children involved.

11 Listening and Juggling in Philosophical Space

The previous chapter discussed the value of disagreement and risk-taking in the classroom and suggested that democratic processes in trusting communities of enquiry give courage to tackle troublesome questions. We connected this claim to the way that philosophical enquiry through picturebooks creates a space for novel thinking. In philosophy with children (P4C), the possibility of being authentic depends on being able to share responsibility for the content and direction of dialogue. We do not under-estimate the difficulties with democratic practice, authenticity, and autonomy. There is always the danger that we delude ourselves, replace one system of authority with another, or err too often on the side of harmony and consensus, no matter how hard we strive for 'real' dialogue.

Trust and inclusiveness in any community are not characteristics to be taken for granted. They are elusive and precarious qualities and must be constantly sought after and re-invigorated. Authentic learning is sometimes possible when we can successfully bring together the openness of a teaching space, democratic processes, and philosophical facilitation. As Kohan has argued, philosophy with children as a project needs to be approached philosophically, 'with as few non-thinkable points as possible' (Kohan, 2009:23). We argue that thinking about listening is at the heart of facilitation, whilst fully accepting the impossibility of final words on the subject of listening in education.

This section of the book explores the ethics of listening as an overlooked dimension of educational practice. An earlier dialogue (1999) is included in this chapter to provide a sense of the evolution of our practice. Subsequent chapters discuss what is involved in learning to listen to child in philosophical enquiry. Children's philosophising makes a distinctive contribution to debate about respectful listening. Before presenting our dialogue, we briefly outline the direction of recent work on listening in the field of childhood studies.

LISTENING AS THE ORDER OF THE DAY

What does it mean to listen and what prevents listening to children? Recent theorising about relations between adults and children has taken an explicitly ethical orientation (Garber, Hanssen, & Walkowitz, 2000). Political critiques of neo liberalism have set out to challenge historical and current discourses in which the child is described as an object to be developed (developmentality) and governed (governmentality) and to present alternative perspectives more consistent with an understanding of children as persons (Fendler in Hultqvist & Dahlberg, 2001; Dahlberg & Moss, 2005). We distance ourselves from constraint, fear, risk aversion, and mistrust in public debate about child and childhood. We are critical of practice where terms such as 'appropriate/inappropriate', ready/not ready', 'mature/immature', 'advanced/behind', 'safe/upsetting', along with countless goals and targets seem to rule the everyday lives of adults and children. Our approach is born of a desire to (re)build trust and to work with greater freedom, tact, care, and optimism. Our voices are among many to explore the meanings of 'child' and 'adult'. We resist timeless answers, whilst sensing that 'child' and 'time' are somehow connected, but not in ways that lock the meaning and experience of child into a pre-scribed life phase of certain temporal duration, namely childhood. Without relying on empty political slogans that hearken to abstract or universal visions of childhood, what are the conditions in which we can make claims to be listening to children?

Much current work in the field of childhood is founded on growing interest in children's lived experiences and situated perspectives[1] and, through paying due regard to children's views, aims to extend policy and practice of listening beyond the narrow sense of 'consultation'[2]. Where consultation is the sole aim of listening, we often find tokenism: every now and again children's views might be canvassed about a particular issue, for example the playground, school dinners, the rules, raising money for charity (Whitty & Wisby, 2007), through systems in which a few children may well be speaking on behalf of others and within processes that are not necessarily friendly to children's preferred modes of expression. Consultation on a range of matters in educational settings is important, and there are many practitioners who take this seriously and work at making practice more democratic, by exploring new processes and forms of representation, so that children are properly included in policy and decision-making (for example Cox & Robinson-Pant et al, 2003; Haynes 2009a; Leeson, 2007; Rudduck & McIntyre, 2007). But there is much more to listening than consultation.

LISTENING BEYOND CONSULTATION

Some of those who work with children and young people have begun to reflect on the limitations of their insights into children's lives and to express concern with more effective inclusion, for example Fielding (2006, 2007). Clark, McQuail, and Moss (2003) offer some definitions of listening and participation to reflect these theoretical understandings. Consultation is an element of, but not synonymous with, participation. Participation is more than being periodically consulted about one's views. Participation implies active involvement in decision-making and some ownership of the decision-making process itself, along with the introduction of processes that allow for various modes of representation, including those that are sympathetic to the current interests and communicative strengths of the particular children concerned. It implies opportunities to question, represent ideas, and initiate action. Listening, Clark et al suggest, is an active process involving 'hearing, interpreting and constructing meanings' (Clark, McQuail, & Moss, 2003). It is not limited to the spoken word and is fundamental to participation in everyday life. From such perspectives children are not regarded only as 'becomings' but also as 'beings' whose thoughts, choices, relationships, and concerns are of interest in their own right (James & Prout, 1997).

LISTENING AND CRITICAL ENGAGEMENT

Children's participation is problematic, particularly in areas such as compulsory schooling (Fielding & Rudduck, 2006) or the curriculum, even in a climate in which talk of voice and rights trips easily off the tongue. A more fundamental shift in thinking is needed. A central function of schooling is enabling a 'handing on' of accumulated public knowledge to the incoming generation, a process that necessarily puts educators in a role of authority. It does not have to turn them into authoritarians. Human society can benefit when the best of such acquired wisdom is sensitively imparted, whilst maintaining a stance of openness to re-interpretation and revision. Part of the public contract with school teachers is that they should attend to the 'becoming' of children, to their economic and social futures. This does not need to be at odds with questioning the assumptions associated with such 'futures', nor with taking children seriously as 'beings'. There does not need to be a contradiction between the exchange of public knowledge and participatory pedagogy.

Much of the 'work' of education consists of drawing on ideas from the past and on public knowledge of the wider world to help make sense of the 'here' and the 'present'. It is in the process of sense-making and critical interrogation of knowledge and culture that teachers can choose to behave in ways that make a positive difference to the experiences of learners, not as 'missionaries' but as social critics. History suggests that there can be many dangers in the relationship between the state and education, including in contemporary democracies. For those who work in the public education system, what is required is collective as well as individual reflection about what it means to be 'authoritative', along with critical awareness of the dangers of political goals for education. These include education for human rights or political literacy, or overly confident definition of concepts such as citizenship, which remain contested: critical engagement is essential to avoid the tyranny of indoctrination (Gearon, 2010:130).

Adults should be prepared to be influenced by their interactions with children, as they would expect to be by other adults *and* because of the positioning of children and young people, historically and today. It could be argued that children have been a political 'minority', and we have to find a way out of this, that neither mimics the trajectories of liberation movements of adult minorities nor follows the perpetual pendulum swing associated with education policy development. We need some ways forward that are sensitive to the care of young and growing human beings, that neither rest on old assumptions and generalisations nor pander to the fashion for innovation for its own sake. Our practice-based knowledge tells us that philosophy with children can be helpful here because of the force of experience that being child entails and, as Kohan puts it, 'philosophy, democracy, citizenship and politics are things to be questioned, not end points of its practice' (Kohan, 2009:23).

LISTENING AS EMBEDDED PRACTICE

In the world of childhood studies, listening is increasingly being understood as a much wider and embedded practice of ongoing conversation between adults and children, mutual and reciprocal encounters where listening is understood as fundamental to ethical relations (Clark & Moss, 2001:10). In contemporary writings the concept of 'encounter' is informed by the work of philosophers such as Derrida, Deleuze, and Levinas. The events of the twentieth century, and the debates about ethics to which they have given rise, have thrown up the notion of 'radical openness' to the Other, whilst positing the 'ungraspability' of the Other. Such ethics imply effort and attention to the particularity of the Other, to the plurality of Others, alongside the idea that a unifying narrative or method will not be discovered and should be resisted.

For Levinas, responsible ethics precedes thought, and encounter is only possible when we accept the unknowability of the Other; when hospitality is respectful, rather than grasping (see Dahlberg & Moss, 2005). Perhaps the portrayal of adult–child worlds and the symbolic encounter between Max and the Wild Things in Sendak's story *Where the Wild Things Are* provide an illustrative flavour of such 'unknowability' (although the film of this book is reported to have 'filled in some of the gaps' in the original text). Oram Kitamura's book *In the Attic* (2004) conveys this sense in the illustration of the boy and the tiger, each speaking their own unfathomable languages, as does the illustrator of The Island, in portraying the reception given by the island community to the naked stranger who arrives on their shore, disturbing their thoughts and dreams and exposing the cruel limits of their receptiveness to newcomers (Greder, 2007).

Such an idea of encounter arises when we are confronted by something from the outside. Kohan (after Deleuze) describes philosophy as an unrepeatable experience of thinking arising from 'the encounter with what forces us to think, with what puts us into doubt, with what takes us out of our conformity, our naturality' (Kohan, 2002:9). This is not philosophy as an exercise but as lived experience: palpable acts of engagement and translation. Such upheavals of thought catch us unawares. In Velthuijs' picturebook *Frog in Love* (1989), discussed in Chapter 5, the profound uncertainty that the character Frog experiences when trying to make sense of his physical 'symptoms' (feeling feverish, distracted, and agitated), along with the questions he asks himself, might be an example of thinking thus provoked.

PHILOSOPHICAL LISTENING AND UNCERTAINTY

Clark (2004) argues that respectful listening is central to learning, helping to challenge assumptions about children made by early years' practitioners and to raise expectations of young learners. She suggests that working with children in a more democratic way can relieve adults from the 'burden' of needing to know *all* the answers. Relinquishing this 'burden' and the certainty that often accompanies knowing all the answers is at the heart of our interpretation of listening in philosophy with children (Haynes, 2005b), where uncertainty and hesitancy are called for in the process of making sense of the world. We would not have responded to Frog as Hare does so categorically, in Velthuijs' *Frog in Love* (1989), assessing his symptoms and looking them up in a medical book to confidently make the diagnosis that Frog must be in love. As philosophers we make conscious efforts and instigate certain steps to dismantle this position of certainty and knowing the answers, asking for example, 'Just because Hare has read this diagnosis in a book, is he right?' or 'Does this combination of 'symptoms' necessarily mean that frog is in love?' or 'Should we always believe what we read in a book?' Certain things need to be put in place to enable us to adopt such a facilitation stance and to put into question the everyday authority we often assume in our 'transmission' role as educators. Other things need letting go, like the idea that dialogues should necessarily follow a particular trajectory in order to qualify as philosophical.

The dialogue that follows is an examination of what it means for practitioners to listen to contributions that some children make in philosophical enquiry. Are we prepared to treat our knowledge as contestable? Are we willing to inhabit the perplexity of children's questions when we think we already have the answers? Do we expect to be changed by young children's philosophical perspectives? Are we willing to play inside the narrative ground created by fictional characters?

THREADS OF DIALOGUE

We are concerned about the tendency to prematurely shape what we hear. Our experience leads us to believe that creativity is impeded by over direction, by pre-occupation with a normative sense of 'truth', or a linear notion of 'progress', in a community of enquiry. The direct experience that children bring to enquiry gives practical significance to their learning. It's playful and it's also useful. The facilitator needs to understand and fuse emotional and cognitive, literal and metaphorical dimensions in philosophical enquiry. Metaphors and analogies offer valuable ways to explore ideas, emotions, and experience.

As the dialogue unfolds we explore aspects of listening in the classroom such as the extent of children's power and authority in philosophical enquiry, safe-keeping and risk-taking as aspects of thinking and discourse, and what's involved in 'changing one's mind'. We present the need for a particular kind of effort, attention, and presence in listening to children's contributions and in sensing the direction of the emergent enquiry. Ideas concerning 'effort' and 'cost' in thinking infiltrate our dialogue from our reading of Corradi Fiumara (1990, 1995).

The dialogue took place as we prepared for a keynote presentation at a conference (see Haynes & Murris, 2000)[3]. Given the conference theme, it occurred to us to adopt dialogue as the form for our presentation. The dialogue format (often the format for philosophy) is challenging to the listener or reader, deliberately so in a way. It's a bit like eavesdropping—there are pieces missing. There is some obscurity, and issues remain unresolved. This happens when 'following a thread', when building on each other's ideas. The structure of philosophical enquiry is dialogical. There are many interpretations and characterizations of dialogue and dialogical teaching (for example Alexander, 2004; Burbules & Bruce, 2001; Wegerif, 2010). 'Dia' means 'through', and dialogue can be understood as 'a stream of meaning flowing among and through us and between us' (Bohm, 1996:6).

CHILDREN'S EVALUATION OF PHILOSOPHICAL ENQUIRIES

Our email dialogue begins with our response to a video extract in which a group of nine and ten year olds are evaluating philosophical enquiry[4]. In the episode the children are talking to a journalist about what they get out of doing philosophy in the classroom:

> Claire: *I hate maths because . . . you're not allowed to talk at all when we're doing it, in philosophy you can talk anytime apart when someone else is talking, but like in English and things, I enjoy writing and doing art and everything, but philosophy is one of my favourite subjects to do it in.*
> Journalist: *But don't you come to school to learn, to listen and not to. . . ?*

Claire: Well you are learning. Well, it's like a lesson, but just dif-
          ferent—not writing or drawing or anything. The only time
          you're drawing it is when you're drawing it in your mind.
Lucy: I think maths is just as hard as philosophy, because, hum
          ... you might think maths is really hard and philosophy
          is really easy, because you just have to say things, but you
          have to use your think, you have to use your brain. Well
          both of them really, you think a lot.

                                                (Channel Four, 1994).

DIALOGUING

Karin

What really strikes me is the journalist's question: 'Don't we come to school
to learn and to listen?' Would it be reasonable to assume that she means the
children should listen to the teachers, that is, the adults?

Joanna

*I'm not sure we can assume that the journalist means that children should
listen to the teacher/adult but in her question to the children there is an
implicit notion of what listening in school usually means. Does the 'we'
in the question include the teachers? Do teachers also come to school to
listen and to learn?*

*Listening is central to any educational enterprise, but what this means
remains hidden. As teachers we know very little about the conditions that
make listening possible in school. What exactly do we intend when we
plan for the development of children's 'listening skills'? Comparatively
little attention is paid to the development of 'speaking and listening' in
either initial or continuing training for teachers. When training addresses
classroom discussion this often entails teacher-mediated discussion and
emphasis is on the 'conversion' of children's contributions towards the
teacher's objectives for a lesson. It is rare for the emphasis to be put on
teachers learning to hear what children say or learning to achieve a diffu-
sion of listening among a group.*

*Teachers frequently implore children to listen. Often this means: listen
so that you will know what to do or listen to follow some instructions or
rules of behaviour. Do we usually work on the assumptions that listening
requires considerable effort, that listening somehow 'costs' the listener,
and that children find it more difficult than adults do?*

Karin

My tentative answers to your questions are that listening does require considerable effort, that listening costs the listener, and that children do not
find listening harder than adults, on the contrary.

However, I would like to claim that listening is not just a necessary condition for thinking, but listening *is* thinking. I don't just mean that in order to think well I have to listen to the Other (i.e. hear what someone says) or listen to myself (i.e. what I say and how I say it). The kind of listening involved in dialoguing is more like paying 'thoughtful attention', to use one of Corradi Fiumara's phrases (1990:31). I interpret this as: an openness when paying attention to the Other thoughtfully, and this takes a great deal of effort. Corradi Fiumara explains that listening is only an effort when 'both accepting and critical, trusting and diffident, irrepressible and yet consoling' (Corradi Fiumara, 1990:90).

Research in philosophy with children (Dyfed County Council, 1994) suggests that more than half of the teachers involved in the project resisted the central idea of children setting the agenda for discussion and the idea of allowing the children's enquiry to take its own course. Resistance to authentic listening to children is crucial in this, I believe.

Joanna
I am interested in what you say about the research on teachers' 'resistance' to letting children determine the agenda for and direction of enquiry. I think this has partly to do with accounting—in the sense of justifying results and the way time is spent. All lessons are expected to have very specific pre-defined goals. The teacher is expected to steer the children towards these goals. This must have a profound influence on the nature and qualities of classroom discourse. These conditions can inhibit contemplative or meditative thinking. They do inhibit listening. They make it difficult for teachers and for children to listen, both to one another (child–child, child–teacher, teacher–teacher) and each to his or her inner voice. The curriculum chatters so loudly. It clamours and claims us.

When I have asked children what advice they would want to give to teachers beginning philosophical enquiry they have emphasised that teachers need to give children choice, give more time to think and to explain things. One girl said, 'If a child has something to say, let them feel that they can say it to the teacher and not think to themselves "I'd better not tell her"'. The right to this time and space seems paramount.

Karin
I believe that pupils and teachers have the right to 'play' with knowledge. What we regard as 'knowledge' is, after all, the product of previous enquiries (but seldom conducted by ourselves), and what counts as knowledge changes all the time. It all depends on how we perceive knowledge. If I assume that 'our' knowledge 'grasps' reality *immediately*, then it seems to make sense to try and 'transmit' this knowledge to our less experienced and informed youngsters. Acquiring knowledge is then, metaphorically speaking, like putting buns (facts) in the oven (brain/mind). However, if I accept the view that knowledge is a *mediated* grasp of reality, a space (literally) opens up for philosophical enquiry. After all, it is through language that we

make sense of ourselves, the world, and others. To let children and adults play in this philosophical space is not just fun but opens up possibilities we do not know the boundaries of. It takes a great deal of effort and courage to move around in this creative space in which new language is generated and new ways of looking and listening emerge. In my experience young children thoroughly enjoy travelling in philosophical space.

I'm not sure that travelling in philosophical space doesn't necessarily fit in nicely with a curriculum with pre-determined objectives. Does it depend on how we formulate those objectives? It is fascinating to observe how children resist fixed objectives. In the children's evaluation, for example, Claire remarks:

> *we started it yesterday and it took us ages on one questions and then we moved on—because we had to—because we were talking so long on the first question, and it was really interesting all the things that we came up with, and Lisa came up with one, and it took at least half an hour to get off the subject of what she said.*

Claire reports that they 'had to move on' because they were taking 'too long'. In all fairness to the teacher, on this occasion this move was voted for. What is interesting is that Claire experienced it in this way.

Joanna
Perhaps the kind of effort (as sacrifice or self-restraint) associated with listening in the classroom is the product of resistance, by teachers and pupils, to fixed outcomes. The teacher's effort to steer the course and the children's effort to conform is costly.

The effort of listening in philosophical enquiry is rather different. The teacher relaxes her omnipotent role (in terms of the direction of learning) and responsibility is shared. Authority is assumed by <u>all</u> the participants. Listening in P4C is an effort, as we think 'otherwise', as we listen thought-fully, as we are drawn towards new pathways of thought. The children testify to this when they say: 'It's making my brain hurt'.

However, I have also noticed that our work in P4C can seem effortless! This happens when the dialogue takes on a natural and flowing dynamic because we are 'letting' each other think, because it is so compelling. In these episodes, there is profound evidence of 'listening as thinking'. What would be the opposite of 'thinking aloud'—that term we use when we want to express the process of thinking through talking? 'Thinking through the ears' perhaps? You can see this flickering across the children's faces. One obvious sign of this is the ease with which the children change their minds and the pleasure they take in it:

Louise: In philosophy sessions we do . . . especially this morning we had people that were disagreeing with someone, when they said something else they were kind of thinking . . . oh . . .

well . . . actually I've changed my mind. In philosophy you
don't have to stick to the same. There's never a time when
you've got to stick to what you said first. You can always
change your mind.
Journalist: What is good about changing your mind?

*That journalist's question is interesting: 'What is good about changing
one's mind?'*

Karin

I hadn't thought about this interplay of effort and effortlessness before,
but I agree. When the enquiry takes off, i.e. when the children start to
build on each other's ideas, I as a teacher become almost invisible. There is
excitement, curiosity, and involvement in the classroom. You can see it in
their eyes. You can feel it in their bodies. The 'only' effort I experience as
a teacher is to restrain myself from guiding them into areas of thinking I
myself feel comfortable with. . . . I'm not talking here about sensitive issues,
such as sex or child abuse, but typical Western philosophical topics I myself
am so familiar with. Letting *them* speak and listening to what *they* find
important is effortless when I let go of wanting to control their thinking.
That includes the philosopher's agenda too. For example when Lucy said,
in her comments on the video: 'You have to use your think, you have to use
your brain, well both of them really . . .', I would have immediately asked
for clarification because I '*know*' it could lead into a fascinating area of
philosophical enquiry.

The journalist's question is an intriguing one. But I'm not so sure that
the children quoted here mean the same with changing one's mind as what
I understand it to mean. When I say I have changed my mind there seems
to be more permanence to the change. Considering ideas offered by others
doesn't mean for me changing my mind. Do you agree?

Joanna

*Yes, I agree: the effort of listening in P4C for me, as the teacher, is more
to do with resisting my own tendency to steer the discussion, or the effort
to lose pre-conceptions about the way the enquiry might go, or the effort
of giving up my own philosophical interests in favour of the children's, or
the effort of worrying about whether we are 'getting anywhere'! When the
children say things like: 'I think I've changed my mind' they seem pleased
with the new possibilities for thinking that this state offers them and it's
as if the 'fluidity' of mind in itself is pleasurable. The loss of certainty or
continuity does not appear to represent a threat.*

Karin

I agree. I am learning all the time, especially when working with very young
children, especially not feeling threatened by this loss of certainty you are

referring to. The lack of boundaries, the sensation of freedom, and the confusion make philosophical enquiry with children not just a sheer pleasure, but is also intellectually very challenging for me. I believe that making one's self vulnerable in this way to the Other is necessary in dialogue, whether this takes place in the classroom, the boardroom, or one's counselling practice. To have your own pre-conceptions challenged can be very painful, but it seems less painful or, on the contrary, fun for young children. What I find so exciting about young children's thinking is how they enjoy 'starting from scratch', analysing and defining concepts as *they* perceive them. For me, that is creative thinking. This kind of thinking emerges in the classroom when teachers and children exercise courage, trust each other, and when teachers accept that children are their own epistemological authorities. When 'we' listen to 'them', children offer us other ways of looking and listening, but children do need the philosophical space for this to happen.

Joanna

The children's evaluations describe the pleasure of changing your mind as not being obliged to stick to your first idea. What does that conjure up for you 'sticking to an idea'? Sounds uncomfortable!

I have noticed that children might change their minds during enquiry and sometimes come back to an original view, having 'visited' the other possibilities—but for the duration, they will embrace those other possibilities wholeheartedly. For example, in one of my classes, Lauren was puzzled by a toy bear that was moving in a film we watched. She said this did not usually happen. When Anna reported that her teddy bear often moved and that we couldn't be certain that toy bears don't move when we're are not watching (perhaps they don't want us to know) . . . Lauren fully entertained this possibility. At the end of the first session she said she was going to be more watchful of her teddy bears in future. When the group came back to the story again and the children were reviewing their learning, Lauren said, 'I don't think toy bears do move, like they do in the video'. This is a powerful example because of the way, as you say, the children make creative use of the space to play with possibilities . . . and this is why it is a pleasure—as long as we, as teachers, do not misunderstand what is going on.

Karin

The way in which young children embrace wholeheartedly other ideas is impressive. Both or more ideas could be right, but also they seem to *really* leave open the possibility that their original idea could be wrong or inappropriate. Not being too concerned about making 'mistakes' is central to philosophical enquiry, I think. Or, even stronger, learning through and from so-called 'mistakes' could be viewed as essential in reaching a greater understanding. This is, surely, more promising than 'sticking' to our first, possibly 'mistaken' standpoint. The more 'mistakes' we make, the more varied and challenging it is for our own thinking. 'Sticking' to an idea sounds uncomfortable—like bubble-gum on a train-seat—but at the same time it is very comfortable to stick to certain ideas, e.g. that I'll still 'be' tomorrow. I'll stick to that one—provisionally!

Joanna
I have been re-reading some of the evaluations I have had from children. I came across this reference to thinking and changing one's mind:

> Philosophy helps me . . . well, juggling things in my mind really to think about what I am thinking. Like if there is a question like 'do you believe in aliens, don't you believe in aliens' . . . you might think you don't believe in them and then a question comes up that tells you more about it, so you change (Justin, age ten).

Many things strike me in this contribution. I am caught by the metaphor of juggling in the mind. How many thoughts can I juggle? I sometimes drop one, stop, pick it up again. Others might throw thoughts to me and I can reciprocate. The rhythm changes. When I juggle it absorbs me and demands my utmost attention.
I think the misunderstanding we were thinking about may arise in the teacher's premature desire to identify the direction of discussion in order to take the wheel and drive. My own efforts as a teacher of P4C are increasingly towards not trying to anticipate or push for direction. I am trying to slow down to ambling pace.

Karin
The direction teachers want to steer pupils towards is that of the accepted answers. But knowledge is always based on acknowledgement! Knowledge develops and changes over time. It is a laborious process and a relational process. Making errors is part of this process. It makes you wonder what the purpose of knowledge is. Is it to achieve certainty and control? Or, is it genuine creativity? It is not so much the answers teachers should be focusing on, but on the questions the answers are trying to answer, and on the questions that haven't been asked but should be asked.
I very much like the juggling metaphor. It describes really well how I often feel in an enquiry. Young children are excellent at generating their own metaphors—also metaphors about 'thinking'. I worry about the lack of space given by teachers to children offering refreshing perspectives on these matters.

Joanna
Teachers must find space and courage. In the search for knowledge an 'error' marks a vital moment. An 'error' comes into existence in con-sciousness in the moment that the belief/idea is called into doubt by

other possibilities. It signifies therefore the moment of receptiveness to thinking otherwise.
 (Dialogue ends)

LISTENING MOVES

There is a wealth of literature concerning the teacher's role in philosophical enquiry. In reading it might be tempting to grasp techniques mentioned, such as questioning, probing, and challenging; encouragement to give reasons or make connections. There is no doubt that 'technique' is significant, but it is often more subtle moves and the disposition of the facilitator that are key markers of experience. A lightness of touch and an intuitive sense of how and when to intervene are preferable to over-dependence on procedure.

Not knowing the direction of enquiry enables a spontaneous, rather than a scripted response. Philosophical facilitation charges us to stay with uncertainty, to listen attentively, to tune into participants' engagement, to notice concepts that surface, to observe the unexpected. These moves are difficult to pinpoint. P4C is not constructed from building blocks of technique. We are uneasy about P4C introduced to children via 'skills practice', for example first you learn how to ask questions and then you do exercises in making connections. P4C is not a rehearsal for something else in the future but an experience of thinking in the present.

In the dialogue, Joanna talks of conditions that inhibit listening, and Karin speaks of the particular challenge and necessity of making one's self vulnerable to the Other. A major challenge of facilitation is not to *mimic* uncertainty or *pretend* to be 'at a loss' but to relinquish the position of *always* knowing what to do to be in control of enquiry, to respond to what comes up. Another is to be genuinely engaged with children's questions but to maintain some detachment from the direction in which they might lead; to support children's awareness of their thinking but not to focus on their 'performance' as thinkers. In our dialogue we allude to 'letting go' and 'giving up' with regard to our position as teachers in P4C. We have come to think of this as a crucial 'move' to open up a gap in which original, creative, and playful thinking might take place.

LISTENING FOR PLAYFULNESS

Children often adopt an experimental stance towards ideas. They are quite prepared to make an imaginary or fantastic situation a philosophically serious context for enquiry, pursuing the question, for example, how come a forest grew in Max's bedroom or how come his supper was still hot when he had been away for so long (*Where the Wild Things Are*)? Or how come the dog could talk in *John Brown, Rose, and the Midnight Cat*? It is not that they do not distinguish reality and fantasy, as discussed in Chapter 8. It is more often the case that the imagination is a great driver, and young learners are usually prepared to envisage all kinds of possible worlds without the need to connect them directly to an actual world. Arguably, this is a characteristic of being child, or 'childing' as Kennedy and Kohan have termed it (Kennedy & Kohan, 2008)[5]. Such playful episodes of exploratory talk may function similarly to those 'thought experiments' deliberately constructed by professional philosophers. Such imaginative thinking is a bonus and something we regard as entirely desirable in classroom philosophy.

We have much to learn from young children's willingness to try thoughts out, or inhabit them temporarily, without worrying about the transience of the ideas or their reputations as thinkers. As described in earlier chapters, many children have been absorbed in the moment by the novelty, humour, or magic of what they say, for example the possibility that their dogs might speak or their teddies move when they are not looking. The imagination is a realm in which children can be powerful. We also read this as evidence of flexibility rather than impressionability because the context is one that encourages exploratory thinking and emphasises the provisional nature of our theories. Children seem less concerned than many adults about making 'errors' and happy to change their minds in the light of what they hear. Being willing to change one's mind when other, or more persuasive, arguments are put forward is a pre-requisite for the reciprocal searching that characterises philosophical dialogue.

SENSITIVITY AND ATTENTIVENESS

In her 'Inquiry Is No Mere Conversation' (1996), Gardner warns against a woolly notion of 'facilitation' and over-emphatic claims about children's natural tendencies to philosophise. She is critical of allowing discussion to follow its own course. She argues that students are sold short by teachers who lack the ability to maintain direction, to guide, and 'to force depth with respect to the philosophical truth toward which the discussion points' (Gardner, 1996:47). She suggests that the facilitator's interest in the perplexity of the question may be the best guide to its philosophical potential. We do not disregard the responsibility to move in the direction of 'truth'. However, the issue of the facilitator's perplexity is contentious, and we would argue that teachers who are serious about listening to young children have to remain open to the perplexity they express to engage in authentic dialogue with them. This is not a case of pretending to be puzzled (a form of 'scholarly ignorance') but being sensitive and attending to the origin of the puzzlement that is being articulated. The ethical move is to assume that children's puzzlement and contributions are genuinely rooted in their experiences, unless there is evidence to the contrary. It is also to be willing and able to move between literal and metaphorical domains in ways that we have illustrated.

JUGGLING AND EFFORT

Playfulness calls for re-collection on the part of adults. We refer to listening as thinking and describe it as both effortful and effortless. We suggest that some of the obstacles to listening in the classroom include: unequal power relationships between teachers and pupils, and indeed among pupils; the breadth of prescribed curriculum objectives which lead to an overwhelming sense of education as the 'formation' and 'development' of the child; misunderstandings of being-child itself; as well as doubts about children as capable meaning-makers and reliable authorities in respect of their experience.

Effortless listening seems possible when control is relinquished and there are episodes of enquiry that achieve momentum, flow, and engagement with the emerging ideas. There is a rhythm to dialogue. It does not progress evenly or smoothly. There are moments of restlessness, ennui, frustration, and elation.

For all participants it can be an effort to remain open or to think differently and otherwise, without repetition, and beyond what we currently 'know'. There is the difficulty presented by language itself. For teachers the effort is sometimes associated with being pulled between the requirement to justify time spent and demonstrate purpose on the one hand, and wanting to follow children's thinking on the other hand. Sometimes the effort is in the attempt to do justice to the sheer range and diversity of voices in the classroom community, to stay with a thread of thinking even though a handful of participants are contributing, or to try and give everyone a say. Our effort may be towards maintaining or resisting control (either of thinking or actions), making quick judgements about the safety or danger of the subject, or whether we deem it philosophical. In a large class it can seem as if we are making a thousand tiny moves a minute: observing, listening, thinking, and responding. It is like juggling. The idea of listening seems to hold a key to understanding the part that philosophical practice can play in education. It is to the 'condition' of listening in schools that we turn in the next chapter.

12 Listening and Not Listening in Schools

This chapter draws on our professional development work in schools, universities, and teacher education programmes during a period of intensive policy change and innovation in education in different countries. It explores experiences of arrival and hospitality in educational settings to develop insights about listening and learning. We identify obstacles and windows to listening and thinking in schools and teacher education settings. When incorporated as part of a critical pedagogical framework, we propose that ideas and methods associated with philosophy as a practice deepen and enrich critical thinking and dialogue in classrooms, for children, young people, and teachers. We acknowledge the contribution made by other disciplines to understanding classrooms and developing pedagogy. As part of learning about facilitation of enquiry with children, we suggest that the discovery of philosophical frameworks for thinking, models, tools, and ideas, significantly extends teachers' repertoires as inclusive educators.

WHITE NOISE

Experience of teaching and discussions with teachers suggest that there are a number of obstacles to listening in classrooms. The culture of innovation, along with a rapid succession of policy initiatives, has made great demands on energy, often without bearing any real fruit. These end to end 'new' ideas create a kind of white noise in the world of education. Teachers speak of feeling distracted by competing voices about curriculum, pedagogy, and children's well-being and hampered from getting on with teaching. Many teachers successfully mediate these competing demands, but there is no doubting their intrusive impact. From a sociological perspective, Furedi (2009) has commented on the damaging, wasting effects on public education that result from perpetual dismissal of the old and hyper-elevation of the new. Listening might become easier in classrooms if politicians and educational innovators left teachers and children some breathing space or waited for their call. The lack of professional autonomy is a serious point: 'To live in the contemporary world of education is often to experience a kind of schizophrenia, to hear voices' (Haynes, 2007a:38). One teacher at a conference in South Africa[1] referred vividly to her experiences of such interference as being professionally 'beheaded'.

Calls on teachers to teach critical thinking might also be read as an example of such educational innovation. Across all sectors of education, including higher education, thinking 'skills' are often presented as an educational commodity whose application enhances the future employability of learners. Less attention is paid to deep conditions and relationships that make listening, challenging each other's ideas, and the critical pursuit of knowledge more likely and natural in classrooms, let alone to exploring the transformative potential of such a project.

The association between listening and learning appears so simple and obvious. However, familiarity with the *disciplinary* call to listen prevents consideration of what listening means, how it is experienced, when it opens up and when it silences, when it angers, soothes, or neutralises, and how some kinds of listening can challenge or transform us. We might remember the unfathomable nature of the conventions of listening experienced in childhood or in moments of being an outsider, yet as educators we often act as if listening is straightforward and uncomplicated. Listen, we urge. Just listen.

Adults often talk about how important it is for children to listen in the classroom, hearkening to a lost time when children were more attentive. Children no longer listen, nor do as they are told, are frequent complaints. Similarly, children and young people report that teachers do not listen to them. Sometimes it can seem as if schools are places of not-listening. Is this deafness the end of the story, something to be accepted as a necessary, even desirable, characteristic of compulsory education? Is it a 'natural part' of learning to be part of a larger group? Stories of being ignored, misrepresented, or humiliated often feature in fictional accounts of schooling; they are part of its folklore, arguably engendering resilience, solidarity, and resistance, or maybe helping to keep the system in place. The picture-book *Michael* (Bradman & Ross, 1990) presents one such tale. Michael is described in the text as 'different' and drawn as a loner, misunderstood by all his teachers as he fails to engage with their lessons and pursues his interests in space travel, finally taking off in his make-shift rocket. Arguably, he is successful *in spite of* his schooling and the disinterest of fellow pupils and teachers[2].

ARRIVALS AND HOSPITALITY

Over the last twenty years we have worked extensively with teachers and children in primary and secondary schools introducing philosophical approaches to teaching, with picturebooks as well as other visual and textual narratives. Much of this work has taken the form of relatively short visits, perhaps a day or series of shorter sessions with staff and three or four periods with children, while teachers observe us in action. One of the most striking things is the frequency with which teachers express surprise about the depth and quality of thought they hear from learners when they observe enquiries with their classes. We are not suggesting that teachers and children have not heard each other before or that they do not want to listen to one another. It's almost as if being puzzled, enlightened, opposed, or surprised by one another is outside the scope of what is expected in a classroom, or that there is normally little room for such critical and reciprocal interaction. There's no doubting the almost tangible opening that is created through philosophical work with children and teachers, when hospitality permits: an atmosphere of being taken up in the moment; a difficult struggle perhaps; a dynamic energy in the room. Like any visit from outsiders, it can prompt intellectual and emotional excitement or disturbance. As educational practitioners we wonder what makes it possible for dissonance and disagreement to be 'normalised'. We are particularly interested in what can generate a much stronger sense of curiosity about one another's thinking in classrooms and the moves that would enable practitioners to open up such a space in their teaching: an outward-facing educational architecture and pedagogy.

An exploration of our itinerant experiences of 'arrival' and 'hospitality' might be illuminating. As relative outsiders and occasional visitors to a school to introduce teachers to philosophical enquiry we often enjoy a luxurious sense of freedom and novelty; however, there can be micropolitical complexities that cast shadows over conversations with children and teachers alike. We have sometimes described this kind of short-term training as 'parachuting in' to a school. This metaphor conveys certain characteristics of our arrival in a school: we 'drop in' for a brief period of work without knowing much about the teachers, children, or neighbourhood, or them knowing much about us, and then we leave again. There can be ambiguity about the circumstances of the 'invitation'—is our offering something teachers really want, or is the impetus coming only from the school principal or head teacher or from advisors outside the school? It is a paradox that much so-called 'professional development' is imposed and arguably 'non-developmental', in the sense that it does not build on knowledge and experience of staff and is not fully embedded into local practice.

Now somewhat seasoned travellers in the world of school-based professional development, we have the feeling that we can almost 'smell' a school's hospitality, or lack of it, as soon as we cross the threshold. As visitors to schools we have experienced warmth and care, envy, courtesy, disdain, and neglect. We have been party to secrets and confidences, been receptacles for private miseries, and been milked for resources and ideas.

Sometimes our offerings are gladly received, other times we certainly miss the mark. Our train and taxi journeys to unfamiliar schools to carry out such work are sometimes long: we eat alone, phone home, watch television, catch up on other work, and sleep fitfully in hotel rooms: the strange life of the travelling educational saleswoman. Through her intimate understanding of cultural politics, Bruno's *Atlas of Emotion* (2002) underlines the corporeality and the moving force of the emotions carried through migrations. What can schools really get out of visits from migrant in-droppers such as ourselves? We often muse about this 'parachutist' model of professional development.

Institutional hospitality is not expressed through superficial gloss. It reveals itself in the face shown to the outside world and in the quality of attention given to the newly arrived, demonstrating an ethical and epistemological stance. It indicates locus of attention as well as the degree of confidence and capacity for care. It is expressed in receptiveness to different ideas or ways of knowing and accommodation to risk. Some schools and classrooms confidently open their doors to outsiders, and others are very wary of strangers. This is not to be judgemental, but to be sensitive to schools as having the potential to be hospitable or inhospitable spaces, for inhabitants and visitors alike. It is to recognise the impact of inhospitality on the growth of knowledge itself. It is to understand its bearing on the listening that can take place, both within the school and between the school and beyond. These things are true of public and private places, but the school must feature as one of the places where the impact of inhospitality must, by virtue of their educative purpose, have enormous consequences. Many a learner will testify to that.

Shaun Tan's exceptional graphic novel *The Arrival* (2006) skilfully draws attention to the complexity and significance of arrival and hospitality (see Figure 12.1). Poignantly and creatively depicting a migrant's arrival in unidentifiable territory, and his experiences of finding his way in a strange and unfamiliar landscape, Tan draws the reader's attention to universal human experiences of arrival: leaving and farewells, fear and loss, journeys and transitions, familiarity and strangeness, sameness and difference, language and (mis)communication, hospitality and hostility, love and belonging. It is easy to recognise the uncertainty of crossing borders or the effort to communicate without a common language. Certain picturebooks, introduced to groups of educators through the medium of philosophical enquiry, draw out questions which seem to have been in-waiting, latent. Such questions stir up enquiries that can be intellectually and emotionally liberating or disruptive. There is no doubting the seductive power of this visual medium and the possibilities it creates for working with troublesome knowledge[3]. Used in this way, the narratives of picturebooks seem to provide a kind of transitional space, in which to push at the boundaries.

Figure 12.1 Drawing inspired by *The Arrival* (Shaun Tan) made by Tim Geschwindt (aged 16).

RE-FRESHMENT

Struggles are likely, but we also experience freedom in our exchanges with children. This may be because we are outsiders passing through—there is a certain novelty value. When teachers explore philosophy with children (P4C) themselves many describe a similar sense of freedom, initially quite intoxicating, as do their learners. At a conference in London[4], a group of ten and eleven year olds from a primary school confidently presented their ideas on philosophy to an audience of educators and fielded questions. The word 'letting' cropped up several times in these accounts of philosophical conversations: letting one's own ideas out, letting go of the pre-determined lesson plan, letting each other speak. For this group, doing philosophy seemed to allow a relinquishing of routine (Haynes, 2007b:231). This 'letting' is not only a releasing of constraint, but also a letting-loose-of-thinking and letting-in-of-listening. Levin suggests that such hearkening requires a disciplined practice of *'letting-go and letting-be'* (Levin, 1989:48). In his critique of skills orientated approaches to thinking in classrooms, Bonnett (1995) prefers the idea of 'letting think', which conveys receptivity rather than grasping.

The sense of re-freshment of thinking through philosophical enquiry, reported by many children and practitioners, strikes us as worthy of further investigation. These anomalies between 'normal practice' and the introduction of P4C might be useful in considering possibilities for listening in the classroom. Is it idealism to think that elusive qualities of interaction, such as challenge, subversion, and playfulness, could be sustained in classrooms through establishing a responsive practice of philosophical enquiry? To what extent, after the initial excitement, can P4C remain a practice of criticality, creativity, and freedom? So much of this depends on a school's hospitality and on teachers' collective confidence, educational values, and experience, as well as their practical expertise in dialogical pedagogy and desire to listen.

THINKING SQUEEZED OUT OF TEACHER EDUCATION?

We should also consider the hospitality of universities and teacher education programmes towards critical, dialogical pedagogies and their preparedness to tackle troublesome or uncertain knowledge. Universities are traditionally associated with independent enquiry and critical thinking but are increasingly driven by broader business or political agendas and world events[5]. Pedagogy increasingly extends beyond the educational setting. The 'pedagogised society' (Bernstein, 2001, cited in Lingard et al, 2003) has translated in many workplaces as 'lifelong learning' and impacted on both university and school programmes. Increasingly, school and teacher education curricula involve much broader social agendas, such as tackling obesity; sex, relationship, and parenting programmes; drugs and alcohol education; and emotional or political 'literacies'. Ecclestone and Hayes (2009) suggest that universities are becoming similarly 'therapeutic' in orientation, seriously undermining their role in the promotion of independent thinking, the growth of knowledge, and the contribution to human progress.

In such a climate, to what extent do candidates for teaching arrive at their place of training expecting to work on critical, enquiry based teaching and learning? In the majority of initial teacher training courses around the world, emphasis is on the transmission of policies, legal requirements, delivery of curricula, learner performance, management of assessment, and psychological techniques for controlling behaviour or inculcating the capacity for lifelong learning. The very language of 'delivery' and skill building seems to be at odds with any call to openly listen to learners, let alone to engage with troublesome knowledge. The teacher training timetable is full to bursting with the latest curriculum change and teaching innovations. Like the two-headed monster of Sesame Street fame, it is in training that classroom novices begin to grow a second head to address the cacophony of voices competing for attention—not the voices of learners in classrooms, but the many public voices contesting education. Educators themselves are part of this evolving story.

Studies in critical thinking, reasoning, and dialogue rarely feature as an essential dimension of pre-service courses for teachers, let alone the study of philosophy itself[6]. When they appear they are often content free, described as transferable. Thinking 'skills' become yet another learning outcome for which the overstretched novice has to plan, couched in instrumental terms of the economic role of education in creating the workforce of the future, or their role in developing healthy citizenship. It is rare to find alternative and critical pedagogies built into the very fabric of subject teaching in training programmes. In our experience critical thinking and dialogical teaching remain marginal, optional activities. Meanwhile, philosophy and ethics have largely been squeezed out of teacher education; as Ilan Gur-Ze-ev put it more than ten years ago, it has been an 'anti-philosophical era' (Gur-Ze-ev, 1998:486).

It is usually teacher *training*, rather than professional education. The focus on a narrow pedagogical repertoire has negative consequences for the quality of thinking and listening in classrooms and for teachers' preparedness to engage with controversial topics. If student teachers are not invited to consider fundamental aims and values in education, encouraged to think critically, and engaged in reciprocal dialogue themselves throughout their preparation for teaching, it is far less likely that they will bring these critical skills and experiences to bear in their classroom pedagogy. There is considerable evidence that where such critical teaching skills are introduced, explicitly focusing on learners' thinking and reasoning, they have lasting and positive impact (Baumfield, 2006, Higgins et al, 2004). Considering the weight of argument to support exploratory talk and dialogical teaching (for example Alexander, 2004; Burbules, 1995; Mercer & Littleton, 2007; Wegerif, 2010) it is curious that teacher education has not caught up. Knowledge about such ways of working, and its benefits, is well established, but has to compete with the latest policy initiatives. In initial teacher education, more attention needs to be paid to cultivating, in the novice practitioner, the confidence and capacity to listen to learners and to engage them through critical thinking and reasoning.

PARADIGMS OF LISTENING

Talk about listening in schools often has an overt or a covert disciplinary tone to it. It is concerned with moulding children and young people and getting them to follow instruction, as one might expect in publicly funded schooling. It is about formation. We somehow have to disentangle *authoritative* pedagogies, which support learners' intelligent acquisition, understanding, application, and extension of public knowledge, from the *authoritarian* versions, whose function is to discipline, control, and silence, rather than educate.

Many pedagogical texts illustrate effective group interaction and articulate theoretical justifications for planned learner to learner talk (for example Mercer, 1995, 2000). There are many outstanding, creative teachers committed to collaborative and exploratory teaching approaches and skilful at mediating competing demands of the curriculum (Woods, 1995; Woods & Jeffery, 1996). Much recent research on pedagogy underlines the centrality of oracy and the importance of a culture of genuine participation, listening, and responding. It does not use the language of 'delivery' that has characterised pedagogic discourse in recent times. In England there have been two major reviews of primary education[7]. *The Cambridge Review*, directed by Professor Robin Alexander (2009), claims that good teachers understand the cognitive power of high quality classroom interaction and orchestrate it effectively. There is growing interest in the nature, communicative purpose, and structure of reciprocal dialogue, as distinct from 'ordinary conversation' or discussion. A report introducing the *Cambridge Review* argues that 'Dialogue is central to pedagogy: between self and others, between personal and collective knowledge, between present and past, between different ways of thinking' (Hofkins & Northen, 2009:19). It refers to philosophy with children as an example of this domain in action (Hofkins & Northen, 2009: 22).

When it comes to learner participation, empirical research in education often reveals the intractable nature of institutions, social groups, and classroom discourses and the unintended consequences of even the best laid plans for greater student-directed learning (Fielding & Rudduck, 2006). Reviews of such studies help to highlight the progress made and the issues still to be addressed (Whitty & Wisby, 2007). Case study approaches across the whole education sector illustrate diverse approaches to engaging learner voice, giving hope about the possibility of transformation (Walker & Logan, 2008).

LISTENING, PSYCHOLOGISING, AND THE THERAPEUTIC TURN

Psychological studies often provide insight into individual and group behaviour and cognition, as well as factors influencing motivation and receptiveness to learning. Whilst sometimes restoring teachers' faith in the possibility of improvement and highlighting the significance of choices made by teachers about the listening 'climate' or relationships in their classrooms, such perspectives can sometimes fail to take power and authority into account or place an impossible burden of 'care' on the shoulders of educators. At best, psychologically informed approaches to learning and the educational setting result in important insights about learners and ways of providing them with effective support in their learning. At worst, they affirm the so-called therapeutic turn and give rise to programmes that operate on the basis of a diminished view of the self (Ecclestone & Hayes, 2009). Furedi (2005) links this turn to a 'politics of fear', a protectionist trend that limits academic freedom and wider public debate.

We share the perception that popular psychology has become part of everyday language and thought, sometimes in ways detrimental to good reasoning and judgement. We are frustrated by the tendency to equate 'being critical' with 'being hurtful', and to avoid challenge or discussion of more thorny and uncertain questions. Social mores seem to court individual disclosure whilst seeking to avoid any risk and conflict that might ensue.

In evaluating the worth of any educational initiative, such as P4C, Ecclestone and Hayes argue that we should ask ourselves, 'What sort of child, young person, adult, what sort of human being, is pre-supposed in this policy or initiative?' (Ecclestone & Hayes, 2009:144). Throughout this book, we have argued that P4C should not trivialise and infantilise children. It is a practice that can engage the voice of self-expression *and* the voice of social action. It is capable of promoting both passionate and dispassionate dialogue: talking about things that matter with children in ways that go beyond a repetition of the given.

As argued in Chapter 9, far from being conceived as vulnerable, the child in P4C literature is regarded as naturally philosophical, disposed to curiosity about the world and to questioning; imaginative and open-minded; capable of dialogue and of self-regulation in the context of sustained participation in a community; morally alert and capable of choice and judgement; interested in the welfare of others; capable of conceptual exploration and analysis; as persons to whom it is worth listening (Matthews, 1980; Lipman, 1993c; Murris, 1993, 1994, 1997; Haynes, 2007a, 2008).

Is P4C therapeutic in the ways suggested by Ecclestone and Hayes? Human flourishing and consolation in the face of suffering and angst have been among the concerns of many philosophers, and it is not surprising that these should be among the questions pursued by children philosophising. As much as they enjoy the adventurous space provided by P4C, they often welcome the opportunity to listen and to be heard and describe the sense of feeling cared for and not alone when others listen to them. Perhaps P4C is a form of 'escape', for children and teachers alike, in the face of prescription, performance, and the climate of fear. While philosophical enquiry does not court disclosure in the way that therapeutic techniques tend to do, children do draw on their experience in their exploration of philosophical questions, so P4C can enable them to attend to matters that concern them and to develop P4C as practical wisdom, transforming of self, of experience, and of the community of enquiry: a form of social action.

Is P4C dangerously therapeutic? We argue that what *is* dangerous is the trivialisation and ritualisation of children's thinking, and P4C practice is not necessarily exempt from these. There are teachers who manipulate what should be a democratic process in P4C to pursue behaviour modification or to hi-jack the topic for enquiry. This is both deceitful and dangerous in making the workings of power relations in classrooms less visible and harder to resist (Dahlberg & Moss, 2005:149). In philosophically inexperienced or unskilled hands P4C is not necessarily dangerous but neither is it worthwhile, leading to frustration and abandonment: hence the urgency of attending to the poverty of teacher education. If anything, P4C needs to become more dangerous and subversive to widen the political space in schools. It is a powerful means to encourage; to challenge anxiety, censorship, and the avoidance of controversy; and to contribute to the much needed re-professionalisation of teaching.

UNDOING KNOTS

Smeyers, Smith, and Standish (2007) have a very different take than Ecclestone and Hayes (2009) on the relationship between therapy and education. They examine the idea, traceable as far back as the time of Socrates, that education involves a concern with how to live well as 'a therapy of desire' (Nussbaum cited in Smeyers et al, 2007:4). They investigate recent developments in educational practice that are associated with 'working on the self' from philosophical perspectives (Smeyers et al, 2007:5). Their aim is to distinguish helpful and unhelpful aspects of therapeutic culture, to extend the terms of reference of the therapeutic, and to explore philosophy and literature as disciplines that 'transfigure the ordinary' (ibid, 2007:238), and to understand education as 'one of the richest kinds of therapy' (ibid et al, 2007:6). The final section of the book is concerned with the alienation consisting of disenchantment with the world. With reference to Wittgenstein's work, Smeyers et al discuss the problem of philosophy's abstraction and divorce from everyday life and the 'remedy' required: exploring ways in which, for Wittgenstein, philosophy is like therapy. Insofar as philosophy is therapy, they write, it is about 'undoing knots in our thinking and understanding' (ibid, 2007:225), and it starts from a real problem that someone is facing. Through attention to faithful description and particulars, rather than explanation, the clarity of philosophy brings a kind of peace. Release from difficulties is the work of philosophers and artists, but also of therapists, colleagues, parents, and friends, argue Smeyers et al (2007:227). They agree with Wittgenstein that there is no single method in philosophy, nor in the study of education, but rather 'education is always something to be struggled with, never comfortably to be settled' (ibid, 2007:227).

WHAT CAN PHILOSOPHY CONTRIBUTE
TO LISTENING IN EDUCATION?

A philosophy of listening in educational settings is informed by a wide range of philosophical work addressing the role of the teacher and the ethics of the teacher–learner relationship. Philosophical approaches are often missing, particularly in teacher education. With a few exceptions, philosophy is a 'stranger' in the school curriculum, and herein lies part of its capacity to transform thinking and to challenge the status quo. Philosophy has a well-established tradition of thought outside of the current mechanistic and performative model of education. Philosophical approaches can strengthen reasoning and argument; extend and refresh thinking, listening, knowledge, and understanding, for example by drawing on the history of philosophical ideas, through practical and imaginative reasoning, through the formation of new concepts, through comparison and de-construction. The sections below provide some examples of philosophical ideas that illuminate teaching, where critical thinking and dialogue are valued[8].

CRITICAL LISTENING AND DE-CONSTRUCTION

When it comes to obstacles to listening such as structural and systemic inequalities in education, both critical theory and de-construction offer ways of making sense of the bigger picture. Critical theory offers frameworks and tools to analyse the wider social forces at work in creating and sustaining inequalities[9]. De-construction (after Jacques Derrida) 'is a way of listening and responding to (and being responsible to, in the name of justice) the subversive, dissident voices from the edges and the margins' (Smeyers et al, 2007:36). Such philosophising draws on both the 'canon' as well as other voices. De-construction denies the possibility of closure, and there is no final word. It 'undermines the stabilising order set up by our best educational [. . .] endeavours, not out of love of chaos, but out of the passion to do justice to what we have not yet understood' (Smeyers et al, 2007:37). It is often the absence of a final word that some find so unsettling and leads others to confusion or the flabby relativism of 'no right or wrong answers in philosophy'[10].

THE VALUE OF DISORIENTATION AND
THE NEED FOR FALLIBILISM

There is so much emphasis on the teacher providing answers and having an authoritative presence that it is easy to forget the educative value of uncertainty and being at a loss. At the cognitive level, doubt has a vital role to play in opening the ground for exploration. At the affective level, it can denote openness to new ideas. The capacity to work creatively with the precarious and tentative ground of uncertainty is particularly important when it comes to investigation of controversial questions. Both ancient and twentieth century philosophy offer helpful precedents for such thinking and conversations, and we encourage teachers to draw on such ideas, not as blueprints but as ideas for collaborative scrutiny[11].

Perplexity is necessary to philosophical listening and an important part of the philosophical approach to be embraced, however uncomfortable at the time. The Greek term *aporia* refers to the sense of puzzlement or impasse that may be a starting point for enquiry or the result of the kind of scrutiny and rigorous questioning in Socratic dialogue, a dialectical method referred to as the *elenchus* (Abbs, 1994). The vulnerability and floundering that result from Socratic style cross examination are all part and parcel of progress in pursuit of 'truth'.

As well as 'normalising' disorientation and uncertainty and provoking disequilibrium through deep questioning, a philosophical approach to teaching tends to display fallibilism. Burbules' conception of fallibilism implies risk, reflection, and the capacity to admit to being wrong (in Kohli, 1995). Biesta and Burbules (2003) explain fallibilism as a major tenet of Dewey's pragmatist perspective on education, a founding influence in P4C. This capacity for change implies a strong affective component. Once again, in the context of adults' traditional role in school, the call to fallibilism exerts a contrary pressure to the expectations that adults in charge should exemplify clarity, certainty, assurance, authority, and the final word.

When it comes to teaching young children, we have come across practitioners who argue that doubt and uncertainty are developmentally inappropriate: adults should be providing definite answers and emotional security first and foremost. Such a perspective conflates emotional insecurity with cognitive doubt. Curiosity and wonder depend on openness and doubt, on the postponement of final resolution. If met with only definite answers, they will soon abate (Haynes, 2005b). Curiously, fallibilism is a reassuring response to difficult and sensitive questions, whose very controversy requires tentative, yet thorough and free dissection. Moral courage is needed in the face of troublesome knowledge.

Among the philosophical influences on the teacher's role in P4C, *aporia* expresses both the puzzlement and de-construction that feature in the enquiry process, *elenchus* the practice of rigorous questioning, whilst the idea of fallibilism conveys a moral, emotional, and intellectual disposition towards the truth-seeking process. The Socratic method is self-critical and dialectical, aiming to arouse a genuine desire for authentic learning, moving the learner from strongly held opinion to floundering uncertainty and loss; from confidence to unease, confusion, or anguish (Abbs, 1994; Matthews, 2003). Among other analogies, Socrates offers the metaphor of the philosopher/teacher as midwife.

LISTENING AND MIDWIFERY?

In the Platonic dialogues, Socrates, himself the son of a midwife, describes a number of possible faces of the teacher, philosopher, truth seeker. In Plato's *Theaetetus*, a dialogue concerning the nature of knowledge, the role he describes is that of the midwife. The midwife's task in this process is to question in ways that help to reveal ambiguities or contradictions that need to be resolved in the pursuit of truth, as Socrates puts it 'the triumph of my art is in thoroughly examining whether the thought which the young man brings forth is a false idol or a noble and true birth' (Plato, 1987).

The maieutic method involves assisting in the birth of ideas. It implies that each birth is unique, although births have things in common. It is the mother who delivers the baby, whose features are unknown to mother and midwife until he/she appears. It involves intensive labour, whose general characteristics are familiar, but whose exact length and process in each case is unpredictable, and so on.

Different cultures of education and childbirth co-exist: the systemic and institutionalised and the so-called holistic or naturalistic. However, many current constructs of pedagogy and of supporting childbirth put greater emphasis on a situated and responsive personalised approach, reciprocal interaction between teacher and learner, or midwife and mother-to-be; the co-construction of knowledge, or partnership in giving birth. Nobody knows for certain what triggers labour, but the baby is also involved: an interesting three way relationship among the 'experts', mothers, and babes.

The midwife is idealised as attentive, allowing 'natural' processes to occur, yet intervening where necessary to safeguard both baby and mother. The emphasis may have shifted from teacher to learner, from midwife to mother-to-be. While the fashion in baby clothing changes, the metaphor of midwifery as a way of conveying the kind of intimate support associated with thinking about or understanding difficult ideas seems to be an enduring one. When birth is more difficult, as in the case of complications (controversial questions) or protracted labour (troublesome knowledge), the midwife remains, offering encouragement and reassurance, alternative approaches, ways of reducing the pain, direct intervention.

Corradi Fiumara further develops Socrates' metaphor of listening as midwifery and the effort associated with labouring and the delivery of newborn thoughts and ideas (Corradi Fiumara, 1990:143–147). The word 'delivery' remains prominent in educational debate and is widely used as a synonym for teaching, particularly where formal courses of curricula are concerned. It conveys the idea of the university or school as a warehouse and the tutor/teacher as an operative, delivering the course/curriculum to learners/children, according to a menu and pre-packed, as a courier might 'deliver' a bouquet or a pizza. By contrast with this commercial imagery of delivery, Socratic listening, or maieutics, calls for a different kind of expertise. Corradi Fiumara's take on the midwife's role refers not only to her attendance at the birth but also to her reputation for wisdom in match-making. The maieutic listener, therefore, is able to support the delivery of newborn thoughts *and* to make connections between thoughts, guided by the experience of assisting at other 'births' and by responding to the unique features of the birth in hand, however awkward or difficult (Corradi Fiumara, 1990; Haynes & Murris, 2000).

P4C is often associated with the Socratic tradition of teaching (see for example chapters by Nelson, Lessing, and Baumgarten in Lipman, 1993c). Plato's Dialogues exemplify a process in which Socrates, as 'midwife', uses a distinctive style of questioning to help the learner reveal the truth. As German philosopher Leonard Nelson explains: 'the Socratic method [. . .] is the art of teaching not philosophy but philosophising, the art of not teaching about philosophers but of making philosophers of the students' (Nelson, 1993:437). This is a kind of passive-provocative role.

LISTENING AND NUMBING?

Baumgarten's discussion of philosophy teaching in universities highlights the ethical responsibilities entailed and the dangers of advocacy, edification, and indoctrination (in Lipman, 1993c:510–517). Such responsibilities are all the more important to consider in the meeting of philosophy and child, and while Socrates appears to be non-directive, arguably his questions lead his 'partners' in dialogue to a particular place of recognising that their original claims to knowledge are unfounded. Kohan argues:

> The so called Socratic dialogues show this path very clearly: while some people knew something at the beginning of the dialogue, nobody knows anything in the end. And this 'knowing nothing' is Socrates' trick, for it is precisely what he does know, and on every occasion it is the same knowledge, his knowledge of (pseudo) ignorance, his wisdom (in Kennedy & Kohan, 2008:18).

Kohan proposes that as a teacher Socrates schools his students persistently in this knowledge (*the* knowledge), leaving no space for invention or creation by the other.

Murris (2008b:667–668) draws attention to another analogy for perplexity, which might cast a different light on Socratic thinking, dialogue, and the pursuit of truth. She cites a passage from Plato's Meno that offers the metaphor of the stingray, numbing anyone with whom it comes into contact. In this dialogue, Socrates tells Meno that the analogy is suitable if the stingray paralyses others only through being paralysed itself. He suggests that he infects others with the perplexity he feels himself. In Chapter 10, we argued that mutual perplexity, rather than feigned ignorance, is necessary for dialogue with children to be respectful and authentic. In discussing the facilitation process with teachers, we have found the analogies of both midwife and stingray to be illuminating.

LISTENING AS DWELLING

Corradi Fiumara's methodology of listening is a response to Heidegger's call to 'take up residence' in language (Heidegger cited in Corradi

Fiumara, 1990:156). This is not instrumental, colonising, or manipulative listening. For Heidegger, dwelling is the basic character of human being. It describes the way humans are in the world *'in dwelling* they persist through spaces by virtue of their stay among things and locations'. He elaborates:

> The way in which you are and I am, the manner in which we humans are on the earth, is Buan, dwelling. To be a human being means to be on the earth as a mortal. It means to dwell (Heidegger, 1971:I).

When it comes to the stance of the teacher, Heidegger uses the expression 'to dwell' when he describes a genuine attempt to listen. Such attempts are not grasping, nor do they seek mastery (Tubbs, 2005:314). Such listening does not claim to understand the other person in advance, rather it is 'an anticipatory reaching out for something that is reached by our call, through our calling' (in Heidegger & Krell, 1993:386). As Corradi Fiumara interprets it, 'in authentically philo-sophical moments a part of our mind seems to remain suspended . . . an attitude of waiting that attracts and promotes the emergence of thought in the other' (Corradi Fiumara, 1990:189).

Dwelling listening and dwelling thinking are akin to what Heidegger describes as 'meditative thinking' which he contrasts with everyday 'calculative thinking' that 'never stops, never collects itself' and, unlike meditative thinking, is 'not thinking that contemplates the meaning that reigns in everything that is' (in Heidegger & Krell, 1993:46). Tubbs suggests that a sense of humility and vulnerability is integral to Heidegger's philosophy of the teacher (Tubbs, 2005:314).

Throughout this book we have argued for challenging constraint and timidity in classrooms, and for constructive use of philosophical enquiry to enable such freedom to be felt. Bonnett underlines the importance of receptivity in Heidegger's conception of thinking. Thinking is at the very heart of our being. It is a demanding thinking that involves deep engagement with what draws us to thinking, that which is thought-provoking or provides food for thought (Bonnett, 1995:304–305). Bonnett argues that how we think expresses our relationship with the world and sense of truth and reality. He argues that instrumental thinking, the notion of a method that can be applied to content, is inert. It is about objects that are given structure by an 'incisive thinker'. Thought conceived as a skill is a form of mastery over content from which truth is manufactured. This thinking expresses a 'disconnection between thinker and world, thinker and truth' (Bonnett, 1995:303) whereas 'thinking in the demanding sense' expresses an awareness of what is concealed but whose presence is sharply felt. This awareness is only possible because of the connection, belonging, and commitment that is dwelling. Its movement is towards co-existence. It is the invitation to voice what is thought-provoking and the commitment to respond with this sense of the unknown that characterises philosophical listening.

EMBEDDED LISTENING

The chapter has focused on aspects of listening in educational spaces. Drawing on the perspectives discussed above, this book espouses a practical philosophy of listening as an embodied and socially embedded process of thinking, feeling, doing, and knowing. Listening to children is possible through the cultivation of attention and effort, through challenging the idea that, by virtue of being an adult, I know in advance who *child* is and will become (Kohan, 2002; Irigeray, 1996); through opening up the metaphorical teaching space (Corradi Fiumara, 1990; Haynes & Murris, 2000); through developing listening as a critical practice of the self (Levin, 1989); through drawing on a range of philosophical ideas to reflect on pedagogy in action. As a radically open and critical practice, listening is so fundamental to philosophising with children that it requires constant attention.

Appreciation of the teacher's listening stance is not an abstract discussion, as we have shown. It emerges from experience and a critical and self-critical orientation towards practice. Our listening 'stance' emphasises the links between the way we think and act as enquiring learners and how we regard the children and young people we teach: a tactful acknowledgement of our important role as guardians and guides within an overarching framework of co-enquiry.

13 Towards a Critical Practice of Philosophical Listening

Throughout this book the community of philosophical enquiry has been proposed as a radical approach to education. The community of enquiry is not something that just describes a set of procedures and routines to be added to the school timetable. It is an educational approach that fundamentally challenges the 'delivery model' of practice. We have exemplified the self-critical and transformative pedagogy of philosophy with children (P4C) through the adoption of picturebooks, as philosophical sources and a playful means to subvert essentialising or marginalising versions of childhood. We aim for classroom communities where claims to knowledge are open to investigation and room is made for previously ignored, diverse, or unheard voices. This chapter begins to explore the constituents of a grounded philosophical approach to pedagogy: constituents such as 'philosophical listening', a critical-reflexive stance on everyday professional practice, the need for experiences of 'being alongside' children rather than 'being in front of' children to be part of teaching and teacher education. To underpin a philosophical approach, we propose a creative action research orientation to listening and teaching: practitioners being alongside one another, sharing and investigating what is salient in their lived experience of teaching (Haynes, 2007a). 'Being-alongside' is a visual and bodily way of describing the epistemological and ethical flavour of respectful enquiry with children.

STAYING AWAKE

Socially inclusive dialogue with learners remains an ideal of critical pedagogy. It is difficult to achieve and stays frustratingly out of reach, particularly in the context of schooling. This is partly because of the socialising role of mass education and its dominant social discourse that describes children as minds to be formed, objects of study, and bodies to be measured (Walkerdine, 1984). We have argued that philosophy *with* children necessitates a shift away from such ideas of measurement

and formation. Critical pedagogy offers hope and a counter to normalising education through engaging dialogically with learners and with
the relationship between knowledge and power (Tubbs, 2005:266–275).
Dialogue is not a 'magic fix' pedagogy. In their review on 'dialogue as
teaching', Burbules and Bruce (2001) articulate its political tensions.
They ask:

> Is dialogue inherently "normalizing," or can it be adapted to broader
> horizons of inclusiveness? On the other hand (perversely), when it does
> succeed at being more inclusive, is this at the cost of requiring partici-
> pants to give up or compromise elements of their difference? (http://
> faculty.ed.uiuc.edu/burbules/papers/dialogue.html).

The ideals of critical pedagogies can in themselves be dangerous. Tubbs
suggests such attempts at critical engagement remain a fragile hope in a
postmodern world because *any* 'vision' of the world runs the risk of using
'the same model of education and teaching that allows for the tyranny of
the enlightened over the apprentice' (Tubbs, 2005:280). There is a need for
watchfulness. When the wolves have been chased away, we start to notice
the elephants, as happens to the family in Gaiman and McKean's dark
but humorous picturebook *Wolves in the Walls* (2003). We recognise the
complexity of education and slipperiness of communication, the interplays
of power that can grind learning and social change to a halt. Allan (2008)
cites Lyotard's important critique of the desire for remedy and simplification which he describes as a process that:

> Threatens to totalize experience, to reduce language to Newspeak,
> to rob thinking of its childhood and pedagogy of its philosophical
> moment. It is the 'demand' for reality (for unity, simplicity, commu-
> nicability) and remedy: remedy for the parcelling and virtualization
> of culture, for the fragmentation of the life world and its derealisa-
> tion into idioms, petit recits, and language games (Lyotard cited in
> Allan, 2008:233).

Like the sleepless and sensitive princess in the well known fairytale, educators need to be kept awake by the philosophical pea underneath all the ideological, policy, and curriculum mattresses. Unlike the princess who (out
of politeness) keeps to herself the nightly disturbance she has experienced,
as educators we should continue to pose the awkward questions (see Figure
13.1). In this somewhat precarious place of hope and resistance then, how
are we to set about learning to appreciate the merits of children's perspectives and claims to knowledge?

The epistemological perspective of this book is embodied, situated,
acknowledging children's diverse experiences. It is also one that values

Figure 13.1   Image from *The Princess and the Pea* by Lauren Child.

playful and imaginative forms of engagement with ideas. As Robertson proposes, in proposing pedagogies of reasoning and dialogue, we need to re-think ideas of rationality and reasonableness:

> Until we can offer a conception of rationality that has room for passionate commitment as well as open-mindedness, emotion in addition

to intellect, rupture as well as consensus, and social justice as both a condition and outcome of rational dialogue, we may not have many takers (Robertson, 1995:125).

In developing 'new' pedagogies, there are epistemological and ethical moves to be made. Classroom experience suggests that where adults are willing to let go, relinquish some power, and embrace the associated risks, the pedagogy of the community of enquiry *can* lead to learning experienced as alive and fresh, rather than as tired, imitative, compliant, and repetitive. A critical pedagogical framework cannot sidestep difficulty, errors, and the arguments and emotions that accompany controversy in lived experience. Philosophical thinking is often thinking that disrupts so there is a need to overcome the antipathy to disruption. In schools disruption is often grounds for exclusion, seldom interpreted as a form of resistance or critique of the social order. In our own attempt to understand the difficult and uncertain movement towards more humane and democratic educational practice, we have emphasised the importance of self-critical listening and P4C practice.

DANCING ON HOT COALS?

Listening in education has often been conceived of as an interpersonal event related to therapeutic and humanist models of education. Levin has called this a 'stage of listening' and referred to it as a 'practice of compassion' (Levin, 1989:47). It is well meaning, can make a positive difference, but also has serious limitations in sometimes failing to recognise or challenge underlying structural inequalities or assuming they are being played out uniformly. In previous chapters, we have also referred to current discourses of listening to children, in the context of policies related to children's rights, noting distinctions made between listening associated with periodic *consultation* and listening associated with concern for deeper *participation*. We believe that arguments about rights can be constructive in helping to argue for opportunities for children to play a more active part in school life and learning, but they can be limiting when methods of developing participation are narrow or lack imagination. Equally, discussion of rights can set up unhelpful conflicts between the rights of children and their parents, when focused solely on individual autonomy and empowerment.

In education, frameworks of listening to children are currently exemplified in a wave of 'well-being' initiatives[1] designed to address concerns about children's unhappiness and poor mental health[2]. Hannah Smith proposes that making schools responsible for children's happiness represents a change to the core purpose of education under the current system. She argues that such interventions expose deeply held and normalising beliefs about childhood, which have the potential to marginalise and exclude, place an impossible responsibility on schools and teachers, and result in methods that simplify difficulties (Smith, forthcoming). She suggests that such educational initiatives risk overlooking structural inequalities and perpetuate a myth that schools can somehow transcend the difficulties of wider society. As discussed in previous chapters, therapeutic models of education have also been critiqued by Furedi (2009) and Ecclestone and Hayes (2009), who argue that they neglectfully mis-educate, by constructing learners as diminished subjects, particularly when they do not conform at school.

We are all too aware that in some cases philosophical enquiry has been rather 'hi-jacked' by proponents of emotional literacy as providing instruments to improve behaviour, strengthen self-esteem, or address other personal and social goals such as well-being. Biesta (2009) suggests such instrumentalisation is also inherent in other claims made by P4C 'advocates' that speak of its positive impact on reasoning, IQ, or democratic skills. What he wants to draw attention to is what seems to be the underlying conception of the human being as a 'developing organism' (Biesta, 2009:5). The result is that education becomes focused on the production of a particular kind of subjectivity. Biesta proposes a conception of subjectivity 'in terms of exposure to otherness and difference rather than in terms of the development of skills and dispositions' could offer alternative ideas for philosophical engagement in education (Biesta, 2009:10). It is important to take such critiques on board in thinking about transformative 'pedagogies of listening'.

Burman (2008b) proposes an approach shaped by interrogation and deconstruction of dominant views of childhood, particularly developmental theories and practices, which fail to adequately address the position of particular children in particular cultural or historical contexts. In her view, such problematic, and potentially excluding, discourses also include those referring to universal interpretations of children's rights. As far as ideas of child are concerned, Burman's cross disciplinary[3] and inter-disciplinary[4] work includes drawing on a range of psycho-analytic theories and practices to make sense of the ways children are positioned, both affectively and politically, to develop analyses at the societal level.

In the light of all these warnings about critical pedagogy and critiques in the field of childhood, for practitioners seeking to approach P4C with some confidence it might seem like stepping across hot coals: it requires some knowledge from others and learning through experience. What kind of framework can be adopted to make the best of existing good will and interest in children's many and diverse perspectives in education, yet remain alert to the limitations of compassion or appeal to rights, and do justice to the complex politics of schooling?

HOW AM I TO LISTEN TO YOU?

Listening is at the heart of such a framework. In this book, through an examination of various episodes of practice with children, we have shown that listening entails an ethics of the self, a notion of the relationship of the listener to the *process* of listening and interpretation, as well as with those who are seeking to be heard. The listener brings her/his identity to listening, and, at the same time, identity is always in the process of formation through listening. Listening turns towards the Other, towards the possibilities of both hearing and not hearing; of silencing or letting speak. Listening has not yet decided. There is an open moment. Listening has not yet arrived; it is on its way. When dwelling on listening there is also the chance of admitting the emotions as a source of knowledge: their expression is audible. These revelations are available in the embodied voice, in the choice of words, in the silences in between. If, by being critical of self, and of the processes and limitations of discourse, listening becomes more of a hearkening, it opens the ground for the previously unspoken and allows itself to make audible the previously unheard (Bonnett, 1995). Levin suggests that this hearkening requires a disciplined practice of 'letting-go and letting-be' (Levin, 1989:48).

When it comes to listening to children, Irigeray's exploration of the question 'how am I to listen to you?' describes the ways in which traditional relationships have assumed that:

> the elder is supposed to know what the younger is and what he or she should become. The elder is supposed to know the younger and only listens to him or her within the parameters of an existing science or truth (Irigeray, 1996:116).

She argues that the kind of language used by adults within such a construction of relationships results in 'paralyzing the freedom of the child's becoming out of a lack of autonomy on the part of adults themselves' (Irigeray, 1996:116).

BEING ALONGSIDE IN CLASSROOMS: RECOVERING PHILO

In this concern to inhabit the existential space of our freedom and to tackle the disturbance in the facilitation of philosophical dialogues with children, we recognise the sense of a lack of autonomy identified by Irigeray. How is it possible to live at the 'contradictory heart' of the educational relationship (Tubbs, 2005:309)? A pedagogy of fallibilism, uncertainty, tact, and openness is suggested. We are not looking for a simple technique. It is more a case of envisaging a way of living with the postmodern risks, loose ends, and ambiguities of teaching described in this book. Educational responses to such 'bewilderment' include giving up a notion of 'straight' teaching, stepping aside, moving into ironic teaching, and treating experience in education as an end in itself, rather than a means to later ends (Tubbs, 2005).

The traditional lay-out of classrooms and culture of knowledge transmission has positioned the teacher mostly at the front and nearly always facing the learner. In some places 'eye-contact' between teacher and students is perceived as characterising the attentive learner absorbing knowledge. In the community of philosophical enquiry, positions are typically characterised as 'being alongside' one another. We are not so naïve as to think that simply sitting in a circle, as opposed to in rows or groups of tables, is of itself transformative of classroom relationships. 'Being alongside' serves here as an image of equality through shared enquiry and of leaving room for disagreement.

The pedagogy of this book emphasises the idea of the educator who is prepared to 'creatively mediate' and take risks associated with tackling the unexpected and broaching the unknown. At the same time as taking this responsibility, respectful teaching means recognising the inherent authority in the teaching–learning relation, and that such authority can be mediated through vulnerability, argues Tubbs (2005, after Weil and Buber). It entails turning one's back on the assumption that older is necessarily wiser and accepting that a child or young person, like any other, can reveal something not yet considered or so far unspoken. Irigeray writes:

> I am listening to you is to listen to your words as something unique, irreducible, especially to my own, as something new, as yet unknown. It is to understand and hear them as the manifestation of an intention, of human and spiritual development (Irigeray, 1996:116).

Considering the professional 'in loco parentis' position of the school teacher, we envisage a form of love partly characterised by willingness to hold and risk the unknown. Corradi Fiumara suggests: 'In the enlightened developments of rational knowledge it is possible that the original loving aspect of research—the first part of philosophy[5]—has been lost' (Corradi Fiumara, 1990:109). To recover the *philo*, Irigeray articulates a number of conditions that make the statement 'I listen to you', in the context of love between subjects, a possibility (Irigeray, 1996). It is to listen in a dimension in which I do not assume that I already know you or what your future is. It is to listen with an encouragement towards the unexpected, towards your initiative and your becoming. It is to listen without presupposition and without implicit demands, with a silence that is a 'space-time offered to you with no a priori, no pre-established truth or ritual' (Irigeray, 1996:117). The silence is a condition for self and mutual respect and assumes that the world is incomplete, still open and capable of revealing itself in many forms, including philosophical ones. We could conceive of the teaching situation with children as a context of caring about and loving something, a context capable of encompassing such conditions (Bonnett & Cuypers, 2003).

What is still possible is a listening response with children that subverts and resists dogma, that turns towards rather than turns away, that involves both passivity (Chinnery, 2003) and effort (Corradi Fiumara, 1990), rather than stock phrases and learned answers that leave no emptiness and squeeze out the possibility of thinking. The surrender might be to silence or to the chance of complications. In years to come, will people discover with a sense of shock the ways that the lives of children are portrayed today? Will they express their disbelief at their treatment? At this point in time, when the idea of 'childism'[6] is still in its infancy, the effort is in conceiving of philosophical work with children not as the giving of form to future persons, but as encounters with persons present in which there is also the possibility that each of us might be influenced (Kohan, 2002).

THOUGHTFUL P4C PRACTICE

Given the obstacles and pitfalls associated with trying to make change in schools, importing teaching ideas or top down professional development, we propose a critical framework for learning about P4C through experience, drawing on action research[7] and practical philosophy. Throughout this book we place ourselves wholeheartedly as practitioners, clearly alongside other practitioners in education, within an open and ongoing enquiry about working philosophically with children. Whilst we willingly share and theorise about our experience with others, we avoid positioning ourselves as 'having the answers' to give to other educators. We aim to reproduce the dialogical principles informing our work with children in classrooms when conversing with colleagues in education, whatever the setting in which they are working. We adopt a critical and self-critical research stance towards what we hope is 'thoughtful practice'. In the paragraphs below we briefly summarise this approach to our own learning as a way of drawing this book to a positive conclusion.

Our enquiry about philosophy in classrooms is a form of ongoing educational research in the sense that Elliott (2006:169) argues when he distinguishes 'educational research' from 'research *on* education' via 'its practical intention to realise educational values in action'. How do we set out to achieve consistency in realising our educational values and what do we mean by 'thoughtful practice'? In describing research as 'thoughtful practice' and drawing on Arendt's notion of 'thinking without banisters', Nixon, Walker, and Clough suggest that to become thoughtful is:

> to climb the stairs without the security of known categories; because for each, the other is different, and the challenge of the other unique. Thinking is a moral necessity, without which right action is unthinkable and the onward rush of events irreversible (Nixon, Walker, & Clough, 2003:89).

What motivates our philosophical work in schools is the desire to remove obstacles to participation and strengthen philosophical enquiry through responsive listening and practical reasoning. We set out to tap our experience in education, along with that of the children and teachers with whom we work, and to put it to work to achieve further pedagogic refinement through practical judgement or phronesis. This influential notion from Aristotle's *Nichomachean Ethics* requires a kind of reason that is personal and experiential, flexible and not formulable (Dunne, 1997:9). For Dunne and Pendlebury, practical reasoning is not just something we *do*, but necessarily involves a certain *character* of the reasoner (Dunne & Pendlebury, 2003:206). Practical reason leads to wise actions only if the thinker exercises various virtues, such as reciprocity, mutual respect, openness, and a willingness to give reasons and to listen to others. The common thread is a willingness to give-and-take. They understand *phronesis* as characterised by a habit of 'salient focusing' (after Amelie Rorty) involving:

> the ability to see fine detail and nuance and the ability to discern the differences between this situation and others that to the inexperienced eye might seem as the same (Dunne & Pendlebury, 2003:207).

Salient focusing is partly constituted by cognitive dispositions, such as a person's perceptions of situations and emotional responses to them (Dunne & Pendlebury, 2003:208). Dunne (1997) explains that experience is the consolidation of meaning out of previously discrete impressions and that phronesis is:

> what enables experience to be self-correcting and to avoid settling into mere routine. If experience is an accumulated capital, we might say then, phronesis is this capital wisely invested (Dunne, 1997:292).

In his characterisation of the 'life of practice' Dunne adopts Wittgenstein's metaphor of 'rough ground' to express the need for flexibility, responsiveness, and improvisation on the one hand and the need for 'rootedness' on the other. Such rootedness is available through a practitioner's history of participation in the community of practice itself, through 'grounding' in its dispositions and the subtleties of its culture. Dunne cautions that this particular notion of a 'field of practice' is questionable in a technique and target orientated world of education (Dunne, 1993:378). Such noise can paralyze us or immunise us against our own sense of freedom and the possibility of listening.

Our argument in this book is that it is possible to create an authentic and humane space in the classroom and to hold onto the sense that practice, of research, philosophising, and teaching, has an 'open texture' (Dunne, 1993:379). Rather than P4C being an approach to teaching that we seek to apply or do to others, and then to evaluate their performance within it, its dialogical enquiry methodology is one that we subscribe to ourselves and internalise, a practical everyday philosophy, extending beyond our P4C 'lessons'. Griffiths (2003:21) argues that practical philosophy is 'with and for' rather than 'about or applied to'. It acknowledges its origins in the concrete communities in which it operates and then seeks to speak 'to something more universal, to something inclusive of, for instance, classroom teachers as well as academics, and young people as well as teachers' (Griffiths & Cotton, 2005).

The significance of personal experience, of 'rootedness' (Dunne, 1997), and of 'situational understanding' (Elliott, 2006) is also expressed in feminist approaches to enquiry, which Greene and Griffiths (2003:77) characterise as 'less a theory—or a set of theories—and more a perspective, a lens, a handle on the world and its ideas, a way of acting and speaking'. For Greene and Griffiths, this perspective is held together by certain preoccupations, not necessarily exclusive to feminism, and 'each philosopher marked by feminism makes her own trajectory' (Greene & Griffiths, 2003:75). Our book provides an account of our 'situated philosophy' of listening—a view from somewhere that has taken its bearings from the guideposts of our lived experience, just as Greene and Griffiths argue 'we cannot be the unmoved movers, or take the view from nowhere' (Greene & Griffiths, 2003:77).

The situated outlook is rooted in our orientation towards social justice in education as well as in feminist perspectives in philosophy (Benhabib, 1992; Greene & Griffiths, 2003). This integration or political and professional concerns expresses connections among passion, imagination, and reason and between private and public domains, shaping our understanding, particularly of what it means to *listen* and what it means for children and young people to *participate* in philosophical dialogues and for us to aim to be alongside them in such dialogues. These ethics are articulated through the exploration of significant moments of practice in this book and through their narrative representation. Benhabib (1992) suggests that female experience tends historically to be attuned to the narrative structure of action and the standpoint of the concrete other or what she terms the art of the particular. The concrete events presented in this book have emerged from many enquiries with children in different settings, as well as several years of training sessions with teachers, mostly in England, Scotland, Northern Ireland, and Wales, but also in other countries, including South Africa.

P4C, TEACHER EDUCATION, AND PROFESSIONAL DEVELOPMENT

P4C courses are very distinctive, mirroring the process adopted in classrooms and enabling teachers to experience participation in a community of enquiry for themselves: the philosophical questioning and reasoning, the disagreement and challenge, and the community building. Teachers benefit from discovering their own philosophical voices. P4C training naturally draws teachers' attention to significant aspects of classroom interaction, highlighted in the kind of critical episodes of educational interaction discussed in this book: the necessity to question, freedom of thought and expression, the meaning of reason, the cultivation of independence of mind, difficulty and controversy, and the conditions that enable thinking and dialogue to flourish. We believe that the P4C professional development process can enable teachers to identify important connections to much wider debates in society about childhood, knowledge, education, power, and democracy: debates that impinge on their public role and professional judgements. It provides an exceptional forum to explore the kinds of risks and responsibilities that are entailed in a professional role and the courage and determination required to bring about a culture change and to work with children respectfully and fairly in everyday life. We would like to see teaching and learning approaches from P4C incorporated into mainstream teacher education and continuing professional development. Given the rapid growth in short courses in philosophy with children and the development of P4C study at postgraduate level at universities in many different countries, there is a need for further evaluation studies on the impact of such developments on teachers' thinking and children's learning.

At the heart of a community of philosophical enquiry is the commitment to listen in a radically open way and to learn collaboratively: a commitment that has to be worked out in cultures of child, schools, and learning. Such an ethics of listening in education must be pursued with a sensitive political will on the part of adults: through relinquishing authority and unlearning assumptions routinely made about children, through dialogue and conversation with children, through giving them the responsibility of thinking together for themselves and the power of decision-making, through individual reflection, through addressing their rights, and through explicit attention to relationships and communication in schools.

This book has challenged current practices involving censorship and avoidance in education and illuminated issues to be addressed, such as the kind of teachers and teacher education needed if school systems are to respond to the challenges of involving children in philosophical enquiry and dialogue. The path ahead is respect for children: listening and letting them be confident, articulate, independent thinkers; removing obstacles to their full and meaningful participation in everyday life at school; and encouraging their agency in their learning, in their lives, and in their communities. The professional task for teachers is to engage reflexively with an examination of the everyday authority they often assume and to adopt approaches to teaching and relationships that will democratise classrooms and include learners' voices in every detail of school life. We have argued that the community of philosophical enquiry is a valuable means to move towards these goals, and teachers themselves need opportunities to build the courage and capacity to open this philosophical space with children.

The framework for teacher education and professional development is one that should mirror the generosity and the demands of the participatory processes of enquiry and dialogue advocated for children in classrooms. To develop authentic and dialogical teaching and to overcome the anxieties and uncertainties expressed in respect of an open space in the classroom, where difficult questions might be asked and where a distinctive range of pedagogical moves are called for, teachers should have access to communities of practice in which their practical wisdom can be developed. Such communities of practice would generate a restructuring of teacher thinking and action through an authentic engagement with the kinds of demands made on teachers' judgements and decisions by:

- allowing teachers to regularly participate in philosophical enquiry themselves to enrich and sustain their own philosophical thinking;
- enabling more experienced practitioners of philosophical enquiry to work with those less experienced;
- listening to and working with teachers' stories and questions emerging from their lives with children at school;
- drawing directly on children's ideas and suggestions for ways in which classroom communities of enquiry, and classrooms and schools in general, could become more participatory, democratic, and encouraging of their voices;
- engaging honestly and courageously with 'hotspots' in teaching and the difficulties of tackling sensitive and controversial issues;
- exploring the imaginative and playful dimensions that young children bring to philosophical thought and reflecting on the sometimes unexpected meanings that surface in classroom dialogues; and
- sharing ideas about approaches that draw on a diverse range of philosophical traditions and provide for work with body, heart, and mind.

As far as initial teacher education is concerned, we propose that it should include multi-disciplinary studies of children and childhood, drawing on student teachers' own sense of child, past, present, and future; exploring current issues; and including direct references to diverse voices of children. It should also include placements in settings other than schools and experience of being in roles with children other than that of teacher. Above all, student teachers need to know what it means to be alongside children, listening to them, happy in their company, able to enjoy mutually enriching conversation and exchanges of experience and perspectives, not immediately seeking to form and shape their futures through direct teaching. Each school needs to learn to express itself as a place not quite like any other, a place where biographies of adults and young people intertwine in the course of learning. Such approaches to teacher education and continuing professional development would provide for a more rounded, just, and inclusive understanding of children living in a wide variety of family, neighbourhood, and community settings: notable and distinctive places and times of which schools themselves can be a living, dynamic, and integral part.

Appendix
List of Picturebooks
Discussed in the Book

Bradman, T. & Ross, T. (1990) *Michael* (London: Andersen Press)
Browne, A. (1985) *Willy the Wimp* (London: Julia MacRae/Walker Books)
Browne, A. (1991) *Willy and Hugh* (London: Julia MacRae/Random House)
Browne, A. (1993) *Zoo* (London: Julia MacRae)
Browne, A. (1995) *Willy the Wizard* (London: Julia MacRae)
Browne, A. (1997) *Changes* (London: Walker Books)
Browne, A. (1997) *The Tunnel* (London: Walker Books)
Burningham, J. (1978) *Would you rather. . .* (London: Jonathan Cape)
Carle, E. (1969) *The Very Hungry Caterpillar* (World Publishing Co.)
Child, L. & Borland P. (2005) *The Princess and the Pea* (London: Puffin)
Gaiman, N. & McKean, D. (2001) *The Day I Swapped My Dad for Two Goldfish* (London: Bloomsbury)
Gaiman, N. & McKean, D. (2003) *The Wolves in the Walls* (London: Bloomsbury)
Greder, A. (2007) *The Island* (Crows Nest, NSW:Allen & Unwin)
Kitamura, S. (2006) *Igor the Bird Who Couldn't Sing.* (London: Anderson Press)
Lionni, L. (1974) *Fish is Fish* (New York: Dragonfly Books)
MacDonald, M. & Riches, J. (1990) *Sam's Worries* (London: ABC)
McKee, D. (1978) *Tusk Tusk* (London: Andersen Press)
McKee, D. (1980) *Not Now, Bernard* (London: Andersen Press)
McKee, D. (1989) *The Monster and the Teddy Bear* (London: Andersen Press)
Sendak, M. (1963) *Where the Wild Things Are* (London: Bodley Head)
Sendak, M. (1970) *In the Night Kitchen* (London: Bodley Head)
Sendak, M. (1981) *Outside Over There* (London: Bodley Head)
Sendak, M. (1988) *Dear Mily*; a Grimm story translated by R. Manheim (Scholastic, Michael di Capua Books)
Sendak, M. (2006) *Mummy?* (Scholastic, Michael di Capua Books)
Strauss, G. & Browne, A. (1991) *The Night Shimmy* (London: Random House)
Tan, S. & Marsden, J. (1998) *The Rabbits* (South Melbourne: Thomas C. Lothian Pty Ltd)
Tan, S. (2006) *The Arrival* (New York: Scholastic Inc)
Thompson, C. (1995) *How To Live Forever* (London: Red Fox)
Ungerer, T. (1971) *The Beast of Monsieur Racine* (New York: Farrar, Straus and Giroux)
Ungerer, T. (1980) *Moon Man* (London: Methuen Children's Books)
Ungerer, T. (1991) *The Three Robbers* (New York: Macmillan Publishing Company)
Velthuijs, M. (1989) *Frog in Love* (London: Andersen Press)
Velthuijs, M. (1991) *Frog and the Birdsong* (London: Andersen Press)
Velthuijs, M. (1992) *Frog in Winter* (London: Andersen Press)

Velthuijs, M. (1993) Frog and the Stranger (London: Andersen Press)
Velthuijs, M. (1993) *Frog Is Frightened* (London: Andersen Press)
Velthuijs, M. (1995) *Frog Is a Hero* (London: Andersen Press)
Velthuijs, M. (1998) *Frog and the Wild World* (London: Andersen Press)
Velthuijs, M. (2001) *Frog Finds a Friend* (London: Andersen Press)
Velthuijs, M. (2003) *Frog Is Sad* (London: Andersen Press)
Wagner, J. & Brooks, R. (1977) *John Brown, Rose, and the Midnight Cat* (Harmondsworth: Viking Kestrel)
Wiesner, D. (2001) *The Three Pigs* (New York: Clarion Books)
Wormell, C. (2004) *The Big Ugly Monster and the Little Stone Rabbit* (London: Random House)

Notes

NOTES TO THE INTRODUCTION

1. Debates about child and childhood are also central to our thinking in this book, and we discuss these in depth in Part II.
2. Detached youthworkers are not attached to a particular institution or place; their informal educational work is mainly on the streets.
3. J. K. Rowling in an interview on BBC's Radio Four (10 December 2005).
4. Some of the varieties of P4C are discussed in Chapter 3.
5. When we use the word 'author' in the context of picturebooks we refer to the creator of the words as well as the images when they are one and the same person. When two or more people created the one picturebook, the word 'author' will refer to the creator of the words and 'illustrator' will refer to the creator of the images.

NOTES TO CHAPTER 1

1. Sociologist Frank Furedi expresses his concern for an increasing tendency in contemporary culture to portray and treat adults as being 'behind' the times, whilst children are seen more to be 'up to date', for example, in technology use or coming home to educate their parents in environmental issues. In *Wasted: Why Education Isn't Working* (2009), Furedi argues that the 'authority' of parents/adults is increasingly undermined through contemporary culture, and that this makes it impossible for adults to 'educate' in the sense of confidently passing on knowledge accrued. In the introduction to the Cambridge Review of Primary Education (Hofkins & Northen 2009:19), Professor Robin Alexander is also keen to preserve the notion that education necessarily involves a dialogue between past and present (see discussion in Chapter 12).
2. For a further development of this argument, see in particular Chapter 2.
3. We will return to this particular characteristic of books that may explain censorship.
4. We speculate that young people engage readily with this ambiguous material because of the postmodern blurring of boundaries and ambiguity that characterises contemporary culture.
5. For a further explanation and visual image of this metaphor of a spiral, see our *Storywise: Thinking through Stories* (2002, 2010).
6. Our experience of working and living with children has made us question the certainty with which some adults claim that particular books are good

or bad for children. How exactly do adults know and control what the child reader has understood?

7. The meaning of the abstract concept 'colour' can be explored philosophically in enquiries (see the *Web of Intriguing Ideas* in our *Storywise: Thinking through Stories* [2002, 2010]).

8. A flip-book has a drawing on each page, and when flicking rapidly through the pages the impression of moving images is created.

9. In *Where the Wild Things Are* the monsters and Max have a party—a 'wild rumpus'.

10. Including an opera composed by Oliver Knussen (on commission from the Opèra National in Brussels) and a movie in 2009.

11. Such cross referencing is a common feature of 'postmodern' picturebooks.

NOTES TO CHAPTER 2

1. Matthew Lipman suggests that complex thinking is 'thinking that is aware of its own assumptions and implications as well as being conscious of the reasons and evidence that support this or that conclusion. Complex thinking takes into account its own methodology, its own procedures, its own perspective and point of view' (Lipman, 1991:23, 24).

2. For biographer Tony Kushner, *Outside Over There* signals a 'seachange' and a new direction in Sendak's art. He groups this book as the first of another trilogy (followed by *Dear Mili* and *We Are All in the Dumps with Jack and Guy*) and identifies it as a 'dark departure' characterised by Sendak's psychological, political and philosophical struggle with despair (Kushner, 2003:14).

3. The ALA also hosts in September of every year the Banned Books Week (BBW) which 'celebrates the freedom to choose or the freedom to express one's opinion even if that opinion might be considered unorthodox or unpopular *and* stresses the importance of ensuring the availability of those unorthodox or unpopular viewpoints to all who wish to read them' (www.ala.org; accessed 20 December 2007).

4. The 'Disneyisation' of modern culture—a construction of child for parent consumer.

5. At the same time people talk of increased 'sexualisation' of children; e.g. the selection of clothes young girls can buy in shops and how they are portrayed in magazines, the internet, and through commercial television channels.

6. See Chapter 1.

7. See Chapter 1.

8. Matthew Lipman explains 'self-correction' as follows: 'Individuals and groups seeking to strengthen their judgment making should practice questioning others and themselves, offering counterexamples and counterarguments and looking for disconfirming evidences or testimonies. They should recognize the potential value of dissent in the community as a possible basis for correction of errors as well as the value of falsification as a method of identifying vacuous truths' (Lipman 1991:64).

9. 'Transcendental' means 'preceding experience', so a transcendental ego is the ego that makes experiences possible (unity of consciousness), but can itself not be experienced.

10. See for example the episode of enquiry in a multi-faith classroom in the London Borough of Newham as reported by Haynes (2005b) 'The Costs of Thinking'.

11. Dialogue means 'through' (*dia*) 'reason' (*logos*). See also p. 192.

12. Diagram 2.3 is inspired by Mike Lake (1990:3).

NOTES TO CHAPTER 3

1. Cartesian dualism refers to the metaphysical ideas of the 'father' of modern philosophy, French philosopher Rene Descartes. He settled the notion of mind—as a separate entity, located in 'inner space'—firmly in Western philosophical tradition, that is, the mind as a *substance* in which mental processes occur. Such dualism has become part and parcel of our everyday language and expresses itself in various dichotomies (e.g. man/woman, feeling/thinking, mind/body, black/white, developed/underdeveloped, thinking/talking) and influence how we define ourselves as a teacher and as a person.

2. For this practice, see e.g. the SAPERE Training DVD *Socrates for Six Year Olds* in *The Transformers* series. Available from SAPERE: www.sapere.org.uk or access at: http://www.youtube.com/results?search_query=Socrates+for+Six+year+Olds&aq=f

3. Lipman and Sharp argue that the use of specially written fiction has an important moral function in education as it makes it possible to portray what they call 'model communities of children'. The novels portray 'models of enquiry, models of cooperation, and models of caring, sensitive individuals'. These models, they continue, stimulate moral imagination and feelings of hope and courage, offering glimpses of what the ideal community of thinkers could be like as an ideal (Lipman & Sharp, 1978).

4. Unlike other Thinking Skills programmes, critical thinking in P4C for us is not about the logical analysis of arguments in isolation from context, the thinker whose argument it is, etc. All arguments are culturally, socially, politically, and morally positioned, whether consciously or subconsciously. The typical form in which argument analysis is presented falsely suggests that the activity has a kind of clean straightforwardness, with the teacher knowing the right answers—as if analysing an argument is like solving a mathematics problem.

5. See Chapter 2.

6. See Chapter 12.

7. Some prefer to guide children in creating their own narratives using objects (see e.g. Liptai, 2005).

8. For the storyline and an example of an enquiry with children using this picturebook, see Chapter 8.

9. Sharon Todd in her paper 'Pedagogy as Transformative Event: Becoming Singularly Present in Context' argues how Hannah Arendt critiques the individualist notion of *Dasein* (introduced by Heidegger) and emphasises *Mitsein*: 'being-in-the-world-with-others' (Todd, 2010). This ontological concept is neither mathematical nor a social aspect of existence, but part of the human condition. We are born into an already populated realm through which action and speech are founded ('natality'), and therefore existence cannot be abstracted from co-existence.

10. The problem here is that it is difficult to ascertain what is cause and effect. Although in other countries, it is in principle possible to purchase the kind of picturebooks we would recommend for philosophical enquiry, booksellers often do not select them. In conversation with a South African bookseller it became apparent that one of the difficulties is the marketing of books such as Shaun Tan's *The Arrival* (2006) or *The Rabbits* (1998). Are they for adults *or* for children? Are they for reading *or* for visual contemplation? On which bookshelf do they belong?

NOTES TO CHAPTER 4

1. In his book *Actual Minds, Possible Worlds* (1986) Jerome Bruner distinguishes between two modes of thinking, that is, the 'logico-scientific' and the 'narrative' . They deserve attention in their own right, though they cannot be separated, in the sense that they cannot function independently. These two modes of thought are distinct ways of ordering experience, of constructing reality, he claims. For Bruner they are irreducible to one another and complementary. As opposed to statement A ('If x, then y'), in the case of statement B, 'The king died, and then the queen died', many explanations are possible, e.g. the queen died out of grief, the queen died as a result of an accident, the king killed himself to punish the queen after which the queen killed herself (see, e.g. Cowley, 2006).

2. We will return to Joseph Dunne's use of the phrase 'back to the rough ground' (borrowed from Wittgenstein) in Chapter 13.

3. See Chapter 3, footnote 2.

4. For a description of the storyline, see Chapter 1.

5. Influenced by Heidegger, for Gadamer, hermeneutics is the most fundamental, pre-scientific mode of being-in-the-world. Understanding anything (including a picturebook narrative) is not the outcome of critical, propositional thinking processes, but includes a pre-reflective, pragmatic know-how that reveals itself through the way in which our bodies orient themselves in the world. See http://plato.stanford.edu/entries/hermeneutics/#Turn (accessed 17 July 2010).

6. The 'in', in 'being-in-time' and 'being-in-space', needs to be understood in an *ontological* and not in a *psychological* sense. Psychology starts with the individual accessing his or her experiences with help of the senses and/or introspection. The profound contribution Heidegger has made to the history of ideas and the development of postmodern thought is the radical idea that *existence* (being) and not the individual (beings) is ontologically prior, that is, individuals always already find themselves surrounded by beings (including others). This shift in thinking has made the development of, for example, (post)structuralist, constructivist and other non-dualist pedagogies possible. See also footnote 5.

7. Gadamer's major influence was philosopher Martin Heidegger, in particular the latter's distinction between *Dasein* and *Mitsein* (see Chapter 3, footnote 10).

8. As will be further explained in Chapter 6. In Part 2, we argue for 'child' as a 'form of life' or mode of being and explore the implications for knowledge construction and reading of texts.

9. It was Gilbert Ryle who introduced the distinction between 'knowing that' (propositional knowledge) and 'knowing how' (practical knowledge), but this problematically assumes that theoretical knowledge is not already *presupposed* in successful practice.

10. A similar argument is put forward by Roger Scruton in Chapter 7.

11. See, for example, Chapter 3, as well as Lipman, Sharp, & Oscanyan (1980).

12. See Chapters 3 and 6.

13. With thanks to one of our postgraduate students and colleague, Lauren Rembach, for these examples of children's questions.

14. These are not their real names.

15. We prefer 'artful' over 'skilful'. Facilitation involves more than a set of skills. It requires complex, intuitive judgements balancing critical, creative, caring, and collaborative thinking.

16. See footnote 4.

17. Picturebook artist Anthony Browne explains in an interview how the discovery of his dad's dressing gown enabled him to go back in time and 'retrieve' how he felt as a child. The object enabled him to portray the 'dads' in his subsequent work more like his own dad (Browne, 2006).

NOTES TO CHAPTER 5

1. *Psyche* is often translated as 'soul', but following Jones (1970), we prefer 'self' as Plato's *psyche* is not a theological, supernatural notion, but natural. I also prefer it to 'mind', which is often used in contrast to the body.
2. See especially Chapter 2.
3. See Plato's metaphor at the beginning of this chapter.
4. It is beyond the scope of this book to explore the complex and controversial interpretation of *phronesis*. For Joseph Dunne and Shirley Pendlebury, practical reason leads to wise actions only if the thinker exercises various virtues, such as reciprocity, mutual respect, openness, and a willingness to give reasons and to listen to others. The common thread is willingness to give-and-take. They understand *phronesis* as characterised by a habit of "salient focusing", which involves "the ability to see fine detail and nuance"—partly constituted by cognitive dispositions and partly by a person's perceptions of and emotional responses to situations (Dunne & Pendlebury, 2003:207–208). Emotions are involved in the perception (*aisthesis*) of the necessary details of a particular situation. Joseph Dunne and Kristjan Kristjansson insist that phronesis is not just the *application* of theories to particular cases (Dunne, 1997:157). The implications for teaching are that the 'teacher's capacity for reasoning cannot first be taught 'in theory' and then applied 'in practice' ' (Kristjansson, 2007:166).
5. How picturebooks can be used for the teaching of philosophy is explained and exemplified in Karin Murris and Joanna Haynes (2002). And an international e-book version (2010) is available on: www.infonet-publications.com.

NOTES TO CHAPTER 6

1. See e.g. the list of questions in the appendices in Arizpe & Styles (2003).
2. For an example of a dialogue with children on this topic, see Chapter 8.
3. For an analysis of Sendak's work, see in particular Chapters 1 and 2.
4. For pictures of Frog, see Figures 0.2, 0.3, 0.4, 1.1, 4.2, 4.3, 4.4.
5. In Chapter 8 we develop the idea that crossing the boundaries between the private and the public, play and reality, real and imaginary creates a philosophical space.
6. For examples of our own use of this picturebook, see our *Storywise: Thinking through Stories* (Murris & Haynes, 2002, 2010).
7. One way would be to argue that children's books are those written for children. However, there are some books, such as *Alice in Wonderland*, which are more appreciated by adults than by children.
8. Not all children's stories are exclusively written by adults. *The Diary of Anne Frank* would be such a counter example.
9. The *content* is not a distinguishing feature of children's books either. In adult books, too, we find children or heroes as main characters. Fantasy often plays a role in adult books (e.g. Tolkien's *Lord of the Rings*), and children's books are not less sad, cruel, or sadistic.
10. See Chapter 3.

11. For a lengthy example of philosophical practice with picturebooks, see the dialogue in Chapter 1.
12. See in particular Chapter 10.
13. For a list of picturebooks, see Appendix A.

NOTES TO CHAPTER 7

1. See Chapter 3.
2. See the Introduction for how such factual inaccuracies about the moon can cause censorship.
3. See Gaiman & McKean (1998).
4. It is worth noting that although most scientists hold fast to a concept of *realism* that assumes that external reality exists independently of observation, quantum mechanics opens up possibilities of thinking about reality as not existing when it is not being perceived. For a clear explanation of this difficult subject matter, see Iredale (1997).
5. See Introduction and Figure 0.1.
6. What is *not* meant here is the popular understanding of imagination as mere 'visualisation'—imagination as the faculty of the mind to create pictures 'in' the mind. See Chapter 3.
7. See also Chapter 4.
8. See Chapter 4.
9. See Chapter 5.
10. For a good argumentation against aesthetic relativism, see Scruton (2002:127).
11. See Chapter 3.
12. See Chapter 3.
13. This thought experiment is taken from Burningham (1978).
14. Inspired by Levi-Strauss, Kieran Egan argues how the body helps mediate abstract concepts such as 'cold' and 'hot'. The initial discriminations of temperature as 'hotter' or 'colder' than one's own body temperature help a learner understand the mediating concept 'warm'. See Egan (1995:120).

NOTES TO CHAPTER 8

1. Defined as 'the interpretation of two closely occurring events as though one caused the other, without any concern for the causal link' (Alcock, 1995, cited in Woolley, 1997).
2. Rollins (1996) offers a detailed analysis of positions on realism and philosophy with children.
3. In service training for teachers and other adults working in schools.
4. In *Primary Understanding: Education in Early Childhood*, Egan (1991) suggests that, in pre-literate phases and in oral cultures, human thinking varies. It does not follow that such thinking is inferior or irrelevant.
5. Used in association with *Teaching Philosophy with Picturebooks* by Karin Murris (1992).

NOTES TO CHAPTER 9

1. In *Exploring Teacher Development through Reflexive Inquiry*, Cole and Gary-Knowles (2000:2) define *reflective* enquiry as a process of examining

and refining practice with reference to the pedagogical, social, political, and ethical contexts that influence professional work, while *reflexive* enquiry incorporates the reflective process *and* is 'situated within the context of personal histories in order to make connections between personal lives and professional careers, and to understand personal influences on professional practice'. They argue that such reflexive enquiries are always rooted in a critical perspective expressed through the 'interrogation of status quo norms and practices, especially with respect to issues of power and control' (Cole & Gary-Knowles, 2000:2).

2. Burbules and Bruce (2001) warn us to maintain a critical perspective on dialogue itself and highlight some of the limitations, particularly where there is a failure to take into account wider inequalities and power relationships. See the discussion in Chapter 13.
3. For a comprehensive and authoritative discussion of philosophical perspectives on childhood and adulthood readers should consult David Kennedy's (2006) *The Well of Being: Childhood, Subjectivity and Education.*
4. Murris (2000a) has published a more extensive and detailed paper 'Can Children Do Philosophy?' in the *Journal of Philosophy of Education.*

NOTES TO CHAPTER 10

1. SAPERE stands for Society for the Advancement of Philosophical Enquiry and Reflection in Education (www.sapere.org.uk). It is a charitable foundation and the British network for educators interested in P4C, affiliated to ICPIC (International Council for Philosophical Inquiry for Children). SAPERE provides information, organises conferences, and runs courses.
2. The philosopher Martin Heidegger talks about dwelling thinking in an essay on the concept of dwelling, including the dwelling place, titled 'Building Dwelling Thinking' (1971). In his *Discourse on Thinking* (1966), he contrasts dwelling thinking with calculative thinking. For Heidegger, dwelling thinking is meditative and contemplative, whereas calculative thinking is computational.

NOTES TO CHAPTER 11

1. As Erica Burman (2008b) has pointed out in *Developments: Child, Image, Nation,* much of the work focuses on children in the Northern Hemisphere and takes a Northern Hemisphere perspective. There is much work to be done to redress the imbalance.
2. In the UK over the last twenty years, the idea of consulting with children about matters affecting their everyday lives has been discussed at policy level in areas such as social care, the justice system, community services, and education. In schools for example, many schools councils exist. Children are elected to represent their class or year and work together with teachers and other staff to raise concerns, solve problems, and take initiatives.
3. 'Thinking through Dialogue the Fifth International Conference on Philosophy in Practice' held at Wadham College, Oxford, England.
4. Broadcast on British television in Channel Four's 'Class Action' in November 1994.
5. See Chapter 9.

NOTES TO CHAPTER 12

1. *Thinking Adults: Thinking Children* conference, held at Roedean School, Johannesburg, 13 February 2010.
2. Storywise (Murris & Haynes, 2002, 2010) provides worked examples using picturebooks and offers a wide variety of classroom activities to enable philosophical discussion of such themes.
3. The term 'troublesome knowledge' is used here to refer to experiences of learning that create political or emotional disturbance and difficulty because they are sensitive, alarming, or controversial for people in particular times and places. Such terminology implies that knowledge is not neutral, but rather it is situated with people and between people.
4. SAPERE/NUT conference on Philosophy for Children held NUT headquarters in London, November 2006.
5. In the UK, some universities now have policies that can position teaching staff in an ambiguous, surveillance role, and the Department for Children, Schools, and Families and the Home Office have commissioned research into teaching methods that help prevent violent extremism.
6. Philosophy of education no longer features in teacher education courses in England. Trainees are taught how children develop and learn and how to manage their behaviour.
7. Professor Robin Alexander directed a very comprehensive and evidence based review of primary education at Cambridge University (2009). Sir Jim Rose was commissioned by the Labour government in England to carry out a review of the primary curriculum, and the final report was also published in 2009. Rose, J. (2009).
8. For broad ranging discussion on philosophical ideas regarding the teacher and teaching, readers are encouraged to refer to the special issue of *Journal of Philosophy of Education* 39 (2) written by Nigel Tubb (2005).
9. As far as critical theory in education is concerned, key writers to consult include Michael Apple, Paulo Freire, Henry Giroux, Peter McLaren, and Bel Hooks.
10. Murris (2008b:680) tackles this common problem among novice facilitators in P4C.
11. This is the intention of the web of intriguing ideas in Storywise (Murris & Haynes, 2002), which offers teachers ideas from the history of philosophy, according to some of the common themes that emerge in enquiries, such as love, punishment, power, freedom, self, and good and bad.

NOTES TO CHAPTER 13

1. In the UK, many schools have been taken up with a new resource pack called Social and Emotional Aspects of Learning (SEAL) Improving Behaviour, Improving Learning, published in 2005, as part of the education department's National Primary Strategy. According to http://nationalstrategies. standards.dcsf.gov.uk/primary/publications/banda/seal, '*This curriculum resource aims to develop the underpinning qualities and skills that help promote positive behaviour and effective learning. It focuses on five social and emotional aspects of learning: self-awareness, managing feelings, motivation, empathy and social skills*'. In our work with teachers, we have found that many are enthusiastic about P4C because they see it as a vehicle for implementing SEAL. One could argue that teachers perceive it as a behaviour

modification programme, but one they feel more comfortable with because it is participatory.

2. For example, the UNICEF report. *Child Poverty in Perspective Report Card 7: An Overview of Child Well Being in Rich Countries* (2007).

3. In this case, traversing and working at the boundaries of human and social science.

4. In this case, challenging, for example, unhelpful dichotomising of women's/gender studies and childhood studies and moving away from treating children as a homogenous group, without reference to social divisions of disability, culture, race, class, and so on.

5. Philosophy (*philosophia*) is widely translated from the Greek as love of wisdom.

6. 'Childism' refers to the idea of children as a political minority and likens the unfair and discriminatory treatment of children to that of people according to either their gender, as in sexism, or their ethnic origin, as in racism.

7. Research begins from what catches our attention. Within the framework of practitioner research, a number of accounts are offered of events that alert the researcher to a 'something' to be questioned. In *Teaching as Learning: An Action Research Approach*, Jean McNiff (1993:33) refers to moments when practitioners identify a concern through a felt gap, or contradiction, between values and action. When acknowledged, such contradictions generate questions that can lead to enquiry and modification of theory and practice. In *Researching your own Classroom Practice: From Noticing to Reflection*, John Mason (2002:33) refers to these moments as 'noticing' and has distinguished 'forms of noticing' as well as practical processes for using these in a disciplined way to inform professional judgment. In *Critical Incidents in Teaching: Developing Professional Judgment*, David Tripp (1993) suggests that incidents in practice become significant when they strikingly appear as an example of a wider social category or dramatically contrast with previous experience. These events stand out and can become turning points in professional life.

Author Biographies

Joanna Haynes is Associate Professor in Education Studies at the University of Plymouth, England. Following undergraduate studies in philosophy at the University of Kent, Joanna taught in primary schools in inner city Glasgow and Bristol, before gradually moving into teacher education and professional development and undertaking a Master's degree in education at Bristol University in the late 1980s. Her PhD (University of Exeter) is in philosophy with children. She is author of *Children as Philosophers* (2002, 2008) and co-author, with Karin Murris, of *Storywise: Thinking through Stories*. Joanna has been actively involved in writing, presenting, teaching, and leading courses in the field of philosophy with children since 1994. Her main research interests are in everyday ethics and critical and transformative pedagogies, and she is currently involved with a project concerning the teaching of unsettling and troublesome knowledge.

Karin Murris is Visiting Professor at the University of Wales in Newport (UK) and senior lecturer at the School of Education, University of the Witwatersrand (Wits) in Johannesburg, South Africa. She studied library science in Amsterdam, philosophy at the University of Leiden (NL), University of London (MA), and completed her PhD in philosophy with children in 1997. Trained under Professor Matthew Lipman, she pioneered the use of picturebooks for the teaching of philosophy and helped to set up the professional development courses in philosophy with children in Britain. As co-director of consultancy *Dialogueworks* she has worked as an integrity consultant and philosophy with children senior trainer with children and adults in schools, businesses, and universities for 20 years. Since starting at Wits School of Education, she has set up a Master's package and other post-graduate courses. She also teaches PGCE students and supervises PhD, Master's, and Honours students. She is the author of *Teaching Philosophy with Picture Books* (1992), and *Storywise: Thinking through Stories* (with Joanna Haynes). Her research interests include philosophy of education, professional dilemmas and ethical issues in educational research, and children's literature.

References

Abbs, P. (1993) 'On Intellectual Research as Socratic Activity' in Peter Abbs (ed.). *Socratic Education. Aspects of Education*, Hull: University of Hull, No. 49, 1993:66–76.

Abbs, P. (1994) *The Educational Imperative: A Defence of Socratic and Aesthetic Learning.* London and Washington DC: Falmer Press.

Adams, R. & Rabkin E. (2006) 'Psyche and Society in Sendak's In the Night Kitchen' in *Children's Literature in Education* 38(4):233–41.

Alexander, R. (2004) *Towards Dialogic Teaching: Rethinking Classroom Talk.* Cambridge: Dialogos UK Ltd.

Alexander, R. (Ed.) (2009) *Children, their World, their Education: Final Report and Recommendations of the Cambridge Primary Review.* London: Routledge.

Allan, J. (2008) *Rethinking inclusion: the philosophers of difference in practice.* Dordrecht: Springer.

Archard, D. (1993) *Children: Rights and Childhood.* Abingdon and New York: Routledge

Archard, D. (2004) *Children: Rights and Childhood,* (2nd edn.). Abingdon and New York: Routledge.

Aristotle. "Poetics"; In: McKeon, Richard (ed.). (1973), *Introduction to Aristotle*; 2nd ed. Chicago, Univ. of Chicago Press, pp. 668–716.

Arizpe, E. & Styles, M. (2003) *Children Reading Pictures: Interpreting Visual Texts.* London: Routledge Falmer.

Bachelard, G. (1958/1994) *The Poetics of Space.* Boston: Beacon Press.

Bachelard, G. (1960/1971) *The Poetics of Reverie.* Boston: Beacon Press.

Baddeley, P. & Eddershaw, C. (1994) Not So Simple Picture Books: Developing responses to literature with 4–12 year olds. Stoke-on-Trent, Trentham Books.

Barnes, P. (2002) Obituaries: 'Peter Bayliss' in *The Guardian* newspaper, 5/8/2002.

Baumfield, V.M. (2006) 'Tools for Pedagogical Inquiry: The Impact of Teaching Thinking Skills on Teachers' in *Oxford Review of Education* 32(2):185–196.

Baumrind, D. (1967) 'Child-care practices anteceding three patterns of preschool Behavior' in *Genetic Psychology Monographs,* 75, 43–88.

Benhabib, S. (1992) *Situating the Self: Gender, Community and Postmodernism in Contemporary Ethics.* Cambridge: Polity Press.

Berger, J. (2000) *King.* London: Bloomsbury.

Bettelheim, B. (1991) *The Uses of Enchantment: The Meaning and Importance of Fairy Tales.* Harmondsworth: Penguin.

Bettelheim, B. & Zelan, K. (1981) *On Learning to Read: The Child's Fascination with Meaning.* New York: Knopf.

Biesta, G. (2006) *Beyond Learning.* Boulder, USA: Paradigm Publishers.

Biesta, G. (2009) 'Philosophy, Exposure and Children: How to Resist the Instrumentalisation of Philosophy in Education', presented at the *British Education Research Association Conference* held in Manchester, England.

Biesta, G.J.J. & Burbules, N. (2003) *Pragmatism and Educational Research*. Lanham

Blackburn, S. (1996) *Oxford Dictionary of Philosophy*. Oxford University Press.

Bohm, D. (1996) *On Dialogue*. Edited by Lee Nichol. London: Routledge.

Bonnett, M. (1994) *Children's Thinking: Promoting Understanding in the Primary School*. London: Cassell.

Bonnett, M. (1995) 'Teaching Thinking and the Sanctity of Content' in *Journal of Philosophy of Education* 29 (3):295–309.

Bonnett, M & Cuypers, S. (2003) 'Autonomy and Authenticity in Education' in *The Blackwell Guide to the Philosophy of Education* edited by Blake, N., Smeyers, P., Smith, R., & P. Standish (Eds). Oxford: Blackwell, pp. 326–340.

Bosch, E. (2001) A Philosophical Approach to Contemporary Art: looking out aloud in T. Curnow (Ed) *Thinking Through Dialogue* (Oxford: Practical Philosophy Press) pp 166–169.

Bosch, E. (2005) *Education and Everyday Life: Short Stories with Long Endings, Philosophy for Children*. Moorabin, Victoria, Australia: Hawker Brownlow Education.

Bradman, T. & Ross, T. (1990) *Michael*. London: Andersen Press.

Brandt, R. (1988) On Philosophy in the Curriculum: A Conversation with Matthew Lipman. In: *Educational Leadership*, 46(1): 34–43.

Brann, E. (1993) Through Fantasia to Philosophy—Review with Reminiscences, in: Lipman, Matthew (ed.). *Thinking, Children and Education*. Montclair, Kendall/Hunt, pp. 287–297.

Browne, A. (1985) *Willy the Wimp*. London: Julia MacRae/Walker Books.

Browne, A. (1990) *Changes*. London: Walker Books.

Browne, A. (1991) *Willy and Hugh*. London: Julia MacRae/Random House.

Browne, A. (1993) *Zoo*. London: Julia MacRae.

Browne, A. (1995) *Willy the Wizard*. London: Julia MacRae.

Browne, A. (1997) *The Tunnel*. London: Walker Books.

Browne, A. (2006) *The World of Anthony Browne*; DvD. Jaromin Publishing; www.childrensauthors.tv.

Browne, A. (2006) *The Retreat of Reason: Political Correctness and the Corruption of Public Debate in Modern Britain*. London: Civitas, Institute for the Study of Civil Society.

Bruner, J. (1986) *Actual Minds, Possible Worlds*. Cambridge, Mass.: Harvard University Press.

Bruner, J. (1996) *The Culture of Education*. Cambridge, Mass.: Harvard University Press.

Bruner, J. (2002) *Making Stories: Law, Literature, Life*. Cambridge, Mass.: Harvard University Press.

Bruno, G. (2002) *Atlas of Emotion: Journeys in Art, Architecture and Film*. London: Verso.

Buckreis, S. (2005) 'Questioning with Derrida', paper presented to the *Philosophy of Education Society of Great Britain Conference*, April 2005. Oxford, England.

Burbules, N. (1995) 'Reasonable Doubt: Toward a Postmodern Defense of Reason as an Educational Aim' in Kohli, W. (Ed.), *Critical Conversations in Philosophy of Education*, New York: Routledge. pp 82–103.

Burbules, N.C. & Bruce, B.C. (2001) 'Theory and Research on Teaching as Dialogue' in V. Richardson & American Educational Research Association (Eds.),

Handbook of Research on Teaching, Vol. 4. Washington, D.C.: American Educational Research Association.

Burkitt, I. (1999) *Bodies of Thought: Embodiment, Identity and Modernity*. London: Sage.

Burman, E. (2008a) *Deconstructing Developmental Psychology*. 2nd Edn. London and New York: Routledge.

Burman, E. (2008b) *Developments: Child, Image, Nation*. London and New York: Routledge.

Burman, E (2009) 'Beyond 'emotional literacy' in feminist and educational research' in *British Educational Research Journal*, 35, 137–155.

Burningham, J. (1978) *Would you rather....*London: Jonathan Cape.

Cahen, D. (2001) 'Derrida and the question of education: a new space for philosophy in Biesta, G.J.J. and Egea-Kuehne, D. (Eds.), *Derrida and Education*. London and New York: Routledge, pp. 12–31.

Cam, P. (2000) 'Philosophy and Freedom' in *Thinking: The Journal of Philosophy for Children*, 15(1):10–13.

Carey, J., (2004) 'Frog and friends' in *The Guardian* newspaper, 11/12/04.

Carle, E. (1969) *The Very Hungry Caterpillar*. Putnam: Hamish Hamilton

Cassidy, C. (2007) *Thinking Children: The Concept of 'Child' from a Philosophical Perspective*. London, Continuum.

Channel 4 (1994) *Class Action*. Documentary broadcast in England, November 1994.

Cherkasova, E. (2004) 'Philosophy as Sideshadowing: The Philosophical, the Literary and the Fantastical' in Carel, H & D. Gamez (Eds) *What Philosophy Is*. London: Continuum, pp 200–211.

Chetty, D. (2008) 'Philosophy For Children And Antiracist Education: To What Extent Does P4c Complement Antiracism?' MA in Education Dissertation, *Goldsmiths College, University of London*, September 2008.

Chetty, D. & Splitter, L. (2005) 'Challenging Philosophy for Children' in SAPERE Newsletter February 2005:3–6.

Child, L., & Borland P. (2005) *The Princess and the Pea*. London: Puffin.

Chinnery, A. (2003) 'Aesthetics of Surrender: Levinas and the Disruption of Agency in Moral Education' in *Studies in Philosophy and Education* 22: 5–17.

Clark, A., McQuail, S. & Moss, P. (2003) 'Exploring the Field of Listening to and Involving Young Children', *Research Report 445*. London: DfES.

Clarke, A. & Moss, P. (2003) *Listening to Young Children: The Mosaic Approach*. London: National Children's Bureau.

Clark, A. (2004) *Listening as a Way of Life: Why and How We Listen to Young Children*. London: National Children's Bureau: www.ncb.org.uk.

Clark, M. (1993) Writing for Children. London: A&C Black.

Cole, A.L. & Gary-Knowles J. (2000) *Exploring Teacher Development through Reflexive Inquiry*. Boston: Allyn and Bacon.

Corradi-Fiumara, G. (1990) *The Other Side of Language. A Philosophy of Listening.*London: Routledge.

Corradi-Fiumara, G. (1995) *The Metaphoric Process: Connections between Language and Life*. London: Routledge.

Cowley, C. (2006) 'Narrative and the Personal in Ethics' in *Practical Philosophy*, 8, (1):8–17.

Cox A., & Robinson-Pant S. et al, (2003) *Empowering Children through Visual Communication*. Norwich: University of East Anglia: School of Education and Professional Development www.uea.ac.uk

Cunningham, H. (2006) *The Invention of Childhood: with The Voices of Children by Michael Morpurgo*. London: BBC Books.

Curley, T.V. (1993) 'The Right to Education: An Inquiry Into Its Foundations' in Lipman, M. (Ed.) *Thinking, Children and Education*. Duboque, Iowa: Kendall/Hunt, pp 17–26.

Dahlberg, G. & Moss, P. (2005) *Ethics and Politics in Early Childhood Education*. London: Routledge.

Daniel, M-F. (2005) 'Learning to dialogue in kindergarten: a case study' in *e-Analytic Teaching* 25(3):25–52.

Davis, A. (2001) 'Do Children Have Privacy Rights in the Classroom?' in *Studies in Philosophy and Education* 20, pp.245–254.

De Haan, C. (1995) Deweyan aesthetics in the philosophy classroom: finding a voice in philosophy. *Thinking* 3(1), pp 1–8.

De Rijke, V. & Hollands, H. (2006) 'Leap of Faith: An Interview with Max Velthuijs' in *Children's Literature and Education*, Vol 37:185–197.

Dewey, J. (1978), "Thinking in Education"; In: M. Lipman and A. M. Sharp (eds.). *Growing up with Philosophy*. Philadelphia:Temple Univ. Press, pp. 40–50.

Dewey, J. (1991) 'Art as Experience' in Wilkinson, R. (Ed.) *Theories of Art & Beauty*. Milton Keynes: Open University Press. pp 232–248.

Dewey, J. 'My Pedagogic Creed' first published in *The School Journal*, Volume LIV, Number 3 (January 16, 1897), pages 77–80.

Doonan, J. (1993) *Looking at Pictures in Picture Books*. Stroud: Thimble Press.

Donaldson, M. (1993) *Human Minds: An Exploration*. London: Penguin.

Dunne, J. (1997) *Back to the Rough Ground: Practical Judgment and the Lure of Technique*. Notre Dame and London: University of Notre Dame Press.

Dunne, J. & Pendlebury, S. (2003) 'Practical Reason' in Blake, N. et al (Eds.) *The Blackwell Guide to the Philosophy of Education*. Oxford: Blackwell, pp 194–212.

Dyfed County Council (1994) *Improving Reading Standards in Primary Schools Projects: Final Report GEST 1993–94*. Dyfed County Council, Camarthen, South Wales.

Ecclestone, K. and Hayes, D. (2009) *The Dangerous Rise of Therapeutic Education*. London: Routledge.

Egan, K. (1988) *Teaching as Storytelling. An Alternative Approach to Teaching and the Curriculum*. London Ontario: University of Western Ontario.

Egan, K., (1991) *Primary Understanding: Education in Early Childhood*. London: Routledge.

Egan, K. (1992) *Imagination in Teaching and Learning; ages 8–15*. London: Routledge.

Egan, K., (1993) 'The Other Half of the Child' in Lipman, M. (Ed.) *Thinking, Children and Education*. Montclair, Kendall/Hunt, pp 301–305.

Egan, K. (1995) Narrative and Learning: A Voyage of Implications, in H. McEwan & K. Egan (Eds) *Narrative in Teaching, learning, and Research*. New York: Teachers College Press, pp 116–124.

Egan, K. (1997) *The Educated Mind: how cognitive tools shape our understanding*. University of Chicago Press.

Egan, K. (1999) *Children's Minds, Talking Rabbits and Clockwork Oranges: Essays on Education,* with a foreword by Elliott W. Eisner. New York and London: Teachers College Press.

Egan, K. & Ling, M. (2002) We Begin as Poets, in L. Bresler & C.M. Thompson(Eds) *The Arts in Children's Lives: Context, Culture and Curriculum*. Dordrecht: Kluwer, pp 93–101.

Elliott, J. (2006) 'Educational Research as a Form of Democratic Rationality', *Journal of Philosophy of Education*, 40(2):169–85.

Ende, M. (1993) 'Literature for Children?' in Lipman, M.(Ed.) *Thinking, Children and Education* (Montclair: Kendall/Hunt) pp 281–286.

Feary, V. (2005) 'Art and the good life: The role of literature and the visual arts in philosophical practice' in: *Philosophical Practice*, July 2005, 1(2): 95–112.

Fendler, L. (2001) 'Educating Flexible Souls: the construction of subjectivity through developmentality and interaction' in Hultquist, K. & Dahlberg, G. (Eds.) *Governing the Child in the New Millenium*. New York and London: RoutledgeFalmer, pp. 119–142.

Fielding, M. (2006) 'Leadership, radical student engagement and the necessity of a person-centred education' in *International Journal of Leadership and Education* 9(4):299–313.

Fielding, M. (2007) 'Beyond 'voice': New roles, relations and contexts in researching with young people' in *Discourse* 28(3):301–310.

Fielding, M. & Rudduck, J. (2006) Student voice and the perils of popularity in Educational Review 58 (2):219–31.

Fisher, R. (1998) Teaching Thinking: Philosophical Enquiry in the Classroom. London: Cassell.

Freeman, D. (1976) *Corduroy*. Harmondsworth: Picture Puffins, Penguin.

Friquegnon, M.L. (1993) 'Children's Responsibilities' in Lipman, M. (Ed.) *Thinking, Children and Education*. Duboque, Iowa: Kendall/Hunt, pp 45–58.

Friquegnon, M.L. (1997) 'What is a Child' in *Thinking, American Journal of Philosophy for Children*, 13(1):12–16.

Foreman-Peck, L. (2005) 'How Should We Understand the Teaching of Controversial Topics?' in *Prospero*, 11(4):12–19.

Fox, G. (1996). Reading Picture Books...How to? In: Styles, M & E. Bearne (Eds) *Voices: Texts, Contexts and Readers*. London: Cassell.

Fox R. (2001) 'Can Children Be Philosophical?' in *Teaching Thinking*, Issue 4, Summer 2001, pp.46–49.

Furedi, F. (2005) *The Politics of Fear*. London: Continuum.

Furedi, F. (2009) *Wasted. Why Education isn't Educating*. London: Continuum.

Gadamer, H-G. (1975) *Truth and Method*; translated by G. Barden & J. Cumming. New York: Seabury.

Gardner, H. (1999) *Intelligence Reframed: Multiple Intelligences for the 21ˢᵗ Century*.New York: Basic Books.

Gaiman N. & McKean, D. (1998) *The day I swapped my dad for two goldfish*. Clarkston, GA: White Wolf Publishing.

Gaiman N. & McKean, D. (2003) *The Wolves in the Walls*. London: Bloomsbury.

Gaita, R. (2002) *A Common Humanity: Thinking about Love and Truth and Justice*. London: Routledge.

Gaita, R. (2004) *The Philosopher's Dog*. London: Routledge.

Garber, M., Hanssen, B. & Walkowitz, R.L. (2000) (Eds.) *The Turn to Ethics*. London and New York: Routledge.

Gardner, H. (1999) *Intelligence Reframed: Multiple Intelligences for the 21ˢᵗ Century* New York: Basic Books.

Gardner, S. T. (1996) 'Inquiry is no mere conversation (or discussion or dialogue): facilitation of inquiry is hard work!' in Analytic Teaching, 16(2):41–47.

Gearon, L. (2010) *Education, Politics and Religion*. London and New York: Routledge.

Glover, J. (2005) 'Dialogue is the only way to end the cycle of violence' in *The Guardian* newspaper 27/7/2005

Goldie, P. (2010) Love for a Reason. In: *Emotion Review* 2010; 2; 61.

Goldstone, B. (2008). 'The Paradox of Space in Postmodern Picturebooks' in L.R. Sipe & Pantaleo, S. (Eds) *Postmodern Picturebooks:Play, Parody and Self-referentiality*. London: Routledge. pp 117–130.

Goleman, D. (1996) *Emotional Intelligence: Why it Can Matter More Than IQ*. London: Bloomsbury.

Goodson, I., Biesta, G.J.J., Tedder, M. & Adair, N. (2010) *Narrative Learning*. London: Routledge.

Graham, J. (1990) *Pictures on the Page*. Sheffield: National Association for the Teaching of English.

Greder, A. (2007) *The Island*. Crows Nest, NSW: Allen & Unwin.

Greene, M. (1995) 'What counts as Philosophy of Education' in Kohli, W. (Ed.), *Critical Conversations in Philosophy of Education*, New York: Routledge, pp 3–23.

Greene, M. & Griffiths, M. (2003) 'Feminism, Philosophy and Education: Imagining Public Spaces' in Blake, N., Smeyers, P., Smith, R. & Standish, P. (Eds.), *The Blackwell Guide to the Philosophy of Education*. Oxford: Blackwell. pp.73–92.

Gregory, M. (2008) 'On Philosophy, Children and Taboo Topics'. Statement by the I.A.P.C. discussed at SAPERE conference Birmingham June 2005 and published 2008 in *Philosophy for Children Practitioner Handbook* edited by M. Gregory. Montclair State University: Institute for the Advancement of Philosophy for Children (IAPC).

Griffiths, M. (Ed.), (2003) *Action for Social Justice in Education: Fairly Different*. Maidenhead and Philadelphia: Open University Press.

Griffiths, M. & Cotton, T. (2005) 'Action Research , Stories and Practical Philosophy', paper presented at conference of Collaborative Action Research Network/ Practitioner Action Research *Quality of Practitioner Research/Action Research: What's it about, what's it for and what next?* Utrecht, The Netherlands. 4–6th November, 2005.

Griswold, C.L., (1986) *Self-knowledge in Plato's Phaedrus*. New Haven: Yale University Press.

Gur-Ze-ev, I. (1998) 'Toward a non-repressive critical pedagogy' in *Educational Theory* 48 (4):463–486.

Hannam, P. & Echeverria, E. (2009) *Philosophy with Teenagers: nurturing a moral imagination for the 21st century*. London: Continuum.

Haynes, J., (2005a) 'Secrets and Boundaries in Classroom Dialogues with Children: From Critical Episode to Social Enquiry' in *Childhood and Philosophy*, Online journal of the International Council for Philosophical Inquiry for Children, 1(2) July-December, 2005 www.filoeduc.org/childphilo/n2/JoannaHaynes.pdf.

Haynes, J. (2005b) 'The costs of thinking' in *Teaching Thinking and Creativity* Autumn 2005, Issue 17, pp32–38. Birmingham: Imaginative Minds.

Haynes J. (2007a) *Listening as a Critical Practice: Learning from Philosophy with Children*, PhD thesis submitted for examination to University of Exeter.

Haynes, J. (2007b) 'Freedom and the Urge to Think' in *Gifted Education International, Special Issue on Philosophy for Children*, 22(2/3):229–237, edited by Belle Wallace and Guest Editor: Barry Hymer.

Haynes, J. (2008) *Children as Philosophers*, 2nd Ed. London: RoutledgeFalmer.

Haynes, J. (2009a) 'Listening to the Voice of Child in Education' in Gibson, S. & Haynes, J. (Eds.) *Perspectives on Participation and Inclusion: Engaging Education*. pp 27- 41. London: Continuum.

Haynes, J. (2009b) 'Freedom, Inclusion and Education' Chapter 5, in Gibson, S. & Haynes, J. (Eds.) *Perspectives on Participation and Inclusion: Engaging Education*. pp 76–89. London: Continuum.

Haynes, J. (2009c) 'Dialogue as a playful and subversive space in communities of philosophical enquiry' in online journal *Critical and Reflective Practice in Education*, 1 (1). http://www.marjon.ac.uk/research/criticalandreflectivepracticeineducation/volume1issue1/

Haynes, J., & Murris, K. (2000) 'Listening, juggling and travelling in philosophical Space'   in *Critical and Creative Thinking, Australasian Journal of Philosophy for Children*: 8 (1):23–32.

Haynes, J. & Murris, K. (2004) 'What If Heaven Is Full?' in *Teaching Thinking and Creativity*, Spring 2004, Issue 14: 66–68. Birmingham: Imaginative Minds.

Haynes, J & Murris, K. (2009) 'The Wrong Message: risk, censorship and the struggle for democracy in the primary school' in *Thinking*, 19(1):2–12.

Haynes, J. & Murris, K. (2011) 'The Provocation of an Epistemological Shift in Teacher Education through Philosophy with Children' in *Journal of Philosophy of Education Special Issue on Philosophy for Children* 45 (2): 285–303.

Heidegger, M. (1966) *Discourse on Thinking*. New York: Harper and Row.

Heidegger, M. (1971) 'Building Dwelling Thinking' in *Poetry, Language, Thought*, translated by Albert Hofstadter. New York: Harper Colophon Books.

Heidegger, M. & Krell, D.F. (Ed.) (1993) *Martin Heidegger: Basic Writings*. London: Routledge.

Higgins, S., Baumfield, V., Lin, M., Moseley, D., Butterworth, M., Downey, G., Gregson, M., Oberski, I., Rockett, M., & Thacker, D. (2004) 'Thinking skills approaches to effective teaching and learning: what is the evidence for impact on learners?' in *Research Evidence in Education Library*. London: EPPI-Centre, Social Science Research Unit, Institute of Education, University of London.

Hochschild, A. (1983) *The Managed Heart: Commercialization of Human Feeling*. Berkeley: University of California Press.

Hofkins, D. & Northen, S. (Eds.) (2009) *Introducing the Cambridge Primary Review*. Cambridge University Faculty of Education: Cambridge. www.primaryreview.org.uk

Hollindale, P. (1988) *Ideology and the Children's Book* (Stroud: Thimble Press)

Hughes, J. (1995) 'The Philosopher's Child' in *Thinking, American Journal of Philosophy for Children* 10 (1):38–44.

Hultqvist, K. & Dahlberg, G. (Eds.), (2001) *Governing the Child in the New Millenium*. New York and London: RoutledgeFalmer.

Hunt, P. (Ed) (1992) *Literature for Children: Contemporary Criticism.*London: Routledge.

Hunt, P. (1999) Introduction: The World of Children's Literature Studies. In: P. Hunt (Ed) *Understanding Children's Literature* (London, Routledge)

Hunt, P. (2001) *Children's Literature*. Oxford: Blackwell Press.

Iredale, M. (1997) 'Different way of not being real' in *The Philosophers Magazine*, Issue 39, pp 25–6.

Irigeray, L. (1996)) *i love to you: Sketch for a Felicity Within History*. Translated from the French by Alison Martin. New York and London: Routledge.

James A. and Prout A. (Eds.), (1997) *Constructing and Reconstructing Childhood: Contemporary Issues in the Sociological Study of Childhood*. London and Washington DC: Falmer Press. 2nd Edn.

Janks, H. (2010) *Literacy and Power*. New York: Routledge.

Jaynes, J. (1990) *The Origin of Consciousness in the Breakdown of the Bicameral Mind* (new ed.) Boston: Houghton Mifflin.

Jones, W. T. (1970) *The Classical Mind*, 2nd Ed. New York: Harcourt Brace Jovanovich.

John, M. (2003) *Children's Rights and Power: Charging Up for a New Century*. London: Jessica Kingsley.

Johnson, M. (1987) *The Body in the Mind; the Bodily Basis of Meaning, Imagination, and Reason* (Chicago: University of Chicago Press)

Johnson, M. (2007) *The Meaning of the Body: Aesthetics of Human Understanding*. Chicago University Press.

Kelly, A.V. (1995) *Education and Democracy*. London: Paul Chapman.

Kennedy, D. (1992) 'Why Philosophy for Children Now?' in *Thinking, American Journal of Philosophy for Children* 10(3):2–6.

Kennedy, D. (1998) 'Reconstructing Childhood' in *Thinking, American Journal of Philosophy for Children* 14(1):29–37.

Kennedy, D. (1999) 'Philosophy for Children and the Reconstruction of Philosophy', paper presented at the *Conference of the Society of Consultant Philosophers*. Wadham College: Oxford, 27th-30th July 1999.

Kennedy, D. (2006) *The Well of Being, Childhood, Subjectivity and Education.* Albany: State University of New York Press.

Kennedy, D. & Kohan, W. (2008) 'Aión, Kairós And Chrónos: Fragments Of An Endless Conversation on Childhood, Philosophy and Education' in *Childhood & Philosophy*, Rio de Janeiro, 4 (8) July, 2008. www.periodicos.proped.pro.br/index.php?journal=childhood&page=index

Kitamura, S. (2006) *Ignore the Bird Who Couldn't Sing.* London: Anderson Press.

Kitamura, S. & Oram, H. (2004) *In the Attic.* London: Andersen Press.

Kohan W. (1998) 'What Can Philosophy and Children Offer Each Other?' in *Thinking, American Journal of Philosophy for Children* 14(4):2–8.

Kohan W. (2002) 'Education, philosophy and childhood: The need to think an encounter' in *Thinking, American Journal of Philosophy for Children* 16(1): 4–11.

Kohan, W. (2009) 'Philosophizing with children: the meaning of an experience' in *Farhang, Journal of the Institute for Humanities and Cultural Studies, Tehran, Iran. Special Edition on Philosophy for Children* 22 (69): 13–29, published in English and Farsi.

Kohli, W. (1995) 'Educating for Emancipatory Rationality', in Kohli,W. (Ed.), *Critical Conversations in Philosophy of Education.* New York and London: Routledge, pp.103–115.

Kristjansson, K (2005) 'Can We Teach Justified Anger?' in *Journal of Philosophy of Education*, 39 (4):671–89.

Kristjansson, K. (2007) *Aristotle, Emotions, and Education.* Aldershot: Ashgate.

Kristjansson, K. (2010) 'Emotion Education without Ontological Commitment?' in *Studies in Philosophy of Education* 29:259–274.

Kuier, G. (1981) *Het Geminachte Kind.* Amsterdam: Arbeiderspers.

Kushner, T. (2003) *The Art of Maurice Sendak.* New York: Harry N. Abrams Inc.

Lake, M. (1990) *Primary Thinking Skills Project: Houses and Homes.* Birmingham: Questions Publishing Co.

Lakoff, G. & Johnson, M. (1980) *Metaphors We Live By.* Chicago: University of Chicago Press.

Lakoff, G. & Johnson, M. (1999) *Philosophy in the Flesh: the Embodied Mind and its Challenge to Western Thought.* New York: Basic Books.

Lanes, S. (1980) *The Art of Maurice Sendak.* New York: Harry N. Abrams Inc.

Law, S. (2006) *The War for Children's Minds.* London and New York: Routledge.

Leeson, C. (2007) 'Going round in circles: key issues in the development of an effective ethical protocol for research involving young children' in Campbell, A. and Groundwater–Smith, S. (2007) *An Ethical Approach to Practitioner Research*, Oxon: Routledge, pp. 129–143.

Lesnik-Oberstein, K. (1999) Essentials: What is Children's Literature? What is Childhood? In: P. Hunt (Ed) *Understanding Children's Literature.* London: Routledge.

Letwin, L. (1993) 'Education and the Constitutional Rights of Children' in Lipman, M. (Ed.) *Thinking, Children and Education.* Duboque, Iowa: Kendall/Hunt, pp 6–16.

Levering, B. (2006) 'Epistemological Issues in Phenomenological Research: How Authoritative Are People's Accounts of their own Perceptions?' in *Journal of Philosophy of Education*, 40, (4):451–462.

Levin, D.M. (1989) *The Listening Self: Personal Growth, Social Change and the Closure of Metaphysics.* London and New York: Routledge.

Lewis, D. (2001) *Reading Contemporary Picturebooks: Picturing Text*. London: Routledge.

Lewis, L. (2007) 'Philosophy and the Emotions' in *Teaching Thinking and Creativity*, 8(1) Issue 22:61–66. Birmingham: Imaginative Minds.

Linders, J. (2003). *Ik Bof Dat Ik Een Kikker Ben: Leven en Werk van Max Velthuijs*Amsterdam: Leopold.

Lingard, R. Hayes, D. & Mills, M. (2003) 'Teachers and Productive Pedagogies: contextualising, conceptualising, utilising' in *Pedagogy, Culture and Society* 11(3) 2003: 399–424.

Lionni, L. (1974) *Fish is Fish*. New York: Dragonfly Books.

Lipman, M. (1988a) *Elfie*. Montclair, New Jersey: Institute for the Advancement of Philosophy for Children.

Lipman, M. (1988b) *Philosophy Goes to School*. Philadelphia, Temple University Press.

Lipman, M. (1991) *Thinking in Education*. Cambridge, Mass.: Cambridge University Press.

Lipman, M. (1993a) 'Developing Philosophies of Childhood' in Lipman, M. (Ed.) *Thinking, Children and Education*. Duboque, Iowa: Kendall/Hunt, pp. 143–148.

Lipman, M. (1993b) 'The educational value of philosophy' in *Critical and Creative Thinking*, 1, (1): 1–6. Birmingham: Imaginative Minds.

Lipman, M. (Ed.) (1993c) *Thinking, Children and Education*. Duboque, Iowa: Kendall/Hunt.

Lipman, M. (1997) 'Philosophical Discussion Plans and Exercises' in *Critical and Creative Thinking*, Vol. 5, March 1997, pp. 1–17. Birmingham: Imaginative Minds.

Lipman, M. (2003). *Thinking in education* (2nd Ed) .Cambridge: Cambridge University Press.

Lipman, M. & Gazzard, A. (1988) *Getting our Thoughts Together: Instructional Manual to Accompany Elfie*. Montclair, New Jersey, Institute for the Advancement of Philosophy for Children, with University Press of America.

Lipman, M. & Sharp, A.M. (1984) *Looking for Meaning: Instructional Manual to Accompany Pixie*. Montclair, New Jersey: Institute for the Advancement of Philosophy for Children, with University Press of America.

Lipman, M. & Sharp, A.M. (1985) *Ethical Inquiry: Instructional Manual to Accompany Lisa*. Montclair, New Jersey: Institute for the Advancement of Philosophy for Children, with University Press of America.

Lipman, M. & Sharp, A.M. (1986) *Wondering at the World: Instructional Manual to Accompany Kio and Gus*. Montclair, New Jersey: Institute for the Advancement of Philosophy for Children, with University Press of America.

Lipman, M., Sharp, A.M. & Oscanyan, F.S. (1980) *Philosophy in the Classroom*; (2nd Ed.). Philadelphia: Temple University Press.

Lipman, M., Sharp, A.M. & Oscanyan, F.S. (1984) *Philosophical Inquiry: An Instructional manual to Accompany Harry Stottlemeyer's Discovery*; (2nd Ed.). Montclair, New Jersey: Institute for the Advancement of Philosophy for Children.

Lipman, M., Sharp, A.M. & Oscanyan, F.S. (1980) *Philosophy in the Classroom*; (2nd Ed.). Philadelphia: Temple University Press.

Lipman, M. (1982) *Harry Stottlemeyer's Discovery*. Montclair, New Jersey, Institute for the Advancement of Philosophy for Children.

Liptai, S. (2005) 'What is the meaning of this cup and that dead shark? Philosophical inquiry with objects and works of art and craft' in *Childhood & Philosophy*, 1(2), Jul./Dec. 2005.

Long, F. (2005) 'Thomas Reid and Philosophy with Children' in *Journal of Philosophy of Education*, 39(4):599–615.

Lyotard, J-F. (1992) 'The Postmodern Explained to Children', *Correspondence 1982–1985*. Translation by Pefanis, J. and Thomas, M. London: Turnaround.

McCall, C. (2006) *Laura and Paul*, 3rd Ed. Oxford: Trafford Publishing at www.trafford.com

McCall, C. (2009) *Transforming Thinking: Philosophical Inquiry in the Primary and Secondary Classroom*. London: Routledge.

Maccoby, E.E. (1992) 'The role of parents in the socialization of children: An historical overview' in *Developmental Psychology*, 28, 1006–1017.

MacDonald, M. & J. Riches (1990) *Sam's Worries*. London: ABC.

MacIntyre, A. (1985) *After Virtue: a study in moral theory*, (2nd Ed). London: Duckworth.

McKee, D. (1978) *Tusk Tusk* .London: Andersen Press.

McKee, D. (1980) *Not Now Bernard* . London: Andersen Press.

McKee, D. (1989) *The Monster and the Teddy Bear*. London: Andersen Press.

McNiff, J. (1993) *Teaching as Learning: An Action Research Approach*. London and New York: Routledge.

Mason, J. (2002) *Researching your own Classroom Practice: From Noticing to Reflection*. London and New York: RoutledgeFalmer.

Matthews, G. (1978) 'The Child as Natural Philosopher' in Lipman, M. & Sharp, A. M. (Eds.). *Growing up with Philosophy*. Philadelphia:Temple University Press, pp. 63–77.

Matthews, G. (1980) *Philosophy and the Young Child*. Cambridge, Mass.: Harvard University Press.

Matthews, G. (1984) *Dialogues with Children*. Cambridge, Mass.: Harvard University Press.

Matthews, G. (1992) 'Thinking in Stories' in *Thinking, American Journal of Philosophy for Children*, 10 (2):1.

Matthews, G. (1993a) 'Childhood: The Recapitulation Model' in Lipman, M. (Ed.). *Thinking, Children and Education*. Duboque, Iowa: Kendall/Hunt, pp. 154–160.

Matthews, G. (1993b) 'Philosophy and Children's Literature' in Lipman, M. (Ed.). *Thinking, Children and Education*. Duboque, Iowa: Kendall/Hunt, pp. 274–280.

Matthews, G. (1994) *The Philosophy of Childhood*. Cambridge, Mass.: Harvard University Press.

Matthews, G. (2003) *Socratic Perplexity: And the Nature of Philosophy*. Oxford University Press.

Matthews, G. (2006) 'Thinking in Stories' in *Thinking, American Journal of Philosophy for Children*, 18(1):3.

Matthews, G. (2009) Getting Beyond the Deficit Conception of Childhood in: M. Hand & C. Winstanley (Eds). *Philosophy in Schools*. London, Continuum. pp 27–41.

Mawdsley, J. (1990) Picture Book of All Ages in Wallen, M. (Ed). *Every Picture Tells….*Exeter: National Association for the Teaching of English.

Meadows, S. (2006) *The Child as Thinker: The Development and Acquisition of Cognition in Childhood*, (2nd Ed). London: Routledge.

Mercer, N. (1995) *The Guided Construction of Knowledge: talk amongst teachers and learners*. Clevedon: Multilingual Matters.

Mercer, N. (2000) *Words and Minds: how we use language to think together*. London: Routledge.

Mercer, N. & Littleton, K. (2007*) Dialogue and the Development of Children's Thinking: a sociocultural approach*. London: Routledge.

Miller, A. (2009) A Critique of Positive Psychology—or 'The New Science of Happiness' in Cigman, R. & Davis, A. (Eds). *New Philosophies of Learning*. Oxford: Wiley-Blackwell, pp 221–239.

Moss, E. (1988) *Picture Books for Young People 9–13*. Stroud: Thimble Press.

Murris, K. (1992) Teaching Philosophy with Picturebooks. London, Infonet Publications.

Murris, K. (1993) 'Not Now Socrates...(Part 1)' in *Cogito*, 7(3):236–244.

Murris, K. (1994) 'Not Now Socrates...(Part 2)' in *Cogito*, 8(1):80–86.

Murris, K. (1997) *Metaphors of the Child's Mind: Teaching Philosophy to Young Children*. Phd Thesis, University of Hull.

Murris, K. (1999) 'Philosophy With Preliterate Children' in *Thinking: The American Journal of Philosophy for Children*, 14(4):23–34.

Murris, K. (2000a) 'Can Children do Philosophy?' in *Journal of Philosophy of Education*, 34(2):261–281.

Murris, K. (2000b) 'The Role of the Facilitator in Philosophical Enquiry' in *Thinking, The American Journal of Philosophy for Children*, 15(2): 40–47.

Murris, K. (2001) 'Are Children Natural Philosophers?' in *Teaching Thinking*, Autumn, 2001, Issue 5, pp.46–50.

Murris, K. (2008) 'Autonomous and Authentic Thinking through Philosophy with Picturebooks' in Hand, M. & Winstanley, C. (Eds). *Philosophy in Schools*. London: Continuum.

Murris, K. (2009a) 'Philosophy with Children, the Stingray and the Educative Value of Disequilibrium' in Cigman, R & A Davis, A. (Eds). *New Philosophies of Learning*. Oxford: Wiley-Blackwell, pp 293–311.

Murris, K. (2009b) 'A Philosophical Approach to Emotions: Understanding *Love's Knowledge* through a *Frog in Love*' in: *Childhood and Philosophy*: the official journal of the International Council of Philosophical Inquiry with Children (ICPIC), 5(9) 2009: 5–30. www.periodicos.proped.pro.br/index.php?journal=childhood&page=index

Murris, K. & Haynes, J. (2002) *Storywise: Thinking through Stories*. Newport: Dialogue Works.

Murris, K. & Haynes, J. (2010) *Storywise: Thinking through Stories*. International e-book version. Johannesburg: Infonet. www.infonet-publications.com

Naji, S. (2005) 'Reflections: An Interview with Matthew Lipman' in *Thinking: The American Journal of Philosophy with Children*, 17(4): 23–29.

Neill, A. (2002) 'Fiction and the Emotions,' in Neill, A. & Ridley, A. (Eds) *Arguing about Art: contemporary philosophical debates*. New York: Routledge, pp 250–268.

Nelson, L. (1993) 'The Socratic Method' in Lipman, M. (Ed.), *Thinking, Children and Education*. Diboque, IA: Kendall Hunt, pp. 437–443.

Nikolajeva, M. (2008) Play and playfulness in postmodern picturebooks, in: *Postmodern picturebooks: Play, parody, and self-referentiality*, ed Lawrence Sipe, (New York: Routledge) pp 55–75.

Nikolajeva, M. (2009). *Power, Voice and Subjectivity in Literature for Young Readers*. New York: Routledge.

Nixon, J. Walker, M. & Clough, P. (2003) 'Research at Thoughtful Practice', in Sikes, P. Nixon, J. & Carr, W. (Eds.), *The Moral Foundations of Educational Research: Knowledge, Inquiry and Values*. Maidenhead and Philadelphia: Open University Press.

Nodelman, P. (1988) *Words about Pictures: The Narrative Art of Children's Picture Books*. Athens: The University of Georgia Press.

Nodelman, P. (1999) 'Decoding the Images: Illustration and Picture Books' in Stephens, J. (Ed). *Language and Ideology in Children's Fiction*. London: Longman.

Nussbaum, M. (1990) *Love's Knowledge: Essays on Philosophy and Literature*. Oxford: Oxford University Press.

Nussbaum, M. (2001) *Upheavals of Thought: the Intelligence of Emotions*. Cambridge: Cambridge University Press.

Nussbaum, M. (2004) 'Emotions as Judgments of Value and Importance' in Solomon, R.C. (Ed) *Thinking about Feeling: Contemporary Philosophers on Emotions*. Oxford: Oxford University Press.

Oram H. & Kitamura S. (2004) *In the Attic*. London: Andersen Press.

Ormell, C. (2005) 'The Case for Minimising Controversial Topics in the Curriculum' in *Prospero*, 11(4):3–12.

Paley, V.G. (1987) Wally's Stories. Conversations in the Kindergarten. Harvard University Press.

Paley, V.G. (2005) A Child's Work: The Importance of Fantasy Play. University of Chicago Press.

Pallasmaa, J. (2005). *The Eyes of the Skin: Architecture and the Senses*. Chichester: John Wiley and Sons.

Plato (1995) *Phaedrus*, translation, introduction and notes by Nehemas, A. & Woodruff, P. Indianapolis: Hackett.

Plato (1987) *The Republic*, introduction by Lee, D., (2nd Ed.). London: Penguin.

Plato (1987) *Theaetetus*, introduction by Waterfield, R. H. London: Penguin Classics.

Polkinghorne, D. E. (1988) *Narrative Knowing and the Human Sciences*. New York: State University of New York Press.

Quinn, V. (1997) *Critical Thinking in Young Minds*. London: David Fulton.

Radford, C. (2002) 'How can we be moved by the fate of Anna Karenina?' in Neill, A. & Ridley, (Eds) *Arguing about Art: contemporary philosophical debates*. New York: Routledge, pp 239–250.

Rietti, S. (2009). Emotional Intelligence as Educational Goal: A Case for Caution. In: Cigman, R & A Davis (eds) *New Philosophies of Learning*. Oxford, Wiley-Blackwell, pp 260–273.

Robertson, E. (1995) 'Reconceiving Reason' in *Critical Conversations in Philosophy of Education*, edited by Kohli, W. New York: Routledge, pp 116–127.

Rollins M. (1996) 'Epistemological Considerations for the Community of Inquiry' in *Thinking, American Journal of Philosophy for Children* 12(2):31–40.

Rorty, R. (1980) *Philosophy and the Mirror of Nature*. Oxford: Basil Blackwell.

Rose, J. (1993) *The Case of Peter Pan or The Impossibility of Children's Fiction*. Philedelphia: University of Philadelphia Press.

Rose, J. (2009) *Independent Review of the Primary Curriculum: Final Report*. Nottingham: DCSF Publications. www.teachernet.gov.uk/publications

Rudduck, J. & McIntyre, D. (2007) *Improving Learning Through Consulting Pupils*. London:Routledge.

Sarland, C. (1999) 'The Impossibility of Innocence: Ideology, Politics, and Children's Literature' in P. Hunt (Ed) *Understanding Children's Literature*. London: Routledge, pp 39–56.

SAPERE Training DVD www.sapere.org.uk

SAPERE (2006) *P4C Report: For the Innovations Unit January 2006*.

Scheffler, I. (1983) 'In Praise of the Cognitive Emotions' in *Thinking: the American Journal of Philosophy for Children*, 3(2):16–23.

Schleiffer, M. & McCormick, M. (2006) 'Are We Responsible For Our Emotions and Moods?' in *Thinking: the American Journal of Philosophy for Children*, 18(1):15–21.

Schleiffer, M. (with Martiny, C.) (2006) *Talking about Feelings and Values with Children* Calgary: Detselig Enterprises.

Scruton, R. (2002) The Decline of Musical Culture In: A. Neill & A. Ridley (Eds) *Arguing About Art: Contemporary Philosophical Debates* (2nd Edn). London: Routledge, pp 119–135.

Sendak, M. (1963) *Where The Wild Things Are* .London: Bodley Head.

Sendak, M. (1970) *In the Night Kitchen*. London: Bodley Head.

Sendak, M. (1981) *Outside Over There*. London: Bodley Head.

Sendak, M. (1988) *Dear Mily*; a Grimm story translated by R. Manheim. Harper Collins.

Sendak, M. (2006) *Mummy?* Scholastic, Michael di Capua Books.

Sharp, A-M. (1991) The Community of Enquiry: Education for Democracy in: *Thinking*, Vol. 9, No. 2, pp. 31–38.

Sharp, A-M. (2007) 'Education of the Emotions in the Classroom Community of Enquiry' in *Gifted Education International, Special Issue on Philosophy for Children*, 22(2/3):248–257, edited by Belle Wallace with Guest Editor Barry Hymer.

Sikes, P., Nixon, J. & Carr, W. (Eds.), (2003) *The Moral Foundations of Educational Research: Knowledge, Inquiry and Values*. Maidenhead and Philadelphia: Open University Press.

Sipe, L.R. & Pantaleo, S. (Eds.) (2008), *Postmodern Picturebooks: Play, Parody and Self-Referentiality*. London and New York: Routledge.

Smeyers, P., Smith, R. & Standish, P. (2007) *The Therapy of Education: Philosophy, Happiness and Personal Growth*. Basingstoke: Palgrave MacMillan.

Smith, H. (in press/2011) 'Reading the 'Happy Child': Normative Discourse in Wellbeing Education' in Lesnik-Oberstein, K. (Ed.) *Children in Culture 2*. Basingstoke: Palgrave Macmillan, pp. 73–89.

Solomon, R. C. (1993) *The Passions: Emotions and the meaning of Life*. Indianapolis: Hackett Publishing Company.

Solomon, R. C (Ed.) (2004) *Thinking about Feeling: Contemporary Philosophers on Emotions*. Oxford: Oxford University Press.

Splitter, L. J. & Sharp, A-M. (1995), *Teaching for Better Thinking; The Classroom Community of Enquiry*. Melbourne: ACER.

Sprod, T. (2001) *Philosophical Discussion in Moral Education: The Community of Ethical Inquiry*. London and New York: Routledge.

Standing, E. M. (1957) *Maria Montessori: Her Life and Work*. London: Hollis & Carter.

Standish, P. (2005) '*The Ownership of Learning*', paper presented to the *Philosophy of Education Society Conference* April 2005, Oxford, England.

Stephens, J. (Ed.). (1992) *Language and Ideology in Children's Fiction*. London: Longman.

Strauss, G. & A. Browne (1991) *The Night Shimmy*. London: Random House.

Stroud, S. R. (2008) 'Simulation, Subjective Knowledge, and the Cognitive Value of Literary Narrative' in *Journal of Aesthetic Education*, 41(3) Fall 2008: 19–41.

Styles, M. & Bearne, E. & Watson, V. (Eds.). (1996).*Voices Off: Texts, Contexts and Readers*. London: Cassell.

Tan, S. & Marsden, J. (1998) *The Rabbits*. South Melbourne: Thomas C. Lothian Pty Ltd.

Tan, S. (2001) *The Red Tree*. Melbourne: Lothian Books.

Tan, S. (2006) *The Arrival*. London and Sydney: Hodder Children's Books.

The Transformers: Socrates for Six Year Olds (1990), first broadcast on BBC TV, in *Communities of Enquiry*, DVD produced by SAPERE. www.sapere.org

Thompson, C. (1995) *How To Live Forever*. London: Red Fox.

Tiffany, G. (2008) 'Lessons from detached youth work: democratic education' *Issues Paper 11, July 2008. Nuffield Review of 14–19 Education and Training, England and Wales*. www.nuffield14-19review.org.uk.

Todd, S. (2003) 'A fine risk to be run? The Ambiguity of Eros and Teacher Responsibility' in *Studies in Philosophy and Education*, 22, pp. 31–44.

Todd, S. (2009) Can There Be Pluralism without Conflict? Ingesting the Indigestible in Democratic Education. Paper presented at *PESGB Conference*, Oxford, March, 2009.

Todd, S. (2010) Pedagogy as Transformative Event: Becoming Singularly Present in Context. Paper presented at *PESGB Conference*, Oxford, March 26–28, 2010.

Townsend, J.R. (1996) 'Parents and Children: The Changing Relationship of the Generations, as Reflected in Fiction for Children and Young People' in Styles, M & E. Bearne (Eds) *Voices: Texts, Contexts and Readers*. London: Cassell, pp 77–92.

Trickey, S. & Topping, K. J. (2004) 'Philosophy for Children: A systematic Review' in *Research Papers in Education*, 19(3):365–380.

Trickey, S. & Topping, K.J. (2007) 'Collaborative Enquiry for School Children: cognitive gains at 2 year follow up' in *British Journal of Education Psychology*, 77(4):787–796.

Tripp, D. (1993) *Critical Incidents in Teaching: Developing Professional Judgment* London: Routledge.

Tubbs, N. (2005) 'Philosophy of the Teacher' in *Journal of Philosophy of Education*, 39(2), Special Issue, May, 2005.

Tucker, N. (1981) *The Child And The Book*. Cambridge, Cambridge University Press.

Ungerer, T. (1971) *The Beast of Monsieur Racine*.New York: Farar, Straus and Giroux.

Ungerer, T. (1966) *Moon Man*. London: Methuen Children's Books.

Ungerer,T., (1991) *The Three Robbers* New York: Macmillan Publishing Company.

United Nations Children's Fund (1995) *The Convention on the Rights of the Child*. London: UK Committee for UNICEF.

Van Manen, M. (1991) *The Tact of Teaching: The Meaning of Pedagogical Thoughtfulness*. University of Western Ontario: The Althouse Press.

Van Manen, M. (1997) *Researching Lived Experience: Human Science for an Action Sensitive Pedagogy*. 2ⁿᵈ Edn. University of Western Ontario: Althouse Press.

Van Manen, M. & Levering, B. (1996) *Childhood's Secrets: Intimacy, Privacy and the Self Reconsidered*. New York: Teachers College Press, Columbia University.

Vansieleghem N. (2005) 'Philosophy for Children as the Wind of Thinking' in *Journal of Philosophy of Education* 39(1):19–37.

Velthuijs, M. (1989) *Frog in Love*. London: Andersen Press.

Velthuijs, M. (1991) *Frog and the Birdsong*. London: Andersen Press.

Velthuijs, M. (1992) *Frog in Winter*. London: Andersen Press.

Velthuijs, M. (1993a) *Frog and the Stranger*. London: Andersen Press.

Velthuijs, M (1993b) *Frog is Frightened*. London: Andersen Press.

Velthuijs, M. (1995) *Frog is a Hero*. London: Andersen Press.

Velthuijs, M. (1998) *Frog and the Wild World*. London: Andersen Pres.

Velthuijs, M. (2001) *Frog finds a Friend*. London: Andersen Press.

Velthuijs, M. (2003) *Frog is Sad*. London: Andersen Press.

Vincent, S. (1999) 'A big kid' in *The Guardian* newspaper 20/11/99

Wagner, J. (1979) *John Brown, Rose and the Midnight Cat*. Illustrated by Ron-Brooks. London: Picture Puffins.

Walker, L. & Logan, A. (2008) *Learner Engagement: A review of learner voice initiatives across the UK education sectors*. Bristol:Futurelab. www.futurelab. org.uk.

Walkerdine, V. (1984) 'Developmental Psychology and the Child-centred Pedagogy' in Henriques, J., Holloway, W., Unwin, C., Venn, C. and Walkerdine, V. (Eds.), *Changing the Subject: Psychology, Social Regulation and Subjectivity*. London and New York: Routledge, pp. 148–198.

Walkerdine, V. (2001) in 'Safety and Danger: Childhood, Sexuality and Space at the End of the Millenium' in Hultqvist, K. Dahlberg, G. (Eds.), *Governing the Child in the New Millenium*. New York and London: RoutledgeFalmer, pp 15–34.

Wallen, M. (Ed). (1990) *Every Picture Tells*....Exeter, NATE.

Warburton, N. (2003). *The Art Question*. London: Routledge.

Warnock, M. (1996) 'Moral Values' in Halstead, M. & Taylor, M. (Eds.), *Values in Education and Education in Values*. London:Falmer Press, pp45–53.

Wartenberg, T. E. (2009). *Big Ideas for Little Kids: Teaching Philosophy through Children's Literature*. Lanham: Rowman & Littlefield Education.

Watson, V. (1996) 'Small Portable Galleries: The Picturebooks of Satoshi Kitamura' in Styles, M. & E. Bearne & V Watson (Eds) (1996) *Voices Off: Texts, Contexts and Readers*. London: Cassell, pp 235–248.

Wegerif, R. (2010) 'What does it mean to teach thinking? Children as an example of dialogic education'. [DRAFT for ICPIC 2009 Conference Proceedings] published online http://elac.ex.ac.uk/dialogiceducation/page.php?id=1

Whitty, G. & Wisby, E. (2007) 'Real Decision Making? Schools Councils in Action' *Research Brief DCSF-RB001*. Department for Schools and Families, September, 2007. Published online www.dcsf.gov.uk/research/

Wiesner, D. (2001) *The Three Pigs*. New York: Clarion Books.

Wilson, A. (1983) *Magical Thought in Creative Writing; The Distinctive Roles of Fantasy and Imagination in Fiction*. Stroud: Thimble Press.

Winnicott, D. W. (1971/1991) *Playing and Reality*. London: Routledge.

Winograd, K (2003) 'The Functions of Teacher Emotions: The Good, the Bad, and the Ugly'in *Teachers College Record*, 105(9):1641–1673.

Wittgenstein, L. (1958) *Philosophische Untersuchungen*. Suhrkamp Verlag.

Wittgenstein, L. (1988) *Culture and Value* (translated by P. Winch; edited by G.V. Von Wright in collaboration with H, Nyman) Oxford:Basil Blackwell.

Woods, P. (1995) *Creative Teachers in Primary Schools*. Buckingham: Open University Press.

Woods P. and Jeffery, B. (1996) *Teachable Moments: The Art of Teaching in Primary Schools*. Buckingham and Philadelphia: Open University Press.

Woolley, J.D. (1997) 'Thinking about Fantasy: Are Children Fundamentally Different Thinkers and Believers from Adults?' in *Child Development*, 68(6):991–1011.

Wormell, C. (2004) *The Big Ugly Monster and the Little Stone Rabbit*. London: Random House.

Worth, S. E. (2008) 'Storytelling and Narrative Knowing: An Examination of the Epistemic Benefits of Well-Told Stories' in *Journal of Aesthetic Education*, 41(3) Fall 2008, pp 42–56.

Zembylas, M. (2007) 'The Power and Politics of Emotions in Teaching' in Phye, G.D. & Pekrun, R. (Eds.) *Emotion in Education,* pp. 293–312. Burlington, San Diego and London: Academic Press.

Index

Note: Page numbers ending in 'f' refer to figures. Page numbers ending in 'd' refer to diagrams. Page numbers ending in 't' refer to tables.